Devon Women
in Public and
Professional Life
1900–1950

Devon Women in Public and Professional Life 1900–1950

Votes, Voices and Vocations

Julia Neville, Mitzi Auchterlonie,
Paul Auchterlonie and
Ann Roberts, with Helen Turnbull

UNIVERSITY
of
EXETER
PRESS

First published in 2021 by
University of Exeter Press
Reed Hall, Streatham Drive
Exeter EX4 4QR, UK

www.exeterpress.co.uk

© Julia Neville, Mitzi Auchterlonie, Paul Auchterlonie and Ann Roberts 2021

A CIP catalogue record for this book is available from The British Library.

Neville, J., Auchterlonie, M., Auchterlonie, P. and Roberts, A. 2021. *Devon Women in
Public and Professional Life, 1900–1950: Votes, Voices and Vocations*. Exeter, University of
Exeter Press. https://doi.org/10.47788/KSEU6586

ISBN: 978-1-905816-76-7 (Hbk)
ISBN: 978-1-905816-77-4 (Pbk)
ISBN: 978-1-905816-78-1 (ePub)
ISBN: 978-1-905816-79-8 (PDF)

Cover image: Officers and members of the National Union of Societies for Equal
Citizenship after Royal Assent to the Equal Franchise Act, 2 July 1928. © LSE Library
The group includes Millicent Garrett Fawcett, Ray Strachey, Philippa Fawcett, Agnes Garrett,
Chrystal Macmillan, Miss Macadam, Catherine Marshal, Miss Courtney, Miss Ward.

Typeset in Perpetua 11½ point on 14 point by
Palimpsest Book Production Ltd, Falkirk, Stirlingshire

Contents

Figures

Acronyms Used in the Book

ARMW	Association of Registered Medical Women
BMA	British Medical Association
BMJ	*British Medical Journal*
BWSS	Bermuda Woman Suffrage Society
CC	*Common Cause* [later *The Woman's Leader*]
DACA	Devonian Association for Cripples Aid
DCW	Devon Council of Women on Public Authorities
DHC	Devon Heritage Centre [formerly Devon Record Office]
DEG	*Devon and Exeter [Daily] Gazette*
DPH	Diploma in Public Health
DNA	Devon Nursing Association
E&E	*Express and Echo* [Exeter]
ECA	Equal Citizenship Association
EDACFG	Exeter Diocesan Association for the Care of Friendless Girls
EUA	Edinburgh University Archives
ExJ	*Exmouth Journal*
FRCS	Fellowship of the Royal Colleges of Surgeons
GMC	General Medical Council
HMSO	His Majesty's Stationery Office [now Her Majesty's Stationery Office]
JP	Justice of the Peace
LLA	Ladies Licensed in the Arts
LWSU	Liberal Women's Suffrage Union
MRCOG	Membership of the Royal College of Obstetricians and Gynaecologists
MU	Mothers' Union
MWF	Medical Women's Federation
MWIA	Medical Women's International Association

NCW   National Council of Women
NCWW   National Council of Women Workers
NHS   National Health Service
NSPCC   National Society for the Prevention of Cruelty to Children
NUSEC   National Union of Societies for Equal Citizenship
NUWSS   National Union of Women's Suffrage Societies
ODNB   *Oxford Dictionary of National Biography*
PHC   Public Health Committee
PMS   Plymouth Medical Society
RAMC   Royal Army Medical Corps
RCP   Royal College of Physicians
RD&EH   Royal Devon and Exeter Hospital
SPCK   Society for Promoting Christian Knowledge
UDC   Urban District Council
VAD   Voluntary Aid Detachment
WCA   Women Citizens' Associations
WCG   Women's Co-operative Guild
WDM   *Western Daily Mercury*
WEH   *Western Evening Herald*
WFL   Women's Freedom League
WI   Women's Institute
WL   Wellcome Library
WLF   Women's Liberal Federation
WMN   *Western Morning News* [later *Western Morning News and Western Daily Mercury*; then *Western Morning News and Devon and Exeter Daily Gazette*]
WNLF   Women's National Liberal Federation
WSPU   Women's Social and Political Union
WT   *Western Times*
WWAC   Women's War Agricultural Committee
YWCA   Young Women's Christian Association

Acknowledgements

We would like to thank the three anonymous peer reviewers whose comments helped to reshape and improve the Introduction. We are also grateful to Karen Averby, Ruth Hawker, Sue Rugg and Valorie Mitchell, who assisted in the research on Georgiana Buller; to Tessa Trappes-Lomax for her detailed comments on the draft chapter on Sylvia Calmady-Hamlyn; to Brian Carpenter of the Devon Heritage Centre for providing archival material on Eleanor Acland; and to Hetty Marx of the University of Exeter Press for all her help in seeing this book through the press.

Introduction

PAUL AUCHTERLONIE

Biography and Historical Enquiry

Biography has long been seen as part of history, and as a way to enliven it by rendering the past 'more human, more vivid, more intimate, more accessible, more connected to ourselves'.[1] But its narrative form and its concern with individuals have often resulted in its relegation to the margins of historical study while political institutions or social and economic structures occupy the centre. Now, however, biography is coming to occupy more of this centre ground as it is seen to offer ways of throwing new light on a range of different historical periods and problems, and of bringing individuals and groups who had previously been ignored into the framework of historical analysis.[2]

Both June Purvis and Barbara Caine have shown the significance of recent biographical works for exploring the lives of women, Purvis pointing out that 'biographies of well-known feminists have proliferated in the UK over the last two decades, although they are mainly of white, middle-class women',[3] while Caine has expanded on this, suggesting that there are 'few biographies that explored the lives of the many women engaged in local politics, trade unions, education, philanthropy, or social activism or feminism, who had not attained the standing of a national leader'.[4]

1. A.M. Schlesinger, Jr., 'Editor's note', in *Thomas Jefferson*, ed. by J. Appleby (New York: Holt, 2001), p. xvi.
2. B. Caine, *Biography and History*, 2nd edn (London: Red Globe Press, 2019), p. 1.
3. J. Purvis, '"A Glass Half Full"?: Women's History in the UK', *Women's History Review*, 27 (2018), pp. 92–93.
4. Caine, *Biography and History*, p. 102.

Paul Auchterlonie, 'Introduction' in: *Devon Women in Public and Professional Life 1900–1950: Votes, Voices and Vocations*. University of Exeter Press (2021). © Paul Aucterlonie
DOI: 10.47788/ZJFF9096

Using biography as a medium for exploring the history of Devon,[5] it was decided to compile a group of detailed portraits, through which one could investigate how women have contributed to the public, professional, and civic life of Devon during the first half of the twentieth century. The eight women selected represent four major areas of public and professional activity: national and local politics—Eleanor Acland (1878–1933) and Clara Daymond (1873–1957); medicine and teaching—Mabel Ramsay (1878–1954) and Jessie Headridge (1871–1946); the voluntary sector—Lady Florence Cecil (1863–1944) and Dame Georgiana Buller (1883–1953); and rural life—Jane, Lady Clinton (1863–1953) and Sylvia Calmady-Hamlyn (1881–1962). These women fit the categories defined by Purvis in being white, British and mainly middle class, and by Caine in operating mostly on a restricted, local stage. An earlier project on suffrage had demonstrated how Devon women's struggle for the vote had been integrated into the national campaign but with its own local particularities;[6] the aim of this book is to show to what degree a large rural county, distant from both the metropolis and the industrial heartlands of Britain, reflected the women's movement nationally in the interwar period and to what extent it developed its own patterns of activity.

The Importance of the Local

The suffragist Oliver Strachey (1874–1960) emphasized the importance of the local for the women's movement as early as 1917:

> At present the women's organisations are for the most part national organisations, each with a specific object like our own. The value of these organisations to their members as an educa-tion in political thought and habit of mind is enormous, and certainly need not be laboured with those who attend our annual councils. What we may look forward to, I hope, is a great increase of vitality in local political organisations. It is, after all, only a minority of women whose turn of mind best suits them to belong to these big national unions with a single object. It is the politics

---

5. Caine goes on to suggest that biography is the best form to 'show the great importance of particular locations and circumstances and the multiple layers of historical change and experience' (Caine, *Biography and History*, p. 2).

6. See the *Lives of Devon Women Suffrage Activists, 1866–1918* website for the results of this Devon History Society project <https://www.devonhistorysociety.org.uk/news/lives-of-devons-women-suffrage-activists-1866-1918> [accessed 23 September 2020].

of the parish or the district which most vividly appeal to the majority, and it will be an excellent thing if up and down the country small organisations of the nature of women's interests committees are formed. It will be excellent for their members and excellent for the nation.[7]

Academics working on women's history have also recently highlighted the importance of undertaking in-depth studies of local activity. Catherine Hunt notes that several authors including Steven King, June Hannam and Karen Hunt have shown that 'there is a danger that the more well-known accounts of prominent women whose careers ranged beyond their local communities, can be taken as representative of all women councillors', and that 'the combined employment of a biographical and local focus can advance historical work beyond generalizations and stereotypes, and instead develop an understanding of the full range of women's involvement in local politics'.[8] This view is echoed by Cheryl Law, who bemoans the 'neglect of regional developments in the women's movement in previous secondary sources', which had led to 'an undervaluing of the contribution made by women all over the country',[9] and also by June Hannam, who concludes her study of local women's suffrage campaigns with the words, 'It is to be hoped that an increasing emphasis on local studies will enable historians to trace the negotiations women made between class, sex and party political loyalties beyond the watershed of the First World War into the very different context of the inter-war years.'[10]

This is not to say that studies of women's activism during the interwar period in particular places have not already been published. Esther Breitenbach and Valerie Wright have studied women's involvement in city politics in Glasgow and Edinburgh,[11] while Karen Hunt and June Hannam have examined

---

7. O. Strachey, 'What Next?', The Common Cause of Humanity: The Organ of the National Union of Women's Suffrage Societies, 6 July 1917, p. 167.

8. C. Hunt, 'Success with the Ladies: An Examination of Women's Experiences as Labour Councillors in Inter War Coventry', Midland History, 32 (2007), p. 143. The books Hunt refers to are S. King, Women, Welfare and Local Politics, 1880–1920: We Might Be Trusted (Brighton: Sussex Academic Press, 2006) which focuses on Bolton in Lancashire, and J. Hannam and K. Hunt, Socialist Women: Britain, 1880s to 1920s (London: Routledge, 2002).

9. C. Law, Suffrage and Power: The Women's Movement, 1918–1928 (London: I.B.Tauris, 1997), p. 8.

10. J. Hannam, '"I Had Not Been to London": Women's Suffrage, a View from the Regions', in Votes for Women, ed. by J. Purvis and S.S. Holton (London: Routledge, 2000), p. 242.

11. E. Breitenbach and V. Wright, 'Women as Active Citizens: Glasgow and Edinburgh, c.1918–1939', Women's History Review, 23 (2014), pp. 401–20. Also relevant is S. Innes, 'Constructing Women's Citizenship in the Inter-War Period: The Edinburgh Women Citizens' Association', Women's History Review, 13 (2004), 621–47.

party politics in Manchester and Bristol during the same period.[12] They suggest when looking at political activity

> that interwar women's politics should be reframed. The key is to follow the example of some revisionist suffrage historians, in reconfiguring the national story by focusing on the local to explore the nature of women's networks; how women negotiated multiple and changing affiliations … The connections between women's experiences of formal and informal politics in the interwar period allow us to foreground the extent to which the creation of a new female electorate made a difference to the practice and experience of politics in women's daily lives.[13]

The first full-length regional study of women's activism between the wars was Samantha Clements' 2008 doctoral dissertation on Nottingham; in it Clements claimed that until her research, there had been 'no comprehensive study of a range of organisations operating within a single local environment [in the interwar period]. Such a study is necessary to understand the priorities of a range of women, rather than those who were specifically politicized through membership of political parties.'[14] This was followed shortly afterwards by Ruth Davidson's study of women's organizations in Croydon,[15] which argued that 'many women put their efforts into local campaigning rather than seeking a role within parliament, and built directly on precursors such as the suffrage movement and other political and philanthropic movements to extend their role in public life'.[16]

All these studies emphasize the value of locally focused research, but differ from this book in two essentials: firstly, they are studies mainly of organizations, which throw some light on individuals, while this project is much more focused on individuals and only examines organizations in so far as they were a medium through which the Devon women conducted their public or professional lives.

12. K. Hunt and J. Hannam, 'Towards an Archaeology of Interwar Women's Politics: The Local and the Everyday', in The Aftermath of Suffrage: Women, Gender and Politics in Britain, 1918–1945, ed. by J.V. Gottlieb and R. Toye (Basingstoke: Palgrave Macmillan, 2013), pp. 124–41.
13. K. Hunt and J. Hannam, 'Towards an Archaeology of Interwar Women's Politics', p. 137.
14. S. Clements, 'Feminism, Citizenship and Social Activity: The Role and Importance of Local Women's Organisations, Nottingham, 1918–1969' (unpublished doctoral thesis, University of Nottingham, 2008), p. 48.
15. R. Davidson, 'Citizens at last: Women's Political Culture and Civil Society, Croydon and East Surrey, 1914–1939' (unpublished doctoral thesis, University of London, Royal Holloway College, 2010).
16. Breitenbach and Wright, 'Women as Active Citizens', p. 416.

Secondly, all the above studies look at cities, where activities were concentrated into a relatively small physical space. This book, in complete contrast, looks at England's second largest county, which at the beginning of the twentieth century was sparsely populated apart from the three important conurbations on the south coast—Exeter, Torbay and Plymouth. In 1901, the total number of inhabitants in the county was 660,000, and over the next thirty years, Devon's population grew more slowly than the national average except for Torbay. Devon was also relatively poor by national standards, since by 1914, the heydays of its cloth, mining and shipbuilding industries were behind it, and over a quarter of the employed male population outside the cities of Exeter and Plymouth worked in the agricultural sector, where pay was relatively low.[17] Devon's size, relatively poor road communications, and huge rural hinterland made networking all the more important, but also all the more difficult. Devon also had a reputation for associational life and voluntary organizations. As F.G. Thomas in *The Changing Village: An Essay in Rural Reconstruction* (1939), which dealt principally with Devon, remarked,

A new organisation will find it difficult to find a 'free' night in the [village] hall and equally difficult to discover a possible member in the village who has not already several 'memberships' to finance. The Church, the Chapel, the Women's Institute, the British Legion, the District Nursing Association, the Men's Club, Church Guild, the Buffaloes, and sports associations will be found in most villages, each intent on securing memberships and subscriptions.[18]

This focus on the local is essential in explaining the nature of the activities of the eight women who are studied here and the organizations they worked with. The non-religious and non-political organizations to which the eight women belonged are listed in the Appendix, *Voluntary Organizations in Devon Supported by the Subjects of these Biographies*. Most of the forty-eight organizations listed were supported by only one individual among the eight, but just over one third (seventeen) had more than one supporter, and six organizations had at least four of the eight women as members.[19]

---

17. Most of this information is taken from A.M. Dawson, 'Politics in Devon and Cornwall, 1900–1931' (unpublished doctoral thesis, University of London, London School of Economics and Political Science, 1991), pp. 14–18.

18. F.G. Thomas, *The Changing Village: An Essay in Rural Reconstruction* (London: Nelson, 1939); the book deals mostly with the Devon villages of Lapford and Dartington, but is of county-wide significance.

19. The organizations with the most shared memberships were the Devon Council of Women on

As for sources, an unpublished memoir exists for Mabel Ramsay,[20] and a published one for Jessie Headridge,[21] while a collection of letters written by Eleanor Acland has also been edited and published.[22] There are important organizational archives that shed light on the careers of several of the women mostly held by the Devon Heritage Centre or The Box in Plymouth,[23] but some national collections were used as well, for example, the Wellcome Collection and the British Red Cross archives. Perhaps the most useful overall resources have been the excellent, detailed reports of community events in the local Devon press, which have been invaluable in working out the contours of the women's public and professional lives and their inter-connections. It is worth mentioning that the British Library Newspaper Archive, which contains searchable digitized versions of hundreds of local and suffrage newspapers from the first half of the twentieth century, has made it easier to find information about the Devon women's activities than in the days when microfilms were the main method of access to the local press,[24] though gaps in digital provision mean that some microfilmed newspapers have continued to be necessary for particular dates.

Back to Home and Duty? The Development of the Women's Movement Between the Wars

In 1920, Millicent Garrett Fawcett (1847–1929), President of the National Union of Women's Suffrage Societies (NUWSS) and the acknowledged leader of the non-militant suffrage movement, wrote in the final chapter of her book *The Women's Victory and After: Personal Reminiscences, 1911–1918*:

Public Authorities, Devonshire Association for Cripples' Aid, League of Nations Union, National Union of Societies for Equal Citizenship/Women Citizens' Associations, National Union of Women's Suffrage Societies, and the local Nursing Associations.

20. A copy of M. Ramsay, *A Doctor's Zig-Zag Road*, is held in the archives of Royal College of Physicians in London in File MS87.

21. J. Headridge, *Labuntur Anni* (Exeter: Wheaton, 1932).

22. Most of Eleanor Acland's letters have been published in *Killerton, Camborne and Westminster: The Political Correspondence of Sir Francis and Lady Acland, 1910–1929*, ed. by Garry Tregidga (Exeter: Devon and Cornwall Record Society, 2006); the originals and further unpublished letters are held by the Devon Heritage Centre in Exeter at File 1148M.

23. The Plymouth and West Devon Record Office was incorporated into The Box, Plymouth's new gallery, museum, library and archive complex, in 2019.

24. The significance of the wide array of searchable, digitized newspapers now available is highlighted by Samantha Clements, who explains that, when doing her primary research, although newspapers were a 'rich resource', she was only able to sample a fraction of what was published, and could read on microfilm no more than two days' worth of local daily papers each month, Clements, 'Feminism, Citizenship and Social Activity', p. 52.

Our fifty years struggle for the women's vote was not actuated by our setting any extraordinary value on the mere power of making a mark on a voting paper once in every three or four years. We did not, except as a symbol of free citizenship, value it as a thing good in itself ... but for the sake of the equal laws, the enlarged opportunities, the improved status of women which we know it involved. We worked for it with ardour and passion because it was the stuff of the conscience with us that it would benefit not women only, but the whole community ... it was the cause of men, women and children.[25]

To the women of Devon, including those who form the basis of this book, 1920 must have seemed like the dawn of a new era. The bloodiest war in history was finally over and the Representation of the People Act passed in 1918 had given the vote to propertied women over 30. This act had been closely followed by the Parliament (Qualification of Women) Act 1918, which allowed women to become Members of Parliament, and which had resulted in the landmark election to Parliament of Nancy Astor for the Devon seat of Plymouth Sutton in 1919. Another important piece of legislation in the immediate postwar period was the Sex Disqualification (Removal) Act of 1919, which (theoretically) opened the professions to women and allowed women to become Justices of the Peace (JPs) for the first time.[26] The development and significance of this bill have been studied both by Mari Takayanagi and, from the point of view of women magistrates, by Anne Logan.[27] Pat Thane has pointed out that 'before 1918, any woman on trial had to face a wholly male court: barristers, solicitors, jury, judges, police, clerks, ushers were all male',[28] while this new act, although not prescriptive, opened up the legal (and other) professions to women. It also enabled women such as Eleanor Acland, Sylvia Calmady-Hamlyn and Georgiana Buller

---

25. M. G. Fawcett, *The Women's Victory and After: Personal Reminiscences, 1911–1918* (London: Sidgwick & Jackson, 1920), p. 156.
26. Two hundred women were appointed JPs in 1920; by 1927 there were 1,600 women magistrates in England and Wales out of a total of 25,000. The figures are taken from P. Thane, 'What Difference Did the Vote Make?' in *Women, Privilege and Power: British Politics 1750 to the Present*, ed. by A. Vickery (Stanford: Stanford University Press, 2001), p. 275.
27. M. Takayanagi, 'Sacred Year or Broken Reed?: The Sex Disqualification (Removal) Act 1919', *Women's History Review*, 2020, 563–82; A. Logan, 'In Search of Equal Citizenship: The Campaign for Women Magistrates in England and Wales, 1910–1939', *Women's History Review*, 16 (2007), 501–18. See also H. Glew, *Gender, Rhetoric and Regulation: Women's Work in the Civil Service and London County Council, 1900–1955* (Manchester: Manchester University Press, 2016), which gives in-depth coverage to the issues of equal opportunities, equal pay and the marriage bar.
28. P. Thane, 'What Difference Did the Vote Make?: Women in Public and Private Life in Britain since 1918', *Historical Research*, 76 (2003), p. 272.

to sit as JPs, a position that 'carried significant social prestige' and to which women brought 'pioneering modern ideas'.[29]

In the following decade, a considerable amount of legislation improving the conditions of women and children was passed including the Criminal Law Amendment Acts of 1922 and 1929, which raised the age of consent in cases of indecent assault, and later equalized the legal age of marriage to sixteen; three Property Acts of 1922, 1926 and 1935, which gave women more or less the same rights as men over the owning, inheritance and disposal of property, and the Matrimonial Causes Act of 1923, which reduced the double standards in divorce. In 1924 women were given equal rights with men over the guardianship of children in cases where a marriage broke down, and in the following year the Conservative government of Stanley Baldwin introduced widows' and orphans' pensions,[30] while the Adoption Act of 1926 improved the protection of adopted children who had been born out of wedlock. The legislation of the 1920s culminated in the Equal Franchise Act of 1928, which gave the vote to both men and women at the age of 21.

Yet, despite this profusion of legislation to improve the condition of women and children, some historians writing in the last two decades of the twentieth century have considered the position of women in the interwar period in a negative light. Deirdre Beddoe, paraphrasing Olive Banks in her book *Faces of Feminism*, calls the period 1920–1960 'years of intermission, when for the time at least, feminism seemed to have come to an end'. Beddoe herself, particularly regarding working-class women, considers that 'it would not be going too far to say that the climate in inter-war Britain was anti-feminist'.[31] Beddoe goes on to accuse the women's movement of fragmentation,[32] being divided into 'new'

---

29. Takayanagi, 'Sacred Year or Broken Reed', p. 576. However, it should be pointed out that the picture was not that rosy in Devon. Although Anne Logan claims in 'MP and/or JP: An Examination of the Public Work of Selected Women during the Early Years of Women's Enfranchisement (c. 1920–1931)', *Open Library of Humanities*, 6.2 (2020), p. 25, that 'the woman magistrate quickly became part of the criminal justice system', while this may have been true of the more urbanized parts of England, this was by no means the case for Devon. By 1939, the total numbers of women JPs in Devon had inched up to fifty-nine, for a county with a population of 732,000. This represented less than three women per petty sessions division, and in some parts of rural Devon, there would have been a relatively small chance of finding a woman on the Bench at a police court [note by Julia Neville].

30. 'By 1933 pensions were granted to 725,000 women and 340,000 children', see Thane, 'What Difference Did the Vote Make?' (2001), p. 278.

31. D. Beddoe, *Back to Home and Duty: Women Between the Wars, 1918–1939* (London: HarperCollins, 1989), p. 4; the paraphrase of Olive Banks on page 136 of Beddoe is taken from pages 149–51 of O. Banks, *Faces of Feminism: A Study of Feminism as a Social Movement* (Oxford: Robertson, 1981; repr. Oxford: Blackwell, 1986).

32. Beddoe, *Back to Home and Duty*, p. 140.

feminism, which argued that the movement should be concerned primarily with improving the welfare of women and children, and 'old' feminism, which pursued a more egalitarian policy, and which was more vigorous in challenging male dominance.[33] It is worth pointing out that even some women activists of the interwar period felt gloomy about their own recent achievements; for example, Cicely Hamilton (1872–1952), a stalwart of the suffrage struggle and the Women's Freedom League, wrote in her autobiography in 1935, 'Today, in many quarters of the field, the battle we thought won is going badly against us; we are retreating where once we advanced,'[34] while Mary Willcocks (1869–1952), a Devon novelist and biographer, suffragist and political activist, said in an interview in 1938, 'Are women making the most of the freedom we fought so hard to win? ... They have their freedom, but rarely do we hear of women who are outstanding, who have become leaders.'[35]

This negative view has been seriously challenged, however, from the mid-1990s onwards. In the first comprehensive historiographical analysis of the conflict between the older view and more recent opinion on the interwar women's movement, Joanne Workman has succinctly summarized the supposed division of the women's interwar movement into two camps and concludes that 'the rigidity of the "revisionists" notion of competing feminist camps disallows a consideration of the complexity of the goals of "old" and "new" feminists and the multifarious ways in which these goals overlapped'.[36] In another important survey of the historiography of the women's movement, Maria DiCenzo suggests that 'the narratives of disappointment or defeat are based on a recurring set of themes', which she identifies as a retreat to the domestic sphere; the proposition that in the interwar periods nothing really changed and women's lives remained fundamentally the same as before the war; the idea that the character of interwar feminism is essentially conservative and reformist; and 'the demise of the movement is attributed to its lack of cohesion or focus—with a stress on fragmentation and the conflicts between equalitarian ("old") and welfare ("new") feminists—as well as its failure to attract new and younger women in significant numbers'.[37] The counter-arguments to the four complaints listed by DiCenzo have been addressed by historians such as Cheryl Law, Pat Thane and Caitríona Beaumont. The notion of 'retreat',

33. Beddoe, *Back to Home and Duty*, p. 139.
34. C. Hamilton, *Life Errant* (London: Dent, 1935), p. 251.
35. *Western Morning News*, 6 January 1938.
36. J. Workman, 'Wading through the Mire: An Historiographical Study of the British Women's Movement between the Wars', *University of Sussex Journal of Contemporary History*, 2 (2001), p. 4.
37. M. DiCenzo, '"Our Freedom and its Results": Measuring Progress in the Aftermath of Suffrage', *Women's History Review*, 23 (2014), p. 423.

for example, and the idea that the situation for women was identical before and after the war is contradicted by many of the people who were active suffrage campaigners in the Edwardian era, who could see quite clearly that the problems confronting women in 1918 were different in scale and substance to the struggle for the vote. As the former militant suffragette Sylvia Pankhurst wrote in her history of the suffragette movement:

> The Suffrage movement, which lived through the vast holocaust of peaceful life, was a more intelligent and informed movement than that which, gallant as it was, had fought the desperate, pre-war fight. Gone was the mirage of a society regenerated by enfranchised womanhood as by a magic wand ... Awed and humbled by the great catastrophe, and by the huge economic problems it had thrown into naked prominence, the women of the Suffrage movement had learnt that social regeneration is a long and mighty work.[38]

Welfare work, and the fight to improve conditions for women and children, were also viewed as important a task as the fight for the vote. As Cheryl Law says:

> To dismiss the value of welfare work pursued by all sections of the movement marks a failure to recognise the wretchedness of the poverty, dismal housing and lack of health care which confronted large numbers of women and children in particular ... To get welfare problems addressed had always been a prime motivation for women getting the vote. The concentration on such goals in the 1920s was no dereliction of the feminist credo but a fulfilment if its manifesto.[39]

Different groups formulated different policies to tackle social deprivation, but were often willing to work together. For example, in 1920 when Labour activist Marion Phillips (1881–1932) was preparing a book with Averil Furniss, which was eventually published as *The Working Woman's House*,[40] she received answers to her questionnaire from a wide variety of organizations including the Women's Co-operative Guild, Women Citizens' Associations, the National Council of

---

38. S. Pankhurst, *The Suffragette Movement: An Intimate Account of Persons and Ideals* (London: Longmans, Green, 1931; repr. London: Virago, 1977), p. 608.
39. Law, *Suffrage and Power*, p. 229.
40. A.D.S. Furniss and M. Phillips, *The Working Woman's House* (London: Swarthmore Press, 1920).

Women, the Federation of Girls' Clubs, and Women's Institutes, many of which were neither party political nor part of the supposed old and new divide.[41]

According to Pat Thane and Cheryl Law, 'at least 130 such [women's] organisations were active in the 1920s, almost certainly drawing into public life a larger number and a wider social range of women than ever before'.[42] Among the most actively campaigning groups were NUSEC (the National Union of Societies for Equal Citizenship, the successor to the NUWSS, led by Eleanor Rathbone [1872–1946]),[43] the WFL (Women's Freedom League), the Six-Point Group, the National Council of Women and the (London and) National Society for Women's Service (later the Fawcett Society). Also significant are the Women Citizens' Associations (WCA), formed in 1917 as a result of widespread consultation among the National Union of Women Workers. Open to all women over 16, non-party and non-sectarian, the WCA's role was 'to foster a sense of citizenship in women, encourage the study of political, social and economic questions, [and] secure the adequate representation of the interests and experiences of women in the affairs of the community'.[44] NUSEC, perhaps the most influential group and the one to which earlier historians have devoted the most attention,[45] worked jointly with the National Council of Women and the Consultative Committee of Women's Organizations (to which forty-nine organizations were affiliated),[46] and a range of other organizations such as the Young Women's Christian Association (YWCA) to achieve legal changes.[47]

Caitríona Beaumont is clear that these 'new and egalitarian feminist societies, rather than being in conflict with one another, were in fact able to work side by side representing different, but equally valid, interpretations of how best to campaign for women's rights during the interwar period'.[48] Added to

41. M. Goronwy-Roberts, A Woman of Vision: A Life of Marion Phillips, MP (Wrexham: Bridge Books, 2000), p. 20.
42. P. Thane, 'What Difference Did the Vote Make?' (2001), p. 290. For a list of women's interwar organizations see Law, Suffrage and Power, pp. 232–37.
43. 'By 1918, NUSEC had 126 branches all over Britain, with 142 affiliated women's organisations covering every aspect of women's activities ... [from] the Association for Moral and Social Hygiene ... [to] the National Federation of Women's Teachers', Law, Suffrage and Power, p. 52.
44. Law, Suffrage and Power, p. 113. The WCAs and NUSEC merged in 1924.
45. Workman, 'Wading through the Mire', p. 3.
46. For more information on the Consultative Committee of Women's Organizations, see Pat Thane, 'The Impact of Mass Democracy on British Political Culture, 1918–1939', in The Aftermath of Suffrage: Women, Gender and Politics in Britain, 1918–1945, ed. by J.V. Gottlieb and R. Toye (Basingstoke: Palgrave Macmillan, 2013), p. 61.
47. Thane, 'What Difference Did the Vote Make?' (2001), p. 281.
48. C. Beaumont, 'The Women's Movement: Politics and Citizenship, 1918–1950s', in Women in Twentieth-Century Britain, ed. by I. Zweiniger-Bargielowska (Harlow: Longmans, 2001), p. 264.

these well-established women's political organizations were dozens of single-interest pressure groups, ranging from the Women's Electrical Association and the Women's Local Government Society to the Association for Moral and Social Hygiene. However, as Cheryl Law has shown, membership of a major national organization did not preclude belonging to other societies which had a limited and specific focus, and many women council members of national groups had membership of several other smaller organizations.[49] This multiplicity of membership was mirrored in Devon; in the 1920s, Eleanor Acland, for example, was either chair or on the governing body of the Exeter Branch of NUSEC, the Peacemakers' Pilgrimage, the Exeter Women's Welfare Association, and the National Birth Control Council; she was also involved in the Women's Institutes and Girl Guide movements, served on St Thomas Rural District Council for the parish of Broadclyst and was a JP.[50] This was in addition to her duties for the Liberal Party, which she represented (and chaired) at city, county and national level. As Joanne Workman concludes in her article,

> The inter-war women's movement presents a picture of tremendous pluralism, evident not simply within organisations, but within their individual members also. Contradictions and complexities were contained within this pluralism, but, as recent feminist interpretations have successfully argued, the women's movement of this period should not be judged negatively for displaying the characteristics common to all social movements.[51]

Many women with political interests also joined the Conservative, Liberal or Labour Parties, which all developed significant women's sections. They could therefore campaign through their party organizations and conferences for feminist causes, rather than directly through a feminist society, or, if they wished, through both. There were one million members of the Women's Unionist Organization in 1928, 250,000–300,000 members of the Women's Sections of the Labour Party in the same year, and 88,000 members of the Women's National Liberal Federation in 1926.[52] In addition, women were able

49. Law, *Suffrage and Power*, pp. 4–8.
50. Broadclyst is a village adjoining the Acland family estate at Killerton near Exeter.
51. Workman, 'Wading through the Mire', p. 10.
52. M. Pugh, *Women and the Women's Movement in Britain, 1914–1959* (Basingstoke: Macmillan, 1992), pp. 125, 131 and 140 respectively. To see the sort of work that women's party political sections could undertake, see C. Berthezène, 'The Middlebrow and the Making of a "New Common Sense": Women's Voluntarism, Conservative Politics and Representations of Womanhood', in *Rethinking*

to influence national and local policy in favour of women's issues both at Westminster and in local government. At the 1931 general election, just under 5% of the parliamentary candidates were women, of whom half were elected,[53] while in 1930 there were 1,174 women who had been elected to county, city and borough councils (such as Clara Daymond) and onto urban and rural district councils (for example, Eleanor Acland).[54] And as the examples of Acland shows, being an active member of a political party did not preclude, indeed seems to have positively encouraged, participation in other civic organizations.

One could also argue that the most popular organizations for women in the interwar period were neither political parties, nor ginger groups, but were 'societies representing the interests of wives and mothers working within the home'.[55] As Caitríona Beaumont has shown, 'the largest and most successful voluntary women's organisations during the interwar period were the Women's Co-operative Guild (founded in 1883), the National Federation of Women's Institutes (1915), the National Union of Townswomen's Guilds (1928)[56] and the Mothers' Union (1885)',[57] which together had a combined membership of just under one million in the early 1930s. In her monograph *Housewives and Citizens* (2013), Beaumont argues that organizations such as the Mothers' Union and Women's Institutes transformed the nature of women's activism:

> In spite of their endorsement of domesticity, the Mothers' Union, Catholic Women's League, National Council of Women, Women's Institutes and Townswomen's Guilds insisted that housewives and mothers would be mistaken to devote themselves exclusively to family life. On the contrary, this study will reveal that voluntary

Right-Wing Women: Gender and the Conservative Party, 1880s to the Present, ed. by C. Berthezène and J.V. Gottlieb (Manchester: Manchester University Press, 2018), 104–21; P. Thane, 'The Women of the British Labour Party and Feminism, 1906–1945' in *British Feminism in the Twentieth Century*, ed. by H. Smith (Aldershot: Elgar, 1990), 124–43 and P. Thane, 'Women, Liberalism and Citizenship', in *Citizenship and Community: Liberals, Radicals and Collective Identities, in the British Isles, 1865–1931*, ed. by E.F. Biagini (Cambridge: Cambridge University Press, 1996), 66–92.
53. Pugh, *Women and the Women's Movement*, p. 159.
54. Pugh, *Women and the Women's Movement*, p. 57.
55. Beaumont, 'The Women's Movement', p. 267.
56. 'Strongly influenced by the [Women's] Institutes, the non-feminist Townswomen's Guilds grew up within NUSEC during the late 1920 ... So successful were the Guilds, that in 1932 NUSEC bifurcated into the National Union of Townswomen's Guilds and the National Council for Equal Citizenship,' B. Harrison, *Prudent Revolutionaries: Portraits of British Feminists Between the Wars* (Oxford: Clarendon Press, 1987), p. 8.
57. Beaumont, 'The Women's Movement', pp. 266–67. The Mothers' Union, with over 15,000 local members in 1931, was the largest women's organization in Devon between the wars.

women's groups acknowledged the status of women as equal citizens and continually sought to inform and educate their members about the importance of democratic citizenship.[58]

In a separate publication, Beaumont has shown how 'campaigns actively supported by non-feminist organizations during the 1930s [the five largest voluntary associations listed above plus the YWCA] included the employment of women police, the right of women to equitable state pensions, improved housing and adequate maternity services'.[59] Certainly, the Mothers' Union was Lady Florence Cecil's most pressing concern, as was the Women's Institute for Lady Clinton, while Clara Daymond was a lifetime member of the Women's Co-operative Guild.

Even some of those historians who had once condemned the women's interwar movement as 'moribund' changed their negative stance. Adrian Bingham, in his review essay, has shown how

> Feminists were not merely submitting to conservative discourses on marriage and motherhood, but seeking to improve desperate conditions. Harold Smith, who had previously described feminists as being, by the end of the 1920s, 'a beleaguered band very much on the defensive' seemed to revise his opinion by outlining the success of the London National Society for Women's Suffrage in putting equal pay on the parliamentary agenda in the 1930s. There is, he argued, 'evidence of intense feminist activity and significant achievement in the 1930s and 1940s' which makes it 'misleading to claim that feminism became moribund in the 1930s and did not revive until the late 1960s'.[60]

As the 1920s drew to a close, both international and economic issues became predominant preoccupations. The major questions discussed in the 1930s at

---

58. C. Beaumont, *Housewives and Citizens: Domesticity and the Women's Movement in England, 1928–64* (Manchester: Manchester University Press, 2013), p. 3.

59. C. Beaumont, 'Citizens not Feminists: The Boundary Negotiated between Citizenship and Feminism by Mainstream Women's Organisations in England, 1928–39', *Women's History Review*, 9 (2000), p. 421.

60. A. Bingham, '"An Era of Domesticity?": Histories of Women and Gender in Interwar Britain', *Cultural and Social History*, 1 (2004), p. 228. The citations from Harold Smith are taken from respectively, H. Smith, 'British Feminism in the 1920s', in *British Feminism in the Twentieth Century*, ed. by H. Smith (Aldershot: Elgar, 1990), p. 62, and H. Smith, 'British Feminism and the Equal Pay Issue in the 1930s', *Women's History Review*, 5 (1996), p. 97.

both national and local level were, firstly, unemployment, particularly in the North of England, South Wales and Scotland,[61] and, secondly, the deteriorating international situation and the question of rearmament. The quest for peaceful solutions to international disputes absorbed the attention of many Devon women, Eleanor Acland and Lady Florence Cecil among them.[62] It was also a principal source of debate among the WCAs,[63] to which both Clara Daymond and Mabel Ramsay belonged; indeed, Dr Ramsay, a convinced internationalist, was a longstanding member of the Medical Women's International Association and even, on one occasion, unofficially attended a session of the League of Nations in Geneva. When war finally came in 1939, women again, as they did in the First World War, became exceptionally active—in industry, in the armed forces, and on the Home Front—which had repercussions after 1945, for example, in the campaigns for equal pay and in the demand for women to play a role on policy-making committees.

Maria DiCenzo asserts that '[t]he main tension is between historians who see the glass half empty and those who see it as half full.'[64] Vera Brittain (1893–1970), one of England's most famous interwar women activists, believed the women's movement of the interwar years demanded more from its followers than had the suffrage campaign, because so many issues needed to be campaigned for at the same time.[65] Brian Harrison has noted that achievements of the women's movement 'took place within a most unfavourable political, international, intellectual and economic climate; it must not be judged by some abstract standard but in relation to the difficulties faced'.[66] These achievements were many and varied, and in contrast to the rather gloomy verdicts on the 1920s by Cicely Hamilton and Mary Willcocks quoted above, Eleanor Rathbone, an MP and the leader of NUSEC, pointed out that 'whereas during the twenty years up to 1918 only six laws specifically affecting women were passed, the next seven years saw twenty such laws';[67] Rathbone,

61. Clara Daymond was an active member of the Devon Vagrancy Committee in the 1930s, while both Lady Florence Cecil and Dame Georgiana Buller supported the Devon League of Workfinders.
62. For internationalism, see H. McCarthy, *The British People and the League of Nations: Democracy, Citizenship and Internationalism, c.1918–1945* (Manchester: Manchester University Press, 2011), and H. McCarthy, 'Associational Voluntarism in Interwar Britain', in *The Ages of Voluntarism: How We Got to the Big Society*, ed. by M. Hilton and J. McKay (Oxford: Oxford University Press for the British Academy, 2011), 47–69.
63. Pugh, *Women and the Women's Movement*, p. 242.
64. DiCenzo, 'Our freedom and its results', p. 423.
65. DiCenzo, 'Our freedom and its results', p. 430.
66. Harrison, *Prudent Revolutionaries*, p. 323.
67. Quoted in Harrison, *Prudent Revolutionaries*, p. 302.

in her views on interwar feminism, struck a mainly positive note, considering: 'Speaking generally, the results have exceeded expectations, but in some spheres of effort there have been disappointment … progress has been rapid when it depended on political action and slow when it depended on changes in heart and habits.'[68] This, therefore, is the background against which the eight Devon women worked, campaigned, negotiated and collaborated. Their achievements and those of the national campaign, not only in improving conditions and passing laws, but in engaging so many women in active citizenship, would indicate that the glass was much more full than empty. That was certainly the view of Mabel Ramsay, who, when reflecting on her long life, wrote in her memoir, 'For, perhaps, one of the greatest changes is that of the position of women. The former conventions and taboos have mostly wilted; the legal and political status of men and women is nearly equal, and there are now open to women fields of activity undreamed of before the shattering impulse of two world wars forced the tardy pace of social evolution.'[69]

The Bio-Bibliographical Background

There is remarkably little literature on Devon women who engaged locally in public life during the first half of the twentieth century. The great exception to this is Nancy Astor (1879–1964), the first woman to take her seat in the House of Commons and the only woman who fought every interwar election successfully, who has been the subject of half a dozen biographies.[70] Other relevant full-length biographies have been devoted to Astor's fellow American, Dorothy Elmhirst (1887–1968),[71] the founder of Dartington Hall (a remarkable and progressive educational establishment in South Devon), and Juanita Phillips (1880–1966),[72] an active suffragette (she was chair of the Exeter branch of the Women's Social and Political Union) and eleven times mayor of Honiton. Until very recently, even collective biographies of Devon women were thin on the

---

68. E. Rathbone, 'Changes in Public Life,' in *Our Freedom and its Results*, ed. by R. Strachey (London: Hogarth Press, 1936), p. 16.
69. Ramsay, *A Doctor's Zig-Zag Road*, p. 115.
70. These range in date from M. Collis, *Nancy Astor: An Informal Biography* (London: Faber, 1960) to A. Fort, *Nancy: The Story of Lady Astor* (London: Cape, 2012).
71. J. Brown, *Angel Dorothy: How an American Progressive Came to Devon* (London: Unbound, 2017).
72. J. Neville, *Juanita Phillips: Champion for Change in East Devon between the Wars* (Exeter: Short Run Press, 2012).

ground, comprising Todd Gray's *Remarkable Women of Devon*,[73] which gives a
snapshot of the lives of some early twentieth-century Devon women including
Mabel Ramsay, and a pamphlet entitled *Working Lives: The Careers of Seven Exeter
Women*,[74] which gives brief summaries of the lives of seven women, among
which are Jessie Montgomery (1850–1918), a suffragist and pioneer of higher
education in Exeter, who died too early to be included in this book, and
Georgiana Buller, who does feature in this book. In addition Buller has been
the subject of a short biographical essay by Julia Neville, as has Sylvia Calmady-
Hamlyn,[75] while there are also short entries in the *Oxford Dictionary of National
Biography* for Eleanor Acland by Mitzi Auchterlonie, and for Georgiana Buller
by Catherine Haines.[76] Looking at periodicals, the amount of scholarship on
Devon women (of any period) is equally paltry. The premier journal for Devon
studies, the *Report and Transactions of the Devonshire Association for the Advancement
of Science, Literature and Art* (which commenced publication in 1863) contains
only twenty articles on women in all fields including literature out of more
than 2,500 articles published over 150 years, while, in its fifty-year existence,
one can find only eight articles on women in *The Devon Historian* (which
commenced in 1970), the journal of the Devon History Society.[77]

Prior to the celebration of the centenary of women winning the vote in
1918, information about suffrage activists in Devon was mostly confined to
the two excellent reference works by Elizabeth Crawford,[78] the substantial
article by Margherita Rendel on the early activities of women suffragists in
Devon, and a slighter piece on suffrage in Plymouth by Judith Rowbotham
and Kim Stevenson.[79] The recent commemorations have, however, produced

73. T. Gray, *Remarkable Women of Devon* (Exeter: Mint Press, 2009).
74. Exeter Heritage Project, *Working Lives: The Careers of Seven Exeter Women* (Exeter: Exeter City Council, 1987).
75. J. Neville, 'Noblesse Oblige: Dame Georgiana Buller and Services for Disabled People in Twentieth-Century Devon', in *Aspects of Devon History: People, Places, Landscapes*, ed. by J. Bliss, C. Jago and E. Maycock (Exeter: Devon History Society, 2012), pp. 387–99, and J. Neville, '"They Women Have Done Well": Sylvia Calmady-Hamlyn and Women Working on the Land', in *Food, Farming and Fishing in Devon During the First World War* (Exeter: Short Run Press, 2016), pp. 129–33.
76. M. Auchterlonie, 'Acland (*née* Cropper), Eleanor Mary, Lady Acland', *Oxford Dictionary of National Biography*; C.M.C. Haines, 'Buller, Dame (Audrey Charlotte) Georgiana', *ODNB*.
77. The fact that so few articles on women can be found in these two major Devon journals does not mean that relevant information cannot be found in other periodicals, e.g. Julia Neville, 'Challenge, Conformity and Casework in Interwar England: The First Women Councillors in Devon', in *Women's History Review*, 22 (2013), 971–94.
78. E. Crawford, *The Women's Suffrage Movement: A Reference Guide, 1866–1918* (London: Routledge, 1999), and particularly relevant, *The Women's Suffrage Movement in Britain and Ireland: A Regional Survey* (London: Routledge, 2006).
79. M. Rendel, 'The Campaign in Devon for Women's Suffrage, 1866–1908', *Report and Transactions*

a flurry of new publications dealing with how Devon women organized the suffrage struggle.[80] Two of the books are part of a series entitled *Struggle and Suffrage* (Pen and Sword Press), which takes the story of women beyond the Edwardians and into the interwar period,[81] but of greater importance is the ground-breaking project by Devon History Society mentioned earlier, the *Lives of Devon Women Suffrage Activists, 1866–1918* website,[82] which has created online biographies of varying length and comprehensiveness of over 130 women, and which, hopefully, will enable more detailed analysis of the women and their activities to be undertaken in the future.

The eight women whose careers are described and analysed in this book have all been chosen for their contribution to public, professional and civic life in Devon from the beginning of the twentieth century up to the outbreak of the Second World War. There were several more women who feature in the *Oxford Dictionary of National Biography* (*ODNB*) who might have been included, but Exeter-born Clara Andrew (1862–1939), the founder of the National Children Adoption Association, and Exmouth-raised Edith Pratt (1882–1959), the general inspector of women's agricultural education at the Ministry of Agriculture, spent the interwar years pursuing their careers in London rather than Devon, while Devonport-born Emily Phipps (1865–1943), headmistress, suffragist, parliamentary candidate, barrister and trade unionist, also spent nearly all her adult life far from Devon.[83] Among other Devonian *ODNB* biographees, Margaret Partridge (1891–1967) of Nymet Rowland and Willand,

of the Devonshire Association for the Advancement of Science, 140 (2008), 111–51; J. Rowbotham and K. Stevenson, 'A Point of Justice—Granted or Fought For?: Women's Suffrage Campaigns in Plymouth and the South West', *Plymouth Law and Criminal Justice Review*, 1 (2016), 84–98.

80. For example, P. Vass's book, *Breaking the Mould: The Suffragette Story in North Devon* (Littleham, Bideford: Boundstone Books, 2017), which often extends its reach into the whole of Devon, two short publications by A. Marjoram, *The Women's Suffrage Movement in Exmouth* (Exmouth: Exmouth Historical and Archaeological Society, 2018), and 'Two Suffrage Actresses with Exmouth Connections', *Report and Transactions of the Devonshire Association for the Advancement of Science*, 151 (2019), 179–200, and recent articles by P. Bayer, 'Participation in the Female Community by Women of the Frood Family of Topsham: Gentility, Suffrage, WW1 and Afterwards', *The Devon Historian*, 87 (2018), 71–84 and, 'The Contribution of NUWSS Organisers in Devon to the Campaign for Women's Suffrage', *The Devon Historian*, 90 (2020), 53–67.

81. Relevant books published so far in the series are T. Glasspool, *Struggle and Suffrage in Plymouth: Women's Lives and the Fight for Equality* (Barnsley: Pen and Sword, 2019), and M. Crump, *Struggle and Suffrage in Torbay: Women's Lives and the Fight for Equality* (Barnsley: Pen and Sword, 2019).

82. URL: <https://www.devonhistorysociety.org.uk/news/lives-of-devons-women-suffrage-activists-1866-1918> [accessed 23 September 2020].

83. J. Keating, 'Andrew, Clara', *ODNB*; M. Auchterlonie, 'Pratt, Edith Helen', *ODNB*; H. Kean, 'Phipps, Emily Frost', *ODNB*; Phipps is also one of the four teachers whose lives are described in H. Kean, *Deeds not Words: Lives of Suffragette Teachers* (London: Pluto Press, 1990).

who founded and managed her own electrical engineering company in Devon, was too little involved in public life to qualify,[84] as was Baroness Elsie T'Serclaes (1884–1978), born Elizabeth Shapter in Exeter, who distinguished herself as a nurse in Belgium during the First World War, but whose postwar career, in the words of *ODNB*, 'seemed to lose direction'.[85] Finally, it was also felt that E.M. Delafield (the pseudonym of Mrs Edmée Elizabeth Dashwood, 1890–1943), although a Devon JP and president of her local Women's Institute in Kentisbeare, made her contribution to Devon life mostly in the fields of literature and culture rather than through her public and civic activities.[86]

Devon Women in Public and Professional Life

Of the women selected for study, Clara Daymond was the only one who was working-class (she was the daughter of a Devonport shipwright) and one of only two actually born in Devon (the other being Georgiana Buller, who was born in Crediton). Mabel Ramsay and Jessie Headridge came from the professional middle class, Calmady-Hamlyn inherited money from her mother's family, Georgiana Buller was the only daughter of Devon's best-known and most decorated military figure who had a country estate near Crediton, while Eleanor Acland was connected to the aristocracy through her mother. The final two women whose careers are discussed in this book were aristocrats, being the daughters of earls: Lady Florence Cecil, who married the second son of the 3rd Marquess of Salisbury, Prime Minister and owner of Hatfield House, was the daughter of Edward Bootle-Wilbraham, 1st Earl of Lathom, and Lady Clinton was the daughter of the 5th Earl of Antrim; she married the Hon. Charles Trefusis, who succeeded in 1904 to the title of Lord Clinton, and who, three years later, through inheritance from his uncle, became one of the richest landowners in Devon. Three of the women were educated to graduate level; Eleanor Acland studied history at Oxford, Jessie Headridge studied mathematics at Cambridge and Mabel Ramsay studied medicine at

---

84. A. Locker, 'Partridge, Margaret Mary', *ODNB*. Partridge's life and achievements are also highlighted in J. Robinson, *Ladies Can't Climb Ladders: The Pioneering Adventures of the First Professional Women* (London: Doubleday, 2020).

85. D. Condell and J. Liddiard, 'T'Serclaes, Elizabeth Blackall de (*née* Elizabeth Blackall Shapter; other married name, Elizabeth Blackall Knocker)', *ODNB*; Baroness T'Serclaes's exploits and those of her friend Mairi Chisholm during the First World War are described in D. Atkinson, *Elsie and Mairi Go to War: Two Extraordinary Women on the Western Front* (London: Preface, 2009).

86. N. Beauman, 'Dashwood (*née* de la Pasture), Edmée Elizabeth Monica (pseud of E.M. Delafield)', *ODNB*; see also V. Powell, *The Life of a Provincial Lady: A Study of E.M. Delafield and her World* (London: Heinemann, 1988).

Edinburgh and public health at Owens College, Manchester, while Sylvia
Calmady-Hamlyn attended one of the most progressive and academically
orientated boarding schools in England, without going on to study for a degree.
As was common with the generation born in the 1860s, Lady Clinton and
Lady Florence Cecil both seem to have been schooled at home by governesses,
and both bemoaned their inadequate education.

At least four of the women under study were active in the suffrage movement, some as foot-soldiers, such as Jessie Headridge who was an ordinary
member of the NUWSS,[87] and some in more responsible positions; for example,
Clara Daymond was chair and Mabel Ramsay the very active secretary of the
Three Towns and District branch of the NUWSS,[88] while Eleanor Acland was
on the Executive Committee of the People's Suffrage Federation, Vice-President
of the South-West Federation of the NUWSS, and was instrumental in the
formation of the Liberal Women's Suffrage Union. The latter three undoubtedly
developed their organizational expertise and their competence in public speaking
as they campaigned for the vote, while Clara Daymond praised the Women's
Co-operative Guild (WCG) for 'equipping women for positions of responsibility', and became the first secretary of the St Budeaux branch of the WCG
in 1904.[89] There is no evidence that Sylvia Calmady-Hamlyn was a suffragist,
but before the First World War she was well-known as an energetic breeder of
ponies, exhibiting at all the local agricultural shows and becoming the first
woman president of the Okehampton Agricultural Society in 1912, while
Georgiana Buller was active before the war as Deputy County Director of the
Red Cross Voluntary Aid Detachments. Both Lady Clinton and Lady Florence
Cecil had a strong sense of social obligation and before the First World War
undertook a considerable amount of charitable work, Lady Clinton becoming
the first county commissioner for the Girl Guides, and President of the Budleigh
Salterton Nursing Association, while Lady Florence Cecil was a typical well-
organized rector's wife, performing, as she herself said, the role of 'the best
curate' in her husband's parish of Hatfield in Hertfordshire.

Five of the eight women played a significant role during the Great War. Mabel
Ramsay served as a surgeon with the Belgian and French Red Cross, Eleanor
Acland worked for Belgian refugees and Georgiana Buller became administrator

---

87. There is a reference to a 'Miss Buller' being on the platform of an NUWSS meeting in 1910
    (*Western Times*, 18 March 1910), although her mother, Lady Audrey Buller, was a leading member
    of the National League for Opposing Women's Suffrage.
88. The Three Towns were Plymouth, Stonehouse and Devonport, which joined together in 1914
    to form the borough of Plymouth; Plymouth was elevated to city status in 1928.
89. *Western Chronicle*, 22 November 1907.

of Exeter's seven War Hospitals.[90] Sylvia Calmady-Hamlyn became County Organiser for the Devon Women's War Agricultural Committee, having served as a Board of Agriculture Inspector, while Clara Daymond, already a Poor Law Guardian in Devonport since 1907, was nominated by the WCG to serve on the Food Control Committee in Plymouth in 1917. Jessie Headridge did not undertake specific war work, although she still made a significant indirect contribution to the war effort, through maintaining very high academic standards despite being forced to relocate her school to temporary premises when the original school buildings were requisitioned as a war hospital—indeed, 1914–1919 could even be considered the high point of Headridge's career.[91] Only Lady Clinton and Lady Florence Cecil (who did not arrive in Devon until 1916, and then became immediately involved in the Exeter Diocesan Mothers' Union) did not contribute significantly to the war effort, although Lady Florence did become Vice-President of the British War Graves Association and Lady Clinton was involved in the short-lived Women Signallers Territorial Corps.

After the war ended, most of the women threw themselves enthusiastically into public life. The NUWSS had become NUSEC, which developed a close relationship with the WCAs that had also evolved out of the local suffrage societies.[92] NUSEC's remit was 'to obtain all such reforms as are necessary to secure a real equality of liberties, status and opportunity between men and women',[93] while WCAs, affiliated to both NUSEC and the National Council of Women, operated as 'non-party, non-sectarian democratic groups, whose objects were to foster a sense of citizenship in women, encourage the study of political, social and economic questions [and] secure the adequate representation of the interests and experience of women in the affairs of the community'.[94]

Eleanor Acland became President of the Exeter and District branch of NUSEC in 1923, while Daymond and Ramsay served at different times as chair and secretary of the Plymouth Citizens' Association from its earliest days in 1918–1919. Acland took a keen interest in issues affecting women as reflected on the national stage, making speeches on divorce reform, widows' pensions, and birth control, while serving as President of the Exeter Women's Welfare Association. She clashed with the Mothers' Union and Lady Florence Cecil in particular on

---

90. She was the *only* woman administrator of a group of military hospitals during the First World War.

91. The Episcopal Modern School for Girls achieved more First Class Honours in the Senior Cambridge Examinations in 1919 than any other girls' school in the country.

92. Law, *Suffrage and Power*, p. 114.

93. Quoted in Beddoe, *Back to Home and Duty*, p. 138.

94. Quoted in Law, *Suffrage and Power*, p. 113; see also pp. 51–52.

the questions of divorce and the establishment of a maternity clinic open to all married women.[95] Eleanor Acland was particularly active in Liberal politics, not just at a local level, but as a valued contributor to the party on policy, standing for the constituency of Exeter as a Liberal in the 1931 election; she also served as a JP, as a local councillor for Broadclyst and as the President of the Women's National Liberal Federation from 1929–1931. The cause of international peace was another of Acland's abiding passions, and her contribution to the Women's Peace Crusade movement of the late 1920s was immense.

A practising Methodist, Clara Daymond was elected to Plymouth Borough Council in 1919.[96] As a result of a conference on 'The Work of Women in Public Life',[97] she joined the Devon Council of Women on Public Authorities, which had been set up in 1922, and in the same year became the first and only woman chair of the Devonport Board of Guardians. Daymond worked tirelessly promoting infant welfare clinics, new housing, and women police among other causes; in 1927 she was appointed Vice-Chair of the Public Health Committee, and following the demise of Poor Law Guardians she became a senior member of the Public Assistance Committee. Mirroring to some extent the concentration of NUSEC on domestic and maternal welfare, Daymond said in 1922, 'We don't want to do men's work; we want to do our own work; it is impudence of the men to want to do everything for us, as they have done in the past. We are fully enfranchised now, and we must see that the things concerning women and girls are done by women themselves.'[98] Although issues concerning local children's homes arose in the 1930s, there is no doubting Clara Daymond's dedication to public service and the welfare of the women and children of Plymouth.

Mabel Ramsay, despite working full-time, was deeply involved in medico-politics through her work with the Medical Women's Federation (MWF),

---

95. The arguments put by both sides are analysed at considerable length in the chapter on Lady Florence Cecil.

96. Although initially sympathetic towards the Liberals, when George and Clara Daymond were both elected as Councillors, they served as independents. However, in 1924, they joined the Conservative Party as a way of combating Socialism.

97. For more information on the Devon Council of Women on Public Authorities see Julia Neville, 'Challenge, Conformity and Casework in Interwar England', p. 988.

98. *Western Morning News*, 12 October 1922. C. Hunt in 'Success with the ladies', p. 173, finds the same engagement with welfare issues by women councillors in Coventry, and quotes Pamela Graves who maintained that women sat 'on those [committees] concerned with education, housing, public amenities and maternal and child welfare', P. Graves, *Labour Women: Women in British Working-Class Politics, 1918–1939* (Cambridge: Cambridge University Press, 1994). Julia Neville has found that both Edith Splatt and Florence Browne, Exeter City councillors in the 1920s, 'acquiesced in this pigeonholing' into committees dealing with maternity and child welfare, public health and housing—see J. Neville, 'Challenge, Conformity and Casework in Interwar England', p. 981.

joining when the MWF was formed in 1917, and serving at various times as secretary, vice-president and president. She was still an active council member at her death in 1954, and the MWF enabled her to play a part on the national stage for almost forty years.[99] She was also equally deeply involved in local politics, being a strong supporter of the expansion of maternity and child welfare services within Plymouth through her membership of Plymouth Citizens' Association. Within Plymouth she supported family planning services, and fundraising for the Women's Hospital Fund. Having been active in the suffrage campaign before the war,[100] Mabel Ramsay vigorously supported Nancy Astor when Astor stood for the parliamentary seat of Plymouth Sutton in 1919, and both Astor and Ramsay worked together in the interwar period, lobbying energetically but without success for women police in Plymouth.[101] In her memoir, Mabel Ramsay said that life was split between her medical practice, her social and political work, and sleep and play.[102]

Jessie Headridge was occupied full-time with her job as a headmistress, expanding the school premises, the staff and student body, while also striving to maintain the highest academic standards. The Exeter Middle School for Girls (later the Episcopal Modern School for Girls and eventually the Bishop Blackall School) had an excellent reputation and during Headridge's tenure regularly achieved more success at getting its girls into university[103] than Exeter High School for Girls (later the Maynard School).[104] Deirdre Beddoe points out that girls' secondary schools were 'autonomous women's worlds, [and that] nowhere else did women have as much power'.[105] However, it should also be emphasized that Headridge, as headmistress, had to negotiate for extra funds for buildings or staff with the male School Governors as well as with

---

99. For example, in 1925 she was nominated by the Medical Women's Federation to serve on the Home Office Committee that enquired into 'Sexual Offences against Young Persons'.

100. Mabel Ramsay also took part in the women's census boycott of 1911, despite the fact that a criminal conviction for refusing to complete the form could have damaged her reputation and career. For more information on the boycott and the hundreds of women involved, see J. Liddington, *Vanishing for the Vote: Suffrage, Citizenship and the Battle for the Census* (Manchester: Manchester University Press, 2014).

101. Women police with the powers of arrest were not appointed in Plymouth until 1945.

102. M. Ramsay, *A Doctor's Zig-Zag Road*, p. 121.

103. 'In 1932, the year in which Miss Ragg became headmistress [and Jessie Headridge retired], twelve former pupils received degrees', M.L.E. Hadden, *Bishop Blackall School, Exeter (1877–1983)* (Exeter: the author, 1983), p. 24.

104. In 1919 'nearly a third of the examination papers were assessed as "bad", with a high failure rate', *The Maynard School: A Celebration of 350 Years, 1658–2008* (Exeter: Maynard School, 2008), p. 31.

105. Beddoe, *Back to Home and Duty*, p. 43.

Exeter City Council; that she was a regular co-opted member of the Exeter's Higher Education Sub-Committee; that she coped admirably with numerous inspections and visits by official bodies (especially the Sadler visitation of 1904[106]); that she formed part of a deputation in 1907 to Reginald McKenna, the President of the Board of Education; and that she had to implement the many changes to the way education was organized both before and after the war.[107] Headridge also engaged in wider civic life, by being a member of Exeter Citizens' Association from its formation, and by ensuring that the girls at her school supported a wide variety of charitable causes. She was also clearly acquainted with many of the leading women in Exeter, as can be seen by the people she persuaded to preside over the annual prize-giving, people such as Jessie Montgomery, Lady Clinton and Lady Florence Cecil.

Lady Florence Cecil's life was dominated by religion, not only by reason of her strong personal faith, but also as a consequence of the position she occupied as a rector's—and later a bishop's—wife. Although she married into one of the most prominent Conservative families in the land, she does not appear to have participated in party politics. Instead she devoted her time in Exeter, from her arrival in 1916 to 1936 (the date she left Devon on the death of her husband), principally to the Mothers' Union, where she stoutly defended the sanctity of marriage and large families. Lady Florence's strong sense of social obligation and her interest in maternal and child welfare also led her to engage vigorously with those she considered less fortunate than herself. She was, for example, very active within the Exeter Diocesan Association for the Care of Friendless Girls and the Waifs and Strays Society (now the Church of England Children's Society). The Diocesan Association set up two new homes for children with learning disabilities, both of which evolved as a partnership between the voluntary and the state sector, another example, as with Dame Georgiana Buller's projects, of the 'new philanthropy'.[108] The chapter on Lady Florence shows that while her continued opposition to birth control and divorce never varied, her

---

106. Michael Sadler (1861–1943) was at the time of the visitation the Professor of the History and Administration of Education at the University of Manchester and had been commissioned by Exeter's Education Committee in 1903 to report on all secondary schools in Exeter. In 1905 Sadler presented his report, which devotes six pages to the Exeter Middle School for Girls. Sadler was an egalitarian who, while Vice-Chancellor of the University of Leeds in the 1920s 'encouraged and supported the careers of a number of women' (C. Dyhouse, No Distinction of Sex?: Women in British Universities, 1870–1939 (London: Routledge, 1995), p. 77).

107. For a description and analysis of the changes, see ch. 10, 'Towards a unified system, 1900–1938', in J. Lawson and H. Silver, A Social History of Education in England (London: Methuen, 1973).

108. For more on this topic, see Elizabeth Macadam, The New Philanthropy: A Study of the Relations between the Statutory and Voluntary Social Services (London: Allen & Unwin, 1934).

attitude regarding 'fallen women' and the most appropriate training for girls did not remain static, but evolved over time.[109] Lady Florence on occasion even agreed with the proposals of NUSEC, for example, joining the Devon Council of Women on Public Authorities in 1929 to lobby for women police. She was a great supporter of Nancy Astor and encouraged women to make the most of their opportunities. She participated in civic life by being on the Executive Committee of the Exeter branch of the National Council of Women (the successor to the National Union of Women Workers), as well as being president, vice-president or a committee member of a host of other local organizations.

The toll taken by Georgiana Buller's war work, for which she had been made a Dame of the British Empire in 1920, was so severe that she withdrew from public life for several years, only returning when she was invited to become President of the Devonian Association for Cripples' Aid in 1925; however, from this point onwards, she devoted the rest of her life to assisting the disabled, being the principal agent behind the creation of the Princess Elizabeth Orthopaedic Hospital in Exeter (founded in 1927), and the St Loye's Training Centre for Cripples, which opened for men in 1937 and for women in 1938. She was adept at negotiating the growing partnership between the voluntary sector and increasing state involvement in health and welfare, a characteristic of the period between the two world wars, often described as the 'New Philanthropy'.[110] Her dedicated, practical work over almost thirty years radically altered the opportunities available to disabled people in Devon and her name will always be associated with the pioneering work of St Loye's.

Lady Clinton, from the same generation as Lady Florence Cecil, showed the same sense of social obligation, and her outlook on life largely embodied the ideals of the Primrose League,[111] of which she was a prominent member, and whose declaration of faith read: 'I declare on my honour and faith that I will devote my best ability to the maintenance of Religion, of the Estates of the Realm, and of the Imperial Ascendancy of the British Empire.'[112] She devoted much of her time to the Girl Guides and to the Devon Federation of Women's Institutes, of which she was elected president in 1920. She was

---

109. She was also active in schemes to improve housing and, with her husband the Bishop, worked to alleviate the condition of homeless men who arrived in Devon looking for work.
110. Macadam, *The New Philanthropy*.
111. The Primrose League was founded in 1883, and, although technically a non-partisan organi-zation open to people of all political persuasions, essentially functioned to support the Conservative and Unionist Party. At its height, in 1910, it had over two million members.
112. The revised declaration is cited in J.H. Robb, *The Primrose League, 1883–1906* (New York: Columbia University Press, 1942), p. 50.

particularly keen on training girls in housekeeping and for service in the Empire. In the rural sphere, she lobbied, as Calmady-Hamlyn did, for better opportunities for women in agriculture and, although a staunch Conservative, Clinton was happy to work across party lines with the leading Liberal politician, Francis Acland, in promoting the cause of women in agriculture to Devon County Council. After the passing of the Representation of the People (Equal Franchise) Act in 1928, she admitted she had become a convert to the enfranchisement of women and talked enthusiastically about women's potential for political work. Her contribution to the voluntary sector in Devon during the 1920s and 1930s was immense, and the *Western Morning News* woman columnist, Devonia, called her in 1924 'easily the busiest woman in Devon'.[113] In 1936, despite being in her mid-seventies, she took on the challenging role of president of the Devon Nursing Association, and guided it through the Second World War. Even more impressively, in 1948, at the age of 85, she cast aside any reservations she had about the state provision of services, and, with a characteristic sense of duty, oversaw the transfer of the Devon Nursing Association's responsibilities to the newly established National Health Service.

Sylvia Calmady-Hamlyn, as befitted a person who lived in the middle of the Devon countryside, spent much of her time in the early years after the end of the First World War on the development of Women's Institutes, becoming Chair of the Devon Federation, a post she resigned in 1924 in protest against the dominance of the 'county lady'. She was among the first women to be appointed a JP in Devon, in 1920, participated in meetings of the Devon Council on Women on Public Authorities, and was also one of the first women to serve on the Council of the Devon County Agricultural Association, being appointed in October 1914.[114] Although from 1920 to 1940 she was a full Governor of Seale-Hayne agricultural college, she argued that it was better to train women in a separate institution for female agricultural education, rather than run a course for women at Seale-Hayne (where women were admitted to full-time study only in 1934). Politically left of centre (she was originally a Liberal, inclined in the early 1920s towards the Labour Party, and stood in 1939 as an independent candidate in a local county by-election), her life was centred on her religion (she was a devout Roman Catholic), her pony-breeding (she established the Dartmoor Pony Society), her role as a JP and her interest in

---

113. *Western Morning News*, 9 July 1933.
114. Council member Mr P.C.M. Veitch, a member of the well-known Exeter firm of nurserymen, Robert Veitch and Sons, 'remarked that it showed the broadmindedness of the members in electing a lady as a member of the Council', reported the *Western Times*, 27 October 1914.

women's agricultural education, a subject on which, as Julia Neville says, 'her expertise was too good to waste'.

When reading the individual chapters it will become clear that the women whose biographies are included in this book participated in the public and professional life of Devon in a way that not only mirrored the activities of national organizations, but also enabled them to make their own choices depending on local circumstances. Seven of the eight women dedicated a large part of their lives to improving the cause of women, in their own different ways, through teaching, agricultural education, greater awareness of citizenship, the improvement of welfare services, political lobbying, and through the fellowship of the Women's Institute or the Mothers' Union. The exception is Georgiana Buller, who devoted her life to a cause in which gender was less prominent, that of disabled people. This book is an attempt to show how, at regional as well as national level, there were significant numbers of female leaders in Devon who saw not only that women's potential was being undervalued by society, but that they intended to do something about this.

CHAPTER ONE

Eleanor Margaret Acland (1878–1933)

MITZI AND PAUL AUCHTERLONIE

Eleanor Acland, *c.*1930

Eleanor Acland was born into an old Westmoreland family in 1878 as Eleanor Margaret Cropper. Sir James Cropper (1823–1900), her grandfather on the paternal side, was the Liberal Member of Parliament for Kendal, while Lord Knutsford (Sir Henry Holland, 1825–1914), her grandfather on the maternal side, was Secretary for the Colonies during the Marquis of Salisbury's Premiership. Her mother, the Hon. Edith Emily Holland (1853–1923) was one of the first women members of a Board of Guardians.[1] Eleanor's father, Charles James Cropper (1852–1924) was High Sheriff of Westmoreland and ran the family paper-making business in Kendal. Eleanor writes affectionately about her childhood in the posthumously published memoir *Good-bye for the Present* (1935), and describes her father as 'the most thrilling of the grown-ups … a handsome

---

1. *Western Times (WT)*, 6 February 1931. From an article announcing her candidature for the parliamentary constituency of Exeter in 1931.

Mitzi Auchterlonie and Paul Auchterlonie, 'Chapter One: Eleanor Margaret Acland (1878–1933)' in: *Devon Women in Public and Professional Life 1900–1950: Votes, Voices and Vocations*. University of Exeter Press (2021). © Mitzi Auchterlonie and Paul Auchterlonie
DOI: 10.47788/KEOH4831

man of boisterous spirits, liable to short sharp flurries of temper and moods of gloom that vanished into geniality as suddenly as they appeared, always on easy terms with every man, woman and child of whatever station in life'.[2] Her father was killed in 1924 while out hunting with Eleanor's 18-year-old son, Richard Acland.

Eleanor claims that she 'could read by the time I was three years old',[3] and was initially taught by her mother and her nurse, but 'from seven years old, began to share a governess with the cousins in the Vicarage'.[4] When she was 18 or so, Eleanor was sent to St Leonard's School in St Andrews in Scotland, described as a 'top-ranking progressive girls' boarding school',[5] 'which had been developed with courage and farsightedness to excel, rather than simply to provide for girls an imitation of the education available to boys at the British public schools'.[6] She stayed at St Leonard's until around 1898, making the acquaintance of Liberal loyalist and suffragist Catherine Marshall (1880–1961), who became a lifelong friend.[7] She entered Somerville College at the University of Oxford in 1898, graduating with a first-class degree in history in 1900.[8] After leaving Oxford, in common with many young women who felt that their 'class privilege entailed responsibility',[9] she worked for some time at the University Women's Settlement in Birmingham.[10]

---

2. E. Acland, *Good-bye for the Present: The Story of Two Childhoods, Milly 1878–88 & Ellen, 1913–24* (London: Hodder & Stoughton, 1935), p. 89.

3. Acland, *Good-bye for the Present*, p. 149.

4. Acland, *Good-bye for the Present*, p. 151.

5. J. Vellacott, *From Liberal to Labour: The Story of Catherine Marshall* (Montreal: McGill-Queen's University Press, 1993), p. 9. Other prominent feminists to attend St Leonard's School during the late nineteenth century who also campaigned for women's suffrage were Louisa Garrett Anderson (1873–1943) who was there from 1886 to 1891, Ida O'Malley (1874–1939), who attended the school from around 1889 to 1892, Chrystal Macmillan (1872–1935), who left St Leonard's in 1891 or 1892, and Margaret Haig Thomas (1883–1958), later Viscountess Rhondda, who was at St Leonard's from 1899 to around 1902. The headmistress of St Leonard's from 1882 to 1896 was Frances Dove (1847–1942), a graduate of Girton College, who was not only 'passionately determined to see girls enjoying the same opportunities for education as boys' (p. 14) but also became a dedicated supporter of women's suffrage and active in the Central Society for Women's Suffrage—for Frances Dove and suffrage, see C. Cartwright, *Burning to Get the Vote: The Women's Suffrage Movement in Central Buckinghamshire, 1904–1914* (Buckingham: University of Buckingham Press, 2013).

6. Vellacott, *From Liberal to Labour*, p. 11.

7. Vellacott, *From Liberal to Labour*, p. 371.

8. *Calendar of the Association for Promoting the Education of Women in Oxford for the year 1909–1910* (Oxford: The Association, 1910), pp. 40 and 64.

9. J. Vellacott, *Pacifists, Patriots and the Vote: The Erosion of Democratic Suffragism in Britain during the First World War* (Basingstoke: Palgrave Macmillan, 2007), p. 12. Other suffragists born around the same time as Eleanor who worked in settlements or similar institutions included Maude Royden (1876–1956) and Kathleen Courtney (1878–1974).

10. *WT*, 6 February 1931. The Birmingham Women's Settlement (later just the Birmingham

In 1905 she married Francis Acland,[11] with whom she had four children: Richard (1906–1990), a prominent Liberal politician and later founder of the Commonwealth Party, Arthur Geoffrey (1908–1964), also active in the Liberal Party, Cuthbert Henry (1910–1979) and Eleanor (1913–1924), known as Ellen, who was tragically killed in a road accident at the gates to their country house of Killerton in Devon, and whose short life is commemorated in the second half of *Good-bye for the Present*. Some family letters survive from the period of Francis and Eleanor's courtship, and it is clear that, at least in Francis's case, they had a more modern relationship than their parents, with Eleanor noting that 'the generation before us allow us to behave so much more naturally that the last generation but one'.[12]

Francis Acland (1874–1939) had been born to aristocratic and politically active parents.[13] After public school and Oxford University, he worked as assistant director of secondary education in the West Riding of Yorkshire.[14] In 1905 he was adopted as the prospective Liberal candidate for the Yorkshire constituency of Richmond and, supported by Eleanor, won the seat from the Tories by 102 votes. He was a man of great energy and conviction and he and Eleanor 'covered the whole of that rough Yorkshire dale constituency on bicycles and only hired a car on polling-day'.[15] Like his wife, he was dedicated to the cause of women's suffrage.

Settlement) was founded in 1899 by wealthy women philanthropists to provide services mainly for women and children in one of Birmingham's most deprived areas. It was initially staffed just by women and would have been a challenging environment for Eleanor. For more information see J. Glasby, *Poverty and Opportunity: 100 years of the Birmingham Settlement* (Studley, Warwickshire: Brewin Books, 1999).

11. *Manchester Courier and Lancashire General Advertiser*, 1 September 1905.

12. Devon Heritage Centre File 1148M/14/Series II/91. Quoted in H. French and M. Rothery, *Man's Estate: Landed Gentry Masculinities, c.1660–c.1900* (Oxford: Oxford University Press, 2012), where the relationship of Francis's father Arthur to both his wife and his son is sensitively analysed on pp. 185, 210–11, 216–20, 224.

13. Francis's father Arthur (1847–1926) was an academic, educationalist and had been Liberal MP for Rotherham from 1885 to 1899. Francis's mother, Alice (1849–1935), known as Elsie, helped her husband politically and had been an active member of the co-operative movement and advocate of women's advancement until her health failed. Both may well have had an influence of Francis's young bride. See A. Acland, *A Devon Family: The Story of the Aclands* (London & Chichester: Phillimore, 1981), M. Purvis, 'Acland (née Cunningham), Alice Sophia, Lady Acland', *Oxford Dictionary of National Biography*, DOI <https://doi.org/10.1093/ref:odnb/56454> and A. Ockwell, 'Acland, Sir Arthur Herbert Dyke, Thirteenth Baronet', *ODNB*, DOI <https://doi. org/10.1093/ref:odnb/30327> for more information on Francis's parents.

14. Francis Acland was a dedicated Liberal politician, who was MP for Richmond (Yorkshire) for 1906–1910, Camborne from 1910 to 1922, Tiverton from 1923 to 1924 and North Cornwall from 1932 to 1939. For more information on him, see the introduction to *Killerton, Camborne and Westminster: The Political Correspondence of Sir Francis and Lady Acland, 1910–1929*, ed. by G. Tregidga (Exeter: Devon and Cornwall Record Society, 2006) and Acland, *Devon Family*, pp. 141–52.

15. Acland, *Devon Family*, p. 143.

Campaign for Women's Suffrage

During the early years of her marriage Eleanor Acland was occupied in bringing up her young family, but from at least as early as 1908 she became politically active in her own right in the cause of Liberalism and particularly in support of women's and adult suffrage. She campaigned for votes for women all over England, from Milnthorpe and Bradford in the North, to Felixstowe in the East and Falmouth in the West.[16] She wrote in a wide variety of newspapers on the subject, from upmarket broadsheets like *The Times* and the *Manchester Guardian*, to the *Daily News*, *Nation* and *Westminster Gazette*.[17] She corresponded with a wide range of politicians and activists on the question of the franchise, including Christabel Pankhurst and Emmeline Pethick-Lawrence of the militant Women's Social and Political Union (WSPU),[18] as well as with her many friends in the Liberal Party and in the non-militant National Union of Women's Suffrage Societies (NUWSS), women like Catherine Marshall and Kathleen Courtney.[19] The WSPU constantly asked how women could continue to be Liberals when it was that party, when in office, which refused to grant women the parliamentary vote. On 19 February 1908, Christabel Pankhurst wrote to Acland:

> I should very much like to know what is the true explanation of the action of those Liberal women who, in spite of the continued refusal of the Government to grant the vote to women, continue to support the Liberal Party? Undoubtedly some of them are women who are not prepared to run the risk of losing the approval of the men of their Party by making a real fight for Women's Suffrage. You suggest that others who are supporting this anti-suffrage Government are acting in perfectly good faith and I understand that you claim to be one of those. I can only say that I think your policy a very unwise one. How can you fail to see that by giving this unconditional support to the Government, you are making it easy for them to continue to withhold the Parliamentary Franchise from Women?

---

16. *Common Cause (CC)*, 16 September 1910, 25 April 1912, and *West Briton and Cornwall Advertiser*, 7 October 1912.
17. Extracts from her letters to the latter three publications are quoted in the issues of *CC* for 28 April 1911, 25 July 1913 and 25 January 1912, respectively.
18. Devon Heritage Centre File 1148M/14/Series II/575–577.
19. Many examples of her correspondence can be found in the Catherine Marshall papers in the Cumbria Record Office, Carlisle, in File DMar/3/5.

Acland belonged to the Women's Liberal Federation (WLF) as well as the NUWSS, and she was also a member of the Executive Committee of the People's Suffrage Federation, which had been founded in October 1909 as a non-party organization and was the outcome

> of a strong belief on the part of the promoters that the enfran-
> chisement of women—being a part of the movement towards a
> truly representative and democratic government—could best be
> carried through in alliance with the progressive forces in politics—
> and could only be realized in a really effective manner by the
> reform of the franchise in the sense of Adult Suffrage.[20]

Her views on suffrage were liberal with both a capital and a small L, and from her many letters and speeches it is clear that she was in favour not only of votes for women, but also general franchise reform and adult suffrage as well, although she was strongly against the use of violent tactics.[21] In early 1910 she can be found addressing Liberal women in Manchester (she was living in London during this period), where she argued against giving the vote to women on the same terms as men because of the 'evils and absurdities of the present electoral law', and that 'the real qualification for the franchise should be tax-paying. Every adult citizen paid taxes. Every married woman paid taxes out of her household expenditure. The simplest and fairest thing to say, therefore, was that all adult men and all adult women should have the vote.'[22] She expanded on her views in a well-argued letter to the *Manchester Guardian* in which she attacked the contention of an anonymous correspondent that allowing women municipal voters the parliamentary franchise would resolve the issue.[23]

Later, in October 1910, she engaged in correspondence with the left-wing intellectual, political journalist and suffragist H.N. Brailsford, over the failure of the Conciliation Bill to pass,[24] claiming that 'the suffrage societies by their

---

20. Quoted in S.S. Holton, *Feminism and Democracy: Women's Suffrage and Reform Politics in Britain, 1900–1918* (Cambridge: Cambridge University Press, 1986), p. 63.
21. Her attitude to the militants can hardly have been improved when her husband opened a 'private and unstamped' letter which contained a noxious substance that blinded him for two hours. *The Cornishman*, 13 February 1913, which reported the incident (it took place in Camborne, the seat for which Francis Acland was MP) assumed it to be the work of suffragettes.
22. *Manchester Guardian*, 9 April 1910.
23. *Manchester Guardian*, 16 April 1910.
24. *Manchester Guardian*, 3 October 1910, 7 October 1910, 11 October 1910. The first Conciliation Bill was introduced in October 1910 and proposed a limited parliamentary franchise for women. Asquith immediately said that the bill would be shelved.

contemptuous and antagonistic attitude to Mr. Howard's Bill[25]... and by their recent activities of abusing Liberal suffragists are making it harder for the Liberal party to take to the question with enthusiasm and on real democratic lines'.[26] Her husband shared her views, and attended a meeting with her in April 1911 when 'Liberal and Labour members in favour of adult suffrage met the executive of the People's Suffrage Federation ... [and] decided to ask the Prime Minister to receive a deputation [on the question].'[27]

Acland also appears to have been active in the NUWSS, and was a vice-president of the South-West Federation, which had been created in 1910 as a result of the revision of the NUWSS constitution.[28] She contributed several letters to the NUWSS periodical *Common Cause*, in one of which she outlined her opinion that the franchise should be based on citizenship not property, and should encompass all classes:

> The only consistently democratic method of doing so [tackling the Women's Suffrage Question] would be by a measure basing the franchise on male and female citizenship, abandoning our absurd property and rent-paying basis ... If any Liberal woman desires the vote for herself but dreads one for her cook, she is failing the Women's Suffrage cause, not by being too loyal to Liberalism, but by a secret disloyalty to the cardinal principles of democracy.[29]

Despite her writing to Kathleen Courtney that 'I hate the militants' methods, but I do admire the way they put ladylike scruples aside',[30] in general Eleanor Acland remained solidly opposed to militancy. In a letter to Christabel Pankhurst in February 1908 she maintained:

---

25. Geoffrey Howard's 1909 bill was an adult suffrage measure, which was dropped owing to the dissolution of Parliament.
26. *Manchester Guardian*, 7 October 1910.
27. *The Times*, 5 April 1911. Francis Acland spelled out his views on adult suffrage in a letter to James Drummond, Prime Minister Asquith's private secretary; for the full text of the letter date November 1912, see Tregidga, *Killerton, Camborne and Westminster*, pp. 59–60.
28. Vellacott, *Pacifists, Patriots and the Vote*, pp. 4–5. According to *CC*, 29 November 1912, page 592, Eleanor accepted the post as one of the three Vice-Presidents of the South-Western Federation at a meeting in Plymouth chaired by Mabel Ramsay.
29. *CC*, 18 August 1910. Most of her other letters to *CC* dealt with the attitude of the Liberal Party to women's suffrage, or the intricate politics of the Conciliation Bills, for example those of 25 August 1910, 20 October 1910, 27 October 1910, 27 July 1911, 3 August 1911, 26 October 1911 and 21 December 1911.
30. Letter from Eleanor Acland to Kathleen Courtney in the Catherine Marshall papers, Cumbria Record Office, quoted by Vellacott, *From Liberal to Labour*, p. 424, note 66.

We believe our own [non-militant] tactics to be much more effective. But for a disastrous demonstration on the part of certain women in the House of Commons when the women's suffrage bill came up for second reading in this Parliament, we should be a great deal nearer getting that bill taken up by the government than we are now.[31]

She later condemned the actions of the WSPU as 'hysterical' (ironically, a common anti-suffragist accusation), arguing that they had lost women the chance of gaining the franchise through violence and that they 'had no idea what was going on in the political world'.[32]

In 1913 Acland was instrumental in the formation of the breakaway Liberal Women's Suffrage Union (LWSU),[33] which campaigned to ensure that anti-suffrage parliamentary candidates were not selected for the Liberal Party. Eleanor wrote to Catherine Marshall, 'Asquith must go and ... the LWSU must work energetically for his resignation ... What we want is a Suffrage party in power. And I believe the Liberal Women's Suffrage Union is in the right lines to get that.'[34] Eleanor then 'embarked on a sustained campaign to wrest control of the WLF policy from those who had exercised it unchallenged since 1892'.[35] She outlined the case for the new organization in a letter in the *Liberal Federation Women's News*[36] and wrote to Lloyd George seeking support in 1913 for the LWSU policy towards Liberal candidates.[37]

Acland resigned her position of Vice-President of the South-West Federation of the NUWSS in June 1914 following the NUWSS's decision

---

31. Devon Heritage Centre File 1148M/14/Series II/576, dated 24 February 1908. The bill referred to is presumably the bill to enfranchise women householders introduced by Willoughby Dickinson in 1907, which was talked out during its second reading in March 1907, following the arrest of over seventy suffragettes who attempted to storm the Houses of Parliament.

32. *West Briton and Cornwall Advertiser*, 10 October 1912.

33. C. Hirshfield, 'Fractured Faith: Liberal Party Women and the Suffrage Issue in Britain, 1892–1914', *Gender and History*, 2 (1990), pp. 186–88, who categorizes Eleanor as 'an ardent feminist'.

34. Letter from Eleanor Acland to Catherine Marshall dated 19 December 1913 in the Catherine Marshall Papers, Cumbria Record Office, quoted by Hirshfield, 'Fractured Faith', p. 196.

35. Vellacott, *From Liberal to Labour*, p. 186. Reports of the meeting of the WLF at Westminster when Eleanor and Eva McLaren tried to wrest control of the Federation from the Countess of Carlisle can be found in the *Dundee Courier*, 7 May 1913 and *Grantham Journal*, 10 May 1913. Reports of the formation of the new organization can be found in the *Manchester Courier and Lancashire General Advertiser*, 14 July 1913.

36. *Liberal Federation Women's News* 4.11 (November 1913); the letter is quoted in full in Tregidga, *Killerton, Camborne and Westminster*, pp. 65–67.

37. Hirshfield, 'Fractured Faith', pp. 188 and 196; Holton, *Feminism and Democracy*, p. 120; Vellacott, *From Liberal to Labour*, pp. 228–29, 260–61; Parliamentary Archives File LG/C/10/2/12, Eleanor Acland to David Lloyd George, 3 November 1913.

to support Labour Party candidates by establishing an Election Fighting Fund, arguing that 'the present policy of the NUWSS is alienating Liberals ... and makes the work I am trying to do among Liberals open to misunderstanding'.[38] She did not, however, stop working with the NUWSS, and once war broke out channelled her energies into supporting the war effort, publishing articles and letters in *Common Cause* on 'The care of mothers and babies', 'Working Women's Clubs' and the 'Foolish tone of fashion articles'.[39] She also spoke at a public meeting chaired by Millicent Fawcett in February 1915 on 'The NUWSS and the War',[40] suggesting that 'when the peace settlement between the different countries was considered, they could say, "We have fought for freedom, let us have real freedom, and put down the militarism which says that men shall have the right to govern women, because they are physically stronger".'[41]

War Work

Despite this collaboration with the NUWSS, most of Acland's activities during the war were non-political and the bulk of her time was spent working for Belgian refugees. She was both a patron of the Chelsea Committee for Belgian Refugees[42] and Committee Secretary of the Belgian Repatriation Fund,[43] where she

> organised fund- and goods-raising and visited Holland to see schemes for housing refugees in Dutch camps. She was aware that the word 'Repatriation' was restrictive and was at pains to explain that it included the type of work undertaken by the British in France after the Franco-Prussian war and in South Africa after the Boer war. The Repatriation Committee worked with the Royal Society of Agriculture, the Friends War Relief Committee, the Belgian Town Planning Committee and the War Refugees Committee as a Joint Committee for mutual information and united action when the time comes ... For her work

---

38. Tregidga, *Killerton, Camborne and Westminster*, p. 70.
39. Published in the issues for 4 September 1914, 9 October 1914 and 19 February 1915 respectively.
40. *Daily Herald*, 30 January 1915.
41. *Walsall Advertiser*, 15 February 1915.
42. K. Storr, *Excluded from the Record: Women, Refugees and Relief, 1914–1929* (London: Peter Lang, 2009), p. 40.
43. *Kent and Sussex Courier*, 30 July 1915.

with Belgians, Eleanor Acland was awarded the *Médaille de la Reine Elisabeth*.[44]

Eleanor Acland and the Liberal Party

Francis Acland's uncle Charles died in 1919, and Francis's father, although he inherited the baronetcy, preferred to remain in London. With no cabinet position, Francis moved from London to Devon 'in order to familiarize himself with the estates'.[45] Initially, he and Eleanor lived at Sprydoncote on the Acland estates, finally moving into the Acland family seat of Killerton near Exeter in 1923.

During the war Francis had been Under-Secretary of State for Foreign Affairs, then Financial Secretary to the Treasury until 1916, and had been made a Privy Councillor in 1915. He had been hoping to become President of the Board of Education,[46] and finally take his place in cabinet, when the Asquith government fell in December 1916 and Lloyd George became Prime Minister of a coalition government. Francis, 'although offering to support the new administration "in any way possible", now went into the political wilderness with the other anti-Coalition Liberals'.[47] Francis was concerned about Asquith's lack of progressive policies and depressed about the state of the Liberal Party as he prepared to fight to retain his parliamentary seat of Camborne in the 1918 election.[48] Eleanor, who had apparently been offered a seat in the forthcoming election herself,[49] proved an effective campaigner for her husband, dealing with hecklers and targeting the new female voters.[50] She was as depressed as her husband about the state of the Liberal Party,

---

44. Storr, *Excluded from the Record*, pp. 53–54.
45. Acland, *Devon Family*, p. 151.
46. Tregidga, *Killerton, Camborne and Westminster*, p. 12.
47. Tregidga, *Killerton, Camborne and Westminster*, p. 12.
48. Tregidga, *Killerton, Camborne and Westminster*, p. 12. In a letter to Eleanor dated November 1917, Francis wrote 'I really think the Liberal party is dead & that one will simply have to think of men and policies after the war—not of parties', *Killerton, Camborne and Westminster*, p. 106.
49. Tregidga, *Killerton, Camborne and Westminster*, p. 25. Tregidga, the editor of the correspondence, does not source this information.
50. Tregidga, *Killerton, Camborne and Westminster*, p. 25. The Representation of the People Act of February 1918 gave a limited number of women the vote, while the Parliament (Qualification of Women) Act of November 1918 allowed women to be elected to Parliament. The first election under the new acts was held in December 1918. Hirshfield suggests that 'with the passage of enfranchising legislation in 1918, the suffrage issue was defused as a source of conflict among Liberals' ('Fractured Faith', p. 188) and there appear to be no letters or speeches by Eleanor that give her reaction to these momentous pieces of legislation.

describing English politics in 1918 as 'so utterly in the gutter', writing to her husband with horror in 1918 about 'the Northcliffe-Lloyd-George caucus',[51] and suggesting that 'the Lloyd-George plot seems to me so vile & so likely to succeed in putting in the Tories ... that I am driven to ask even at this 11th hour, whether it might just conceivably be your duty to stand down.'[52] She goes on to suggest in the same letter that 'we could make distinct headway towards creating a real Lib.Lab coalition not merely for the constituency but for the whole country',[53] concluding, 'The Labour manifesto is splendid I think—far better on international points than the average Liberal dare be'.[54] Eleanor's interest in the possibility of working with the Labour Party can also be seen in two letters written to her by Sir Charles Trevelyan (1870–1958), a Liberal defector to the Labour Party.[55]

Eleanor was, however, not just her husband's main source of support and ambitious on his behalf, but was also heavily involved herself in Liberal politics. Nationally, she was a member of the Central Executive of the Women's National Liberal Federation from 1919, and president from 1929 to 1931. Locally, she was elected president of the Devon Union of Women's Liberal Associations in November 1919,[56] having become president of the Exeter Women's Free Liberal Association earlier that year.[57] Acland defended Asquith's role as Prime Minister during the first two years of the war at a meeting of the Exeter Women's Liberal Association in 1920, arguing that 'the way the Liberal Leader had been insulted and misrepresented during the past few years was a scandal',[58] and was still arguing in 1923 that 'the Liberals who joined the forces of the Conservatives in 1915 [had to make] up their minds to cut

---

51. Alfred Harmsworth (1860–1935) was a major newspaper proprietor and became Baron Northcliffe in 1905. He was appointed head of the British War Mission to the United States in 1917 and as Tregidga says 'by this time, there was growing concern over his erratic behaviour and his claims to influence government policy' (Tregidga, *Killerton, Camborne and Westminster*, p. 105, note 4).

52. Tregidga, *Killerton, Camborne and Westminster*, p. 125. In fact, Francis Acland won Camborne by 532 votes from the Labour candidate, while the Unionist prospective candidate, Captain G.F. Thomas-Peter, who had been stationed in India during the War, failed to return to Britain in time to be nominated.

53. Tregidga, *Killerton, Camborne and Westminster*, p. 125

54. Tregidga, *Killerton, Camborne and Westminster*, p. 126.

55. Tregidga, *Killerton, Camborne and Westminster*, pp. 134–37. Charles Trevelyan had been Liberal MP for Elland in Leeds from 1899 to 1918, but left to join the Labour Party, becoming MP for Newcastle Central from 1922 to 1931.

56. *WT*, 25 November 1919.

57. *WT*, 26 June 1919. The Free Liberals were those who opposed Lloyd George's coalition government.

58. *WT*, 5 March 1920.

themselves off from Conservative money and Conservative support and come back to rely on Liberal support to get them in Parliament again.'[59] When the first Labour government was formed in January 1924 under Ramsay MacDonald, Eleanor commented in a speech to the Devon Union of Women's Liberal Associations that

> The present situation was very interesting and whatever they thought of it, it was a great improvement on the last Parliament. They had the progressive forces in control of the situation. They did not agree with the Labour policy or their whole policy. They did not want Socialism, because they believed in private individual enterprise as being the way of getting the best out of the nation. A great deal of the Labour programme was taken from the Liberal programme, and if Labour tried to do some of the things they were keen on doing, the Devon Liberal members, who were all real democrats, would be pleased to support the Labour Government in power. She regarded the women's position in the new Parliament as very much improved, and she hoped before a new General Election that they would have a simplification of the present electoral system. She wanted to see every man and woman of twenty-one a voter on a simple residential qualification.[60]

However, by May 1924, after just four months of the Labour Party being in government, her position against Socialism had hardened. In a speech at a major conference in Devonport, she said:

> Many people think that the Liberal principles are milk and water Socialism ... She did not believe that the Socialistic idea would lead to progress in this country. What it had done in many places was to hinder progress and the production of wealth. Before we tackle the distribution of wealth we have to make sure that

59. *Western Morning News and Western Daily Mercury (WMN)*, 26 January 1923 and *WT*, 2 February 1923.
60. *WT*, 25 January 1924. Eleanor Acland was not the only Liberal woman to favour increased Liberal-Labour cooperation. Both Margery Corbett Ashby and Eva Hubback argued for a Lib–Lab pact on more than one occasion, and Hubback eventually stood as a Labour candidate for Hendon Borough Council in 1932 (B. Harrison's *Prudent Revolutionaries: Portraits of British Feminists between the Wars* (Oxford: Clarendon Press, 1987), pp. 203–204 and 296). As Harrison says, 'Like so many progressive inter-war intellectuals and feminists, Hubback hovered between Liberals and Labour ... and called herself a Lib.Lab' (p. 296).

whatever plan we try is going to be good for the production side. The Liberal prescription for the troubles at the present time is not a kind of watered-down Socialism, but something quite different. I cannot get away from the thought that Socialism leads right away from liberty and right into a kind of industrial conscription.[61]

Eleanor Acland attributed the Liberal Party's poor showing at the 1924 General Election to the Socialists (her husband lost his seat at Tiverton), writing to her son Richard that 'The Labour Party have done a lot of harm.'[62] At the same time Eleanor also began to look more favourably on Lloyd George, particularly after he developed his rural land policy; this was strongly supported by her husband Francis and was officially launched in September 1925 in front of a crowd of 20,000 at Killerton.[63] In a letter to her son Richard dated January 1926, Eleanor said 'I went and made a Liberal speech at Bath which so impressed myself that I reversed my previous decision which was that politics are a rotten game and I'd have no more to do with them. I now think that if you believe in your party's principles at all, you are most of all bound to work for them when the party is in difficulties,'[64] and in a subsequent letter of February 1926 she complained about attacks on Lloyd George: 'LG is violently abused in letters to the Nation—raking up all his past blunders. People who feel they can't stick to the Liberal party because he is one of their leaders ought to have walked out last year. This useless bickering simply disheartens everyone, LG himself is behaving with extraordinary magnanimity.'[65] Her anger against 'a small coterie whose main idea of Liberal work is to jockey

---

61. *WMN*, 2 May 1924.
62. Tregidga, *Killerton, Camborne and Westminster*, p. 148.
63. M. Dawson, 'Politics in Devon and Cornwall, 1900–1931' (unpublished doctoral thesis, University of London, London School of Economics and Political Science, 1991). Dawson describes Lloyd George's policy document called *The Land and the Nation* (known popularly as the Green Book), which was published three weeks after the Killerton meeting, thus: 'At the centre of the Green Book policy was the concept of "cultivating tenure", in effect the nationalisation of agricultural land with compensation for the landlords. It was argued that landlordism had irretrievably broken down and that, as a result, agriculture was starved of leadership and working capital. Owner occupation was not the answer because the price of land meant that the purchasers over-mortgaged themselves and consequently lacked the money to farm efficiently. Cultivated tenure would give the farmer all the security of ownership, without tying up his working capital' (p. 246). For the number attending the policy declaration, see National Trust, *Killerton, Devon: A Souvenir Guide* (Swindon: National Trust, 2014), p. 19.
64. Tregidga, *Killerton, Camborne and Westminster*, p. 153. The speech was described as 'rousing' by the *Western Daily Press*, 29 January 1926.
65. Tregidga, *Killerton, Camborne and Westminster*, p. 155.

LG out of the party' boiled over in a letter to her son Richard in May 1926, where she even went to far as to say that she would have voted for the Labour Party and against the Liberal candidate in the recent by-election in Hammersmith.[66] In letters to her son Richard in May and June 1926 she suggested that, 'If a new party emerges, led by LG & the more reasonable Labour men, I would rather belong to that,'[67] and it would appear that she was involved, at least occasionally, in the inner circle of Liberals who were involved in Lloyd George's policy discussions: 'Daddy is going to stay the weekend with Lloyd George at his house in Surrey [Churt], together with Maynard Keynes and Ramsay Muir (two other unpaid supporters!). I was asked too but can't go. I suppose they are going to discuss a programme for a new party.'[68]

However, her basic belief in the principles of Liberalism never wavered and she was buoyed by Lloyd George's radical approach to problems in agriculture and especially by the Liberal Party's solution to the spectre of mass unemployment, which was based on *Britain's Industrial Future*, a substantial report produced by Liberal politicians and economists including John Maynard Keynes in 1928. Eleanor was much encouraged by the Liberal Party's showing in the 1929 election when it received five and a half million votes, yet only won fifty-nine seats. In the same year, Eleanor was elected president of the Women's National Liberal Federation, and she aired her post-election views in *The Liberal Women's News*:

> I think we must admit that for some time after 1924, we have been concentrating, on public platforms, too much on criticising the Conservative government; and that is a method which serves very well when there are only two parties; but when there are three parties we may thereby be making converts not only to Liberalism, but to the fiercer form of anti-Toryism, namely 'Labour'. In the light of this survey, let us face the question 'What Now?' Shall we accept the Invitations so patronisingly made to us to merge with the other two parties? We cannot do so without a complete denial of our Liberal faith. It would mean declaring our belief either in Protection or in Nationalisation. Worse still, it would mean abandoning our historic stand for individual Freedom.

---

66. Tregidga, *Killerton, Camborne and Westminster*, pp. 157–58.
67. Tregidga, *Killerton, Camborne and Westminster*, p. 157.
68. Tregidga, *Killerton, Camborne and Westminster*, p. 158.

For the more one gets to know about the driving force of the Tory
or the Labour Party, the more one realises that neither of them
really respect that freedom … Personally it would go against the
grain with me to become party to the bullying methods either of
the Tory or the Labour brand.[69]

Eleanor Acland and Peacemaking

Apart from party politics, one of the main issues that concerned Eleanor
Acland as a Liberal was internationalism,[70] and her obituary in the *Western
Morning News and Devon and Exeter Daily Gazette*, 13 December 1933, said that
'she held that the women's movement and the peace movement were very
closely allied'.[71] She was certainly a firm believer in diplomatic rather than
military solutions to disputes, never losing hope that the League of Nations
would bring peace to the world.[72] In one of her first speeches after the war,
she remarked that 'The great hope of the future of the world lay in the League
of Nations,' which she saw as having a very wide remit:

> The League would have to touch industrial matters as well as
> militaristic and political ones. It would have to induce better condi-
> tions of Labour everywhere, and put an end to sweating, if only
> to save the workers of different countries from the perils of under-
> cutting, or being undercut. No tariffs or preference would prevent
> dumping as long as goods were being produced in any country by
> miserably-paid labourers. The only real remedy was to do away
> with sweating everywhere. As women, many of them mothers,
> they had an enormous incentive to educate themselves in the
> knowledge of all that the League of Nations stood for … because
> it would be their children who would pay the price if the League

---

69. *The Liberal Women's News*, June 1929, republished in Tregidga, *Killerton, Camborne and Westminster*,
pp. 164–66.
70. In the biography of her son Sir Richard Acland in the *Oxford Dictionary of National Biography*,
Eleanor was described as the 'outspoken anti-war daughter of Charles James Cropper'; see A.F.
Thompson, 'Acland, Sir Richard Thomas Dyke, Fifteenth Baronet', *ODNB*, DOI <https://doi.
org/10.1093/ref:odnb/39848>.
71. Eleanor Acland's prescient remark quoted in the same article from the *WMN* that 'The next
war, if there was one, would be fought mainly in the air, and our modern homes had no defence
against such attack' underlines the connection she saw between peacemaking and feminism.
72. It was reported in the *WT*, 6 February 1931, that 'she joined the League of Nations Union
when it was established'.

failed, and the only eventuality became a reign of constant terror all over the World.[73]

She condemned the 'wild expeditions in Russia, pointing out that the cutting off of supplies injured ourselves as much as other countries. Not until there was co-operation between the countries should we have proper supplies, or a reduction in price increases,'[74] while she regarded 'the Treaty of Versailles as a "revenge" treaty and not a "peace" treaty'.[75] A particularly difficult issue was the behaviour of British troops in Ireland in 1920 and 1921. Speaking to the Exeter Women's Liberal Association, she attacked the actions of the British Government in Ireland, claiming that

> It made her utterly miserable to think what the British nation was doing at the present time … . The Irish showed what kind of Government they wanted, and they did it in a perfectly constitutional way, but what happened that when the Irish people asked for a Republic, the leaders of the movement were clapped into prison … She believed that they might still make up the quarrel with the Irish … [but] by refusing to negotiate they [the British] were discouraging the moderate element and encouraging the extremist section. She concluded by moving a resolution condemning the crimes in Ireland and the policy of reprisals, and urging the Government to take immediate steps to negotiate with a view to a settlement of the troubles.[76]

In a strongly worded letter to the local press in April 1921, she stated that 'we pledged our honour … to accept President Wilson's fourteen points', and that one of the principles on which the war had been fought was to allow 'small nations, equally with large nations, the right to self-determination and self-government', claiming that to deny this to the Irish was hypocritical. She concluded that 'it is a matter of history that England has met with contempt

---

73. *WT*, 26 June 1919.
74. *WT*, 5 March 1920. Echoing the sentiments about the British and Allied forces in Russia are Charles Trevelyan's two letters to Acland dated 24 May and 5 June 1919, see Tregidga, *Killerton, Camborne and Westminster*, pp. 134–37. For more information of these 'wild expeditions', see I.C.D. Moffat, *The Allied Intervention in Russia, 1918–1920: The Diplomacy of Chaos* (Basingstoke: Palgrave Macmillan, 2015).
75. *WMN*, 2 October 1923.
76. *WT*, 10 December 1920.

and coercion every Constitutional effort of the Irish people (including the election of an overwhelming Sinn Fein Parliament) to secure the fulfilment of one pledge'.[77] Acland visited Ireland in 1921 as a representative of the Women's National Liberal Federation (WNLF), and said to a meeting of the Devon Union of Liberal Associations in April that year, that 'her experience in Ireland was so terrible that it had completely altered her idea of what we ought to do with regard to that country ... [since] when they got to Ireland they found that everybody had been beaten, ruined, imprisoned, deported, their houses burnt down or injured in some way by the Crown Forces'.[78] At the next meeting of the WNLF, she moved a resolution that 'This Country declares its abhorrence of the British Government's policy and methods of coercion, calls for an immediate amnesty and for the withdrawal of the auxiliary forces in Ireland, and urges the Government to enter into immediate negotiations with the elected representatives of the Irish people.'[79] She and her husband were also very active members of the Peace with Ireland Council, which boasted some powerful names among its members, and which has been described as 'perhaps the most effective and certainly the most committed pressure group to protest against reprisals in Ireland'.[80] The Peace with Ireland Council published Eleanor's report as *Report of a Fortnight's Tour in Ireland*, and 'it was claimed that her report was a factor in the loss of support for the government's Irish policy'.[81] Eleanor Acland was strongly attacked in the press for her views,[82] and was even subject to a libel case, where she and her husband (although he had nothing to do with the matter) had to withdraw an allegation Eleanor had made in the *Westminster Gazette* in May 1921 against Basil Clarke, a government publicity agent based at Dublin Castle.[83]

---

77. *WMN*, 19 April 1921. Woodrow Wilson's fourteen points were significant in determining the eventual post-war peace treaties; they were first enunciated in the President's address to both Houses of Congress on 8 January 1918.

78. *WT*, 21 April 1921.

79. *Manchester Guardian*, 11 May 1921. Tregidga, *Killerton, Camborne and Westminster*, on pp. 139–41 gives further examples of Eleanor Acland's views on Ireland.

80. D.G. Boyce, *Englishmen and Irish Troubles: British Public Opinion and the Making of Irish Policy, 1918–1922* (London: Cape, 1971), p. 71. Boyce discusses the work and influence of the Peace with Ireland Council on pp. 63–71 and 193–95.

81. In Tregidga, *Killerton, Camborne and Westminster*, p. 142, a note on Eleanor's letter to *The Spectator* on Irish matters dated 21 June 1921 quotes the remark in *The Liberal Women's News*, November 1925, pp. 109–10, that 'it was claimed that her report [on her visit to Ireland] was a factor in the loss of support for the government's Irish policy'.

82. For example in a letter to the *WMN*, 19 April 1921 by 'A Victim of S.F.'

83. The case was fully reported in the *WT* and the *WMN*, both 8 December 1921.

Her defeat in the court case did nothing to lessen her passionate belief in the desirability of negotiated settlements as against violent reprisals, and she strongly believed that women could play a vital role in peacemaking. Referring to her husband's victory at a by-election in Tiverton in 1923, she stated: 'The Tiverton election was fought on the question of peace, and she declared that it was wonderful to see women waking up to a realization that the right to vote meant that they really had some power and influence in shaping the affairs of the world and "doing a really good stroke in the cause of peace".'[84] Eleanor's belief in the importance of the role of women in ensuring that 'law not war' prevailed was embodied in the work she did as President of the Peacemakers' Pilgrimage of 1926. The pilgrimage was 'organised by a council composed from a formidable number of organisations',[85] and involved marches towards London along six main routes, which included Penzance, Edinburgh, Cardiff and Carlisle as starting points, with all the separate groups converging on Hyde Park in London on 19 June 1926. The aim of the pilgrimage was, in the words of the feminist author and journalist Evelyn Sharp (1869–1955), 'that law shall be substituted for war, that our own Government shall agree to submit all international disputes to courts of arbitration or conciliation, and shall further take the lead in the proposed disarmament conference of the League of Nations to show that Great Britain does not intend to appeal to force'.[86] Eleanor Acland was the chairman of the organizing council, and, as a follow-up to the pilgrimage, in July 1926 she led a delegation of the Peacemakers to meet Foreign Secretary Sir Austen Chamberlain and in her speech emphasized 'that the object of the pilgrimage was not only merely to speak of the desirability of world peace, but to put before our countrymen ... the need for certain action which England must take here and now in order to throw the full weight of her immense prestige into the scales on the side of international law as against international anarchy'.[87] She continued her work for the Peacemakers' Pilgrimage for several years, writing to the newspapers in favour of 'all-in arbitration treaties',[88] and helping to form (and chair) the Anglo-American Women's Crusade in support of the Kellogg–Briand 'Pact on the Renunciation of War as an Instrument of National Policy', which was signed in 1928.[89] By 1929, when Eleanor Acland spoke at the All-Party

---

84. *WMN*, 2 October 1923.
85. *The Observer*, 2 May 1926.
86. *Manchester Guardian*, 24 March 1926.
87. *Manchester Guardian*, 7 July 1926.
88. *Manchester Guardian*, 3 June 1927.
89. *Manchester Guardian*, 30 April 1928; *WMN*, 16 June 1928. The Pact is named after United States

Demonstration at Central Hall Westminster, there were over ninety Women's Peace Crusade Committees.[90]

Eleanor Acland and Women's Issues

Eleanor Acland's interest in international affairs and the internal politics of the Liberal Party did not prevent her from being heavily involved in domestic and local issues as well. As well as being a Justice of the Peace (she was among the first group of women to be appointed to the Bench in 1920), she served on the St Thomas Rural District Council for the Parish of Broadclyst, topping the poll there in 1925,[91] and was also involved in the Women's Institute and Girl Guide movements in Devon.[92] She also served as the president of the Exeter and District branch of the National Union of Societies for Equal Citizenship (NUSEC) from 1923,[93] and actively supported their aims and objectives, described as 'equal pay for equal work; reform of the divorce law and laws dealing with prostitution and the establishment of "an equal moral standard"; pensions for civilian widows … ; equal rights of guardianship of children; the opening of the legal profession to women'.[94] Acland felt that her involvement with NUSEC meant that it was unnecessary for her to join the Devon Council of Women on Public Authorities, which had been established in 1922 to bring together women in public office such as councillors, JPs and members of Boards of Guardians.[95] However, this did not prevent her from being active on a wide range of national and local issues; for example, at a council meeting of the WLF in 1923, she attacked the current law on divorce claiming that 'the present state of the law was practically a declaration that a

Secretary of State Frank Kellogg and French Foreign Minister Aristide Briand. It was signed by fifteen nations including the United Kingdom, the United States, France and Germany, and came into effect in 1929.

90. *Hull Daily Mail*, 23 May 1929.

91. *Devon and Exeter Gazette (DEG)*, 7 April 1925. Broadclyst is the village bordering the Acland estate of Killerton near Exeter. Eleanor Acland was one of only three women candidates in all twenty-nine rural council elections in Devon in April 1925, and attended the first meeting of St Thomas Rural Council on April 24 (*DEG*, 25 April 1925).

92. *WT*, 2 February 1931.

93. *WT*, 9 November 1923.

94. P. Thane, 'What Difference Did the Vote Make?', in *Women, Privilege and Power: British Politics 1750 to the Present*, ed. by A. Vickery (Stanford: Stanford University Press, 2001), p. 276.

95. The lengthy obituary of Lady Acland in the *WMN*, 13 December 1933, claimed that she was a member of the Devon Council of Women (DCW). However, the newspaper may have confused Acland's membership of the National Council of Women (NCW) with that of the DCW, since the NCW was the parent body of the DCW.

State did not expect the same standard of morality from men as it did from women';[96] she also spoke on widow's pensions at a meeting of the Exeter branch of NUSEC in February 1924,[97] franchise reform at a NUSEC meeting in Exeter in April 1926,[98] and on birth control at a Women's National Liberal Conference in September 1925.[99] Eleanor Acland, who became Lady Acland in 1926, when her husband Francis succeeded to the baronetcy on his father Arthur's death, was also President of the Exeter Women's Welfare Association and a member of the governing body of the National Birth Control Council.[100] At the proposed opening of a family planning advice clinic in Exeter in 1929, she spoke of the necessity of making information on birth control available to married women of all classes.[101] She was also interested in the wider issues of women's citizenship and, despite her fascination with politics, enjoyed discussing more general matters with women, as her article in the February 1924 issue of the Women's Institute magazine, *Home and Country*, makes clear; in the article she declares, 'I think that most strong party women will agree that it is a great pleasure and satisfaction to escape from the atmosphere of party politics and to join with our fellow women of different parties to promote non-party ends, which still, thank goodness, form a large part of our common life.'[102] The writer of her obituary in the local paper summed her up thus:

> a personality of outstanding force and ability, possessing strong convictions and able powerfully to advance and defend them. Lady Acland was every sense a progressive. There can be few places of any importance in the West where she had not spoken in the advancement of some local or national cause. On the platform she

96. *WMN*, 9 May 1923. Eleanor Acland's address to the Divorce Law Reform Union in December 1925 prompted considerable correspondence and she was forced to write letters defending her position from attacks by the Mothers' Union (*WMN*, 21 December 1925) and the Rev. Arthur Lancefield (*WMN*, 28 December 1925).
97. *WMN*, 16 February 1924.
98. *WT*, 16 April 1926.
99. *Manchester Guardian*, 25 September 1925.
100. *The Woman's Leader*, 27 March 1931, p. 63.
101. *WT*, 25 October 1929. Acland's positive support of the family planning advice clinic in Exeter being open to all married women was strongly opposed by Lady Florence Cecil, the wife of the Bishop of Exeter (see the chapter on Florence Cecil). In 1931, Acland's position prevailed and the Ministry of Health issued a memorandum (153/MCW) that allowed maternal and child welfare clinics to issue birth control advice under specific conditions (M. Simms, 'Parliament and Birth Control in the 1920s', *Journal of the Royal College of General Practitioners*, 28 (1978), pp. 86–87.
102. Quoted in J. Robinson, *A Force to be Reckoned With: A History of the Women's Institute* (London: Virago, 2011), p. 106.

was perfectly at home, a ready speaker, splendidly informed and equipped, ready for any emergency, and at all times a match for the political heckler. It was, perhaps, surprising to many that with her great abilities and experience Lady Acland did not appear as a political candidate until she stood for Exeter at the last General Election Altogether her ladyship must have taken part in at least a dozen election campaigns with her husband and her eldest son. But until the Exeter invitation she thought her first duty was to assist them, and she was unsparing in her efforts to advance the cause which they have all conspicuously championed.[103]

The 1931 General Election

Having declined the offer of the Exeter Liberal Party in 1929 to stand against Sir Robert Newman, the former Conservative and now independent MP for Exeter, because she 'found [herself] in general sympathy with his views on public questions',[104] she agreed to be adopted as Liberal candidate for the constituency of Exeter in February 1931, after Sir Robert had stood down. The possibility of winning the seat for the Liberals was remote, since they had trailed the Conservatives in Exeter by large margins throughout the 1920s, while, at the national level, 'by mid-1931, the Liberals were in a hopeless state. Their policy was nonsense, their organization a shambles, their finances almost non-existent and their right-wing on the point of rebellion'.[105] Despite these poor prospects, Eleanor Acland approached the election campaign with typical enthusiasm and conviction, fighting the campaign mainly on a platform of free trade.[106]

Even before her nomination as Liberal Party candidate was accepted in early February 1931 (the election did not actually take place until 27 October 1931), Eleanor had been extremely active in the cause of free trade, probably because 'the severity of the economic situation led many Liberals to question

---

103. WMN, 13 December 1933.
104. *DEG*, 13 October 1931. As President of the Exeter and District branch of NUSEC, Eleanor would undoubtedly have been in favour of the Married Women (Employment) Bill, which was introduced (unsuccessfully) into the House of Commons by Sir Robert Newman in 1927. For more information on Sir Robert Newman, see the chapter on Dame Georgiana Buller.
105. A. Thorpe, *The British General Election of 1931* (Oxford: Clarendon Press, 1991), p. 62. Thorpe's is the standard history of the contest but has little to say on the individual regions.
106. For a regional view, see Dawson, *Politics in Devon and Cornwall*, pp. 284–90, where he claims that the Liberals' aims locally in the 1920s were 'Peace, Retrenchment, Reform' (p. 284) while 'free trade was the chief element of Liberal reform' (p. 285).

the wisdom of their former sacred icon of free trade'.[107] The long-serving Liberal MP for South Molton, the Gladstonian George Lambert, had publicly argued in late 1930 that import duties were now necessary, which no doubt infuriated Eleanor, who never wavered in her belief in tariff-free trade.[108] She sent sixteen letters on the subject to the *Western Morning News and Western Daily Mercury* alone between October 1930 and the end of January 1931, taking on a wide range of opponents including W.A. Wells, the news editor of the Empire Industries Association and Reginald Clarry, the former MP for Newport, defending herself against patronizing remarks by the latter by declaring, 'I may say that I began my study of political economy by taking first-class honours in that, among other subjects at Oxford.'[109] In her acceptance speech, when adopted as the Liberal candidate for Exeter, she said

> I am looking forward to a stern task but a very happy task, along-side of the Exeter Liberals and perhaps others who, while not definitely members of the Liberal Party, support those principles of Free Trade, whole-hearted backing of the League of Nations, individual liberty and private enterprise, for which we shall stand and for which the City has stood for many years.[110]

The article in the Liberal-supporting *Western Times* that contained her speech continues: 'In the struggle for the enfranchisement of women, Lady Acland, while opposed to violent methods of the agitation, took a prominent part. Her interest in the welfare of women has been shown to be not only political but practical.'[111] After her adoption, Eleanor Acland continued to attack protectionism and safeguarding,[112] saying at a meeting in Newquay in February 1931, 'Some of the young people to day have no idea how fine it is to live under a Liberal Free Trade Government. Protection and "jingoism"

107. G. Tregidga, *The Liberal Party in South-West Britain since 1918: Political Decline, Dormancy and Rebirth* (Exeter: University of Exeter Press, 2000), p. 58.

108. Tredidga, *The Liberal Party in South-West Britain*, p. 58, goes on to point out that 'now there was a belief that "something must be done" to remedy the economic situation, there was little to stop them [the Liberals] from leaving the party'.

109. Clarry claimed that 'Lady Acland does not appear to have a very intimate knowledge of the subject [Protectionism]' in a letter to the *WMN*, 17 December 1930; Lady Acland's reply was published on 7 January 1931.

110. *WT*, 2 February 1931.

111. Ibid.

112. Safeguarding is the policy of 'protecting a local product or industry from foreign trade, esp. by the imposition of import duties or quotas' (*Oxford English Dictionary*) [online edition accessed 1 May 2019].

seem to go very much together, they are both based on the theory that the best way to benefit for yourself or your country is to injure or threaten some other country,'[113] while many of the letters Eleanor wrote in the subsequent months referred to Liberal Party views of the Government's Finance Bill.[114]

It is difficult to know how much Acland participated in the complex manoeuvrings of the Liberal Party nationally during 1931. While Lloyd George, the Liberal Party leader since 1926,[115] was willing to collaborate with the Labour government in early 1931, many Liberals led by Sir John Simon wished to accept protectionism and to work instead with the Conservative Party. To complicate matters, Lloyd George fell ill in July 1931, and the main Liberal Party elected Sir Herbert Samuel as its temporary leader. In August 1931, the Labour administration was replaced by a new National Government with a cabinet of Labour, Conservative and Liberal ministers headed by Ramsay MacDonald as Prime Minister, who, on 5 October 1931, decided to go to the country 'for a "doctor's mandate" to introduce any measures which would create economic prosperity and a favourable balance of trade'.[116] This led to a complete split in the Liberal Party, with one group led by Sir John Simon abandoning free trade to stand as Liberal Nationals, Lloyd George standing as the head of a separate 'gang of seven', while the remaining free trade Liberals under Sir Herbert Samuel fought the election as the Liberal Party. The free trade banner is the one under which Eleanor Acland stood in Exeter; indeed, she was one of the signatories (in her capacity as President of WNLF) to the Liberal manifesto, which was published on 10 October 1931.[117] This internal dissension may be the reason why Eleanor Acland ran a relatively low-key campaign, sending far fewer letters to the newspapers than usual. Initially, she became involved in complex offers of horse-trading, whereby if she agreed to withdraw from Exeter in favour of the Conservative candidate Arthur Reed, the Tory candidate for North Cornwall, Mr Williams, would withdraw from that constituency in favour of the Liberal, Sir Donald Maclean; eventually, however, both she and Arthur Reed refused the offer

---

113. *WMN*, 25 February 1931.
114. For example, the letter in the *WT*, 12 June 1931.
115. Asquith relinquished the leadership of the Liberal Party on 15 October 1926; he had been made a peer on 10 February 1925 but suffered a stroke on 12 June 1926; he died on 15 February 1928.
116. Tregidga, *The Liberal Party in South-West Britain*, p. 62.
117. The text of the manifesto and the signatories are taken from the *Dundee Courier*, 10 October 1931.

and stood against each other.[118] In her address to the Electors of Exeter, she declared that she supported the National Government and eschewed a partisan approach:

> We must have National not Party Government ... and I stand in hearty support of the present National Government ... under the Premiership of Mr. Ramsay MacDonald, with Mr. Baldwin and Sir Herbert Samuel and his right and left hand men ... I AM A FREE TRADER... [and] in this Election, I put forward no party programme and no party claims ... From the first day of my adoption ... I declared that if it were possible to form a National joint-party Government, I should support it. To that I adhere.[119]

The election took place less than ten days after Eleanor Acland's address to the electors, on 27 October 1931, and resulted in a landslide win for the National Government, while in Exeter, Acland lost by a majority of 11,789 votes to the Tory candidate, Arthur Reed.[120] Eleanor Acland considered that she had been defeated because

> The Conservative Party in Exeter had played very skilfully on the motive of fear, and the Liberals ... had not worked up a sufficiently complete organisation to combat the egregious rumours that were set going in the city, such as that the Socialist candidate had a real chance of winning and that she herself might turn Socialist if elected to Parliament ... Meanwhile they could rejoice that Mr. Ramsay MacDonald had rightly interpreted the mandate given him by the nation and re-formed his Government on national lines.[121]

---

118. *WT*, 16 October 1931. The *Western Morning News and Exeter and Devon Daily Gazette* in Acland's obituary on 13 December 1933 also claimed that there had been a suggestion that 'Lady Acland and Mr. Reed should stand down if Mr. Baldwin and Sir Herbert Samuel could agree on recommending a candidate for the city'; apparently Lady Acland agreed but 'the Conservatives broke off negotiations'.

119. *DEG*, 19 October 1931.

120. Acland was by no means the only Liberal to fail to defeat a Tory opponent. Stuart Ball, in his analysis of the 1931 election, points out that 'in total, eighty-four of the 109 Samuel [Liberal Party] and six Independent Liberal candidates in the English, Scottish and Welsh constituencies were opposed by Conservatives, and in consequence only nine were successful'. S. Ball, *Portrait of a Party: The Conservative Party in Britain, 1918–1945* (Oxford: Oxford University Press, 2013), p. 141.

121. *DEG*, 16 November 1931.

However, given her support for the National Government, she did not seem too dismayed by the result. After Sir Donald Maclean, who had won North Cornwall for the Liberals in 1931, died in the summer of 1932, Francis Acland was returned to Parliament as the Liberal member for that constituency, a seat he retained until his death in 1939. After the election, Eleanor Acland continued to work for the causes she believed in, writing regularly to the newspapers on disarmament and peace in our time, and taking the Bishop of Exeter to task for his opposition to birth control clinics.[122] Among Acland's last activities was her membership of the organizing committee of the huge National Council of Women annual conference, which was held in Torquay from 9 October to 13 October 1933.[123] She spoke at the conference to a resolution on juvenile delinquency on behalf of the Penal Reform League, claiming that 'the great majority of children who came into contact with the juvenile court broke the law not through any innate depravity, but through environment, under-nourishment, or the overstimulating diet of kinema, and so on'.[124] Her last published document was in November 1933 as a signatory to a declaration in favour of Parliamentary Government, and in support of proportional representation.[125] Shortly after its publication, she was admitted to a nursing home to have her appendix removed, and seemed to be recovering when she suffered a heart attack due to a blood clot on 12 December 1933, and died the same day, aged 55. She was buried at Broadclyst Parish Church, near Killerton, beside her beloved daughter Ellen.[126]

Eleanor Acland as a Liberal Woman

Claire Hirshfield has concluded her study of Liberal women by claiming that the WLF 'survived the war only to experience the ignominy of near total irrelevance in the 1920s'.[127] However, in an important book chapter that examines the lives of numerous Liberal activists in the 1920s and refutes Hirshfield's claim, Pat Thane makes it clear that there was a group of upper- and middle-class women who engaged with both public and political life and who were, with the odd exception, devoted lifelong Liberals.

122. *WMN*, 27 April 1933.
123. *DEG*, 10 October 1933. Lady Florence Cecil, Dame Georgiana Buller and Clara Daymond were also members of the local organizing committee.
124. *WMN*, 13 October 1933.
125. *North Devon Journal*, 23 November 1933.
126. *WMN*, 13 December 1933 (blood clot) and 15 December 1933 (burial).
127. Hirshfield, 'Fractured Faith', p. 188.

There was a similar pattern to the lives of all these women, and they, with others, made a significant and lasting contribution to public life, mainly—though not exclusively—with the aim of improving the relative position of women. Though much of the historiography stresses discontinuities caused by the war and the partial attainment of the vote, they exemplify continuity: in their determination to achieve gender equality; in carrying into the inter-war years, and in many cases, beyond, the late–Victorian commitment to public service ... and in their commitment to liberalism.[128]

Thane begins her survey with Margery Corbett Ashby (1882–1981), devoting over two pages to this major figure,[129] whose career ran parallel to Eleanor Acland's in many ways (Acland is only mentioned a couple of times in passing in Thane's chapter). Both Corbett Ashby and Eleanor Acland went to Oxbridge, both were Anglicans (many other leading Liberal women were Nonconformists, while Eva Hubback was Jewish), both worked with the NUWSS before the war and made enormous efforts to persuade the Liberal Party to support women's suffrage, the mothers of both were pioneer poor law guardians, both initially supported Asquith before moving over to Lloyd George, both were unwavering free traders, both were dedicated internationalists in the cause of peace, both stood for Parliament as Liberals (Corbett Ashby eight times), and both were presidents of the WNLF in the 1920s. Yet, while Corbett Ashby had a high profile and successful career, and is today still highly regarded as a suffragist, an internationalist and as a Liberal activist,[130] Eleanor Acland's achievements remain comparatively unknown. Indeed, Acland surpassed Corbett Ashby in that 'she was invited to become the first woman member of the Advisory Committee of the [Liberal] party'.[131] The writer of her obituary in the local Exeter paper equates the Advisory Committee to a 'Shadow Cabinet', explaining that, 'it was claimed at the time that the invitation to Lady Acland was not extended because she was then president of the Women's National Liberal Federation,

---

128. P. Thane, 'Women, Liberalism and Citizenship, 1918–1930', in *Citizenship and Community: Liberals, Radicals and Collective Identities in the British Isles, 1865–1931*, ed. by E.F. Biagini (Cambridge: Cambridge University Press, 1996), pp. 76–77.

129. Thane, 'Women, Liberalism and Citizenship, 1918–1930', pp. 68–70.

130. Brian Harrison paints a sympathetic portrait of Margery Corbett Ashby in *Prudent Revolutionaries* (pp. 185–208).

131. From Eleanor Acland's obituary in the *Manchester Guardian*, 13 December 1933.

but in recognition of the fact that she was regarded as the most gifted woman Liberal in the country at the time'.[132]

There are various possible reasons why Eleanor did not reach the same heights as some of the other Liberals mentioned in Thane's chapter. Firstly, she died comparatively young; secondly, she spent a great deal of energy looking after her four children; and she was also deeply affected by the death of her daughter Ellen in 1924. Thirdly, once her husband Francis moved into Killerton in 1923, he became one of the largest local land-owners, a major employer and figure of influence in Exeter and East Devon, which meant that Eleanor acquired a much expanded local rather than London-based social role; she was also heavily involved in Devon affairs through her work as a JP and Councillor for Broadclyst. Fourthly, and finally, Francis Acland was extremely active in high politics for the entire period of Eleanor's married life. He was an MP almost continuously from 1906 to 1924, and again from 1932 until his death in 1939, and was a major player in the political struggles of the Liberal Party from before the First World War until his death. After the First World War, he was one of the few Asquithian Liberals to retain his seat in Parliament and came close to achieving leadership of the party. As his biographer, Garry Tregidga, said, 'If Francis had been appointed chairman of the Independent Liberals, in 1919 [which almost happened], it is conceivable that the nature of inter-war British politics might have developed somewhat differently.'[133] Eleanor supported her husband's ambition wholeheartedly (she wrote to him that if he stood down in favour of the Labour candidate in Camborne in 1918, he 'would be Lib-Lab Foreign Secretary in three years' time')[134], as she did that of her son Richard, who contested the first of many elections for the Liberals in 1929. By contrast, many other Liberal women who had prom-inent political careers faced little or no competition from the men in their family; Margery Corbett Ashby had a very supportive husband who 'did not mind being thrown into the shade by his wife',[135] while other Liberal women like Margaret Wintringham and Eva Hubback were widows. Set against the backdrop of these family pressures, Eleanor Acland's local and national achievements seem all the more remarkable. Indeed, despite

132. WMN, 13 December 1933. The WMN of 30 September 1931 also refers to 'Lady Acland, a member of the Liberal Shadow Cabinet'.
133. Tregidga, Killerton, Camborne and Westminster, p. 44.
134. Tregidga, Killerton, Camborne and Westminster, p. 126.
135. Harrison, Prudent Revolutionaries, p. 204.

Francis's closeness to the Liberal political leadership and his decades-long career as an MP, Tregidga sees Francis and Eleanor essentially as equals, since in his view 'both [were] individuals [who] played an important if essentially neglected[136] role in the campaign for female suffrage, the survival of independent Liberalism in the aftermath of the First World War, and the events surrounding Lloyd George's radical crusade in the late 1920s.'[137]

Conclusion

Having been born into a political family and having married into a political family, it is not surprising that Eleanor Acland became a political activist. However, her activism was as much the result of her personality as her upbringing. Highly intelligent, passionate, self-confident and principled, Eleanor Acland upheld Liberal ideals throughout her life,[138] and was an avowed feminist,[139] working both nationally and locally for the advancement of women. She was a born leader, becoming chair of many of the organizations she joined, and also an accomplished writer, authoring three novels—*The Delusion of Diana* (1898),[140] *In the Straits of Hope* (1904)[141] and *Dark Side Out* (1921)—while her memoir *Good-bye for the Present* was published after her death in 1935. She became a highly respected figure in the Liberal Party, involved in policy discussions, sitting on the party's Advisory Committee (the equivalent of a shadow cabinet) and becoming president of the WNLF. Her contribution to political life was significant

---

136. There is still no entry for Sir Francis Acland in the *Oxford Dictionary of National Biography*; the entry for Eleanor Acland was published in 2019.

137. Tregidga, *Killerton, Camborne and Westminster*, p. 44.

138. She would no doubt have echoed the words of another prominent inter-war Liberal, Violet Markham, who wrote to her friend Elizabeth Haldane in 1922, 'I cling, like yourself, to the party, for great though its weakness at the moment and deplorable though the lack of vision in our unsatisfactory leaders, Liberalism as a *faith* and a *principle* is what I cannot give up' (*Duty and Citizenship: the Correspondence and Political Papers of Violet Markham, 1896–1953*, ed. by H. Jones (London: Historians' Press, 1994), pp. 106–107).

139. Eleanor gave a remarkable speech in praise of fellow Liberal activist and suffragist Eva McLaren who had died in 1921 saying that 'she strove for the rights of women as citizens and human beings, and she challenged the Liberal party to make the fight its own, because it was essentially a Liberal movement in the direct line of Liberal progress toward democracy ... she felt the two causes were essentially one' (*Federation News*, May 1922).

140. Written under the pseudonym of Margaret Burneside, Burneside being the name of the village near Kendal where the Cropper family lived. For the attribution of the novel to Eleanor Acland, see the National Trust copy of the book held at Killerton.

141. Written as Eleanor Cropper; Eleanor did not marry Francis Acland until 1905.

both in Devon and in the wider world of British politics, and her deter-mination that women should enjoy all the fruits of citizenship, along with her commitment to Liberalism and her family, were the defining charac-teristics of a remarkable woman, one whose achievements have long deserved greater recognition.[142]

---

142. Eleanor's name features in very few of the historical surveys of Liberal women and Liberal suffragists; she is not mentioned, for example, in M. Pugh, 'The Limits of Liberalism: Liberals and Women's Suffrage, 1867–1914', in *Citizenship and Community: Liberals, Radicals and Collective Identities in the British Isles, 1865–1931*, ed. by E.F. Biagini (Cambridge: Cambridge University Press, 1996), 45–65, nor in L. Walker, 'Gender, Suffrage and Party: Liberal Women's Organisations, 1880–1914', in *Suffrage outside Suffragism: Women's Vote in Britain, 1880–1914*, ed. by M. Boussahba-Bravard (Basingstoke: Palgrave Macmillan, 2007), 77–101, while there is no individual entry for her in E. Crawford, *The Women's Suffrage Movement: A Reference Guide, 1866–1928* (London: Routledge, 1999) (though she is mentioned once in the entry for the 'Liberal Women's Suffrage Union'), nor in C. Law, *Women, a Modern Political Dictionary* (London: I.B.Tauris, 2000).

CHAPTER TWO

Clara Henrietta Daymond (1873–1957)

JULIA NEVILLE

Clara Daymond, cartoon drawn by Bardsley as part
of a series of Plymouth personalities in the 1930s.

Clara Daymond was born Clara Townshend in 1873, the daughter of John
and Mary Townshend. She was born in Devonport, at that time a separate
borough from Plymouth. John had married Mary Futcher in 1866 at the
parish church of Stoke Damerel, although Mary had been baptized in the
Devonport Wesleyan Methodist Church and for most of her life Clara was
herself a non-conformist.[1] Although John Townshend was a shipwright, a
member of the most prestigious trade in the dockyard, housing conditions
in Devonport were such that the address where they were living at the
time of the 1881 census was listed as number 11, 'back of Albert Road',
showing how congestion had led to every scrap of land or building being

---

1. Family history information from www.findmypast.co.uk.

Julia Neville, 'Chapter Two: Clara Henrietta Daymond (1873–1957)' in: *Devon Women in Public
and Professional Life 1900–1950: Votes, Voices and Vocations.* University of Exeter Press (2021).
© Julia Neville DOI: 10.47788/LZQP8976

used for housing. John died suddenly after a ruptured gall-bladder in 1887 when Clara was only 13. By that time the family had moved into slightly more comfortable conditions at 24 Herbert Place, Morice Town. John left over £600 in his will.[2]

Clara and her mother have not been traced on the 1891 census, but they probably remained together at Herbert Place, as Mary is still shown there on the Burgess Roll in 1897. Clara had married George Daymond in 1893, when she was 20 and he was 30. George was a builder–developer in Devonport, working particularly on new developments as housing expanded north from the old heart of the village of Stoke. Though he had been born the son of a bargeman in Saltash, and was trained as a plasterer, he had joined the Salvation Army and gone to work as secretary to Captain King of the Salvation Army in Sunderland, where he was at the time of the 1891 census. Even when he returned to his native corner of England and became a builder he retained the ideal of service he had followed in the Salvation Army. He saw his work as a borough councillor (he was elected to Devonport Borough Council in 1901) as work that he was 'called' to do.[3]

George, Clara and Clara's mother Mary had moved out of Devonport by the time of the census in 1901 to St Budeaux, once a small village on the banks of the River Tamar but by the end of the nineteenth century rapidly being developed as a dormitory suburb for workers in the Devonport dockyard. Some speculative builders in Devonport had a poor reputation and it was alleged that there was a 'builders' clique' on the Devonport Borough Council, but Daymond seems to have been a good and law-abiding one.[4] St Budeaux was formally amalgamated with Devonport in 1899 and George was elected as an Independent councillor to represent St Budeaux on Devonport Council almost immediately after. So began the Daymonds' long joint crusade to improve services for the residents of their area. As the marriage was childless, Clara had time to devote to causes such as the needs of St Budeaux.

It was perhaps through the Salvation Army that George had met Clara, as, though in later life they both practised as Methodists, Clara retained

---

2. A substantial sum representing over £75,000 in 2020.
3. *Western Morning News (WMN)*, 18 September 1936, p. 7. George Daymond was facing his twelfth election.
4. The only court case against him so far identified appears to show him working in partnership with the Borough Council over a property deemed unfit for human habitation, *WMN*, 15 February 1901, p. 4.

an involvement with the Salvation Army.[5] In 1912 she was asked to address the gathering in Devonport Park to commemorate the life of the Army's founder, General William Booth. She paid tribute to Booth's development of opportunities for women, saying that 'he had put women in spheres of usefulness, had given them command of companies, and had offered opportunities for them to work side by side with men to help save the lost'.[6] This seems to speak of personal experience. By that time, however, Daymond was committed to local Methodist congregations and lent her support to the Primitive Methodist Mission Church in Keyham and the Granby Mission in Devonport.[7]

Daymond was also a strong advocate for the temperance movement. She belonged to the Devonport Branch of the British Women's Temperance Association, an organization which, like the Salvation Army, sought to help those perceived as 'unfortunate' out of their misery by offering them support. This led her into a national arena. She is known to have attended the national conference of the British Women's Temperance Association in Newcastle in 1912, the only woman to do so from Devon and Cornwall.[8] She also supported the International Organization of Good Templars, another temperance organization, not merely with money, but presiding at meetings and giving addresses on their behalf, such as the ones she gave at the Art of Love Lodge meeting in 1908, and at the jubilee of Plymouth's First Lodge in 1921, where she spoke in praise of the work of the juvenile lodges, declaring that 'licensed clubs were a national curse, offering special temptations to young men'.[9] Her temperance work was to remain a lifelong commitment even in uncomfortable situations. When, as described below, she became a member of the Devonport Board of Guardians, she found herself at odds on occasion with other members who were brewers or licensed victuallers and who, as she once described, might mutter 'too much blooming temperance' when she spoke.[10] She nonetheless successfully persuaded the Board to subscribe to the Nurses' Fund of the Devonport branch of the British Women's Temperance Association, which suppled nursing services to the sick poor.[11] The nurse was recorded as making over 900 visits in the year 1908–1909.

5. *Western Daily Mercury (WDM)*, 26 March 1912, p. 10. Daymond distributed Sunday School prizes at the Gloucester Street Salvation Army hall.
6. *WDM*, 2 September 1912, p. 10.
7. *WMN*, 28 March 1912, p. 10.
8. *WDM*, 15 June 1912, p. 12.
9. *WMN*, 8 June 1908, p. 7; 30 May 1921, p. 3.
10. *Western Evening Herald (WEH)*, 25 November 1910, p. 4.
11. *WMN*, 3 October 1908, p. 8; 16 October 1909, p. 9.

Into Public Life, 1907–1914

In her work for such charitable causes Daymond was no different from many other wives of skilled tradesmen of the period. As the wife of a borough councillor, she was invited to ceremonial events such as turning the first sod of the St Budeaux allotments, and she went out canvassing on her husband's behalf, or in the Liberal cause, but she was not expected to be politically active in her own right. It seems likely that it was her membership of the Women's Co-operative Guild that took her down this road.

The Women's Co-operative Guild (WCG), founded in 1883 by a Devon woman, Alice Acland, was instrumental in changing the lives of many working- and middle-class women who were members of the Co-operative movement by developing their skills and confidence to enable them to represent their views in public and to stand for and serve in public office. The movement, by the time Daymond joined, had been developed by Margaret Llewellyn Davies on three guiding principles: that women had an aptitude for public service; that they had rights as citizens beyond the domestic sphere; and that they had the knowledge to raise awareness of and plan to tackle exploitation at home.[12] In 1904 Daymond became the founding secretary of the St Budeaux branch of the WCG. A scrapbook made by members of the St Budeaux branch in 1977 contains a facsimile of a copy of the minutes of the formation and first meeting of the branch, held on 21 March 1904, at which Mrs Daymond was elected secretary.[13] The meeting was set up by members of the Devonport branch, and it is possible that Daymond had belonged to that branch at an even earlier date. Daymond is also shown in photographs of the celebrations of the St Budeaux branch silver jubilee in 1929 and golden jubilee in 1954, showing that this was a lifelong commitment. She paid tribute to the Guild for its work in 'equipping women for positions of responsibility on Boards of Guardians, town councils etc.' at a regional meeting in November 1907.[14]

In April 1907 Daymond spoke at the Spring Conference of the West and South Western Sections of the WCG in Gloucester. She moved the motion: 'That this Conference demands the enfranchisement of all Co-operative Women', arguing with humour and in a carefully non-party-political way that the parliamentary franchise was a logical next step now that women had

12. G. Scott, *Feminism and the Politics of Working Women: The Women's Co-operative Guild, 1880s to the Second World War* (London: UCL Press, 1998), pp. 35–58.
13. The Box (Plymouth and West Devon Record Office), 3071/9, St Budeaux Branch Co-operative Women's Guild.
14. *Western Chronicle*, 22 November 1907.

secured votes in municipal politics and in elections to Boards of Guardians. She said:

> She as a canvasser had had more trouble to get men to exercise the franchise than she had had with the ladies who had the power and privilege of doing so. They who had to and who did look after their husbands—(Laughter)—ought to have a vote. If they had the ability and power to look after the home, why should they not be able to exercise the vote: this was a non-political resolution. She was not a Suffragette, but they must remember that the Suffragettes were deeply in earnest and they, too, must be in earnest if they desired to obtain the great benefit of the vote.

Her fellow delegate from Devonport supported her, and the resolution was carried.[15]

Daymond also spoke out as a delegate to the national conference in 1912 when, after a long internal struggle between the central Co-operative Committee and the WCG Committee, the WCG were asked to drop their work to secure divorce law reform. Daymond said they should remain 'determined not to sacrifice principles for money' (referring to the threat to withdraw the grant the WCG received from the Centre) and that she 'knew what the proposed reforms meant for downtrodden women and she could not but raise her voice in protest of the action taken by the Co-operative Union'.[16]

The first recorded step Daymond took in public service was her election to the Devonport Board of Guardians as one of the representatives for Tamerton Ward at the elections in March 1907.[17] There was only one other woman member of the Board at that time, Mrs Smith. Daymond was to remain a member of the Board, re-elected every three years, until its abolition in 1930. The Devonport Guardians were responsible for Poor Law services throughout the borough, with the main institutional centre at an 1850s workhouse for 500 inmates on the edge of the borough, at Ford. Unfortunately the minutes of the Devonport Guardians no longer exist, and Daymond's contribution has to be assessed chiefly from newspaper accounts. The earliest reference to the sub-committees on which she served is from 1910 by which time she was a member

15. *Gloucester Journal*, 27 April 1907, p. 5.
16. Scott, *Feminism and the Politics of Working Women*, p. 143.
17. *WMN*, 9 February 1907, p. 8; 12 February 1907, p. 8.

of the Children's Committee, the Boarding Out Committee and the Infirmary Committee.[18] It is likely that the Children's and Infirmary Committees were the ones on which she was placed upon her initial appointment. The Boarding Out Committee was a new committee created in 1910 in order to implement new national guidance that children would be better looked after in family settings than in institutions. She was diligent in her attendance, which, for 1911–1912, was reported as having been fifty meetings out of a possible fifty-one for Board Meetings, twelve out of thirteen for the Boarding Out Committee and twelve out of thirteen for Children's Committee meetings.[19]

It is evident that Daymond's principal interest lay in services for children, and her election to the Board occurred at a time of considerable change. Edwardian society had begun to view children as a precious resource for the future of the nation, and to seek to promote their well-being. As well as formal legislation such as the Children Act 1908 there was an increasing determination to bring up children in environments where they could thrive, and a national view that for pauper children this would be in smaller-scale establishments than the traditional workhouse could offer. The Local Government Board started to put pressure on Guardians to board children out with foster parents, or to care for them in cottage homes. The Devonport Guardians held out against this because they believed their workhouse services were exceptionally good: even when in 1909 their own committee reported that a boarding out system such as that in neighbouring Plymouth should be adopted, they tried to defer its implementation.[20] However, the Local Government Board then issued a circular requiring Guardians to set up the new system and the Devonport Guardians were compelled to embark on arrangements to create new homes for the seventy children living in the workhouse.[21]

Daymond was appointed to the new Boarding Out Committee and seems to have been the Guardian particularly responsible for finding suitable places. She commented on the difficulty of finding these when the Boarding Out Committee reported to the Board on the first tranche of foster homes in June 1910. Four out of the six homes under consideration had been approved and nine children were to be sent out to them. The allowance made for fostering was five shillings per child per week, a relatively small sum, and Daymond remarked that 'anybody who took them would have to do so for love'.[22] The

18. *WDM*, 15 April 1910, p. 8.
19. *WDM*, 13 April 1912, p. 9.
20. *WEH*, 1 October 1909, p. 4.
21. *WMN*, 24 June 1910, p. 8.
22. Ibid.

inspector from the Local Government Board, present at the meeting to rein-
force to the Guardians the new regulations, pointed out that the intention
was not that people should make a living out of fostering children, but that
they should be people who desired 'to see children running about' and who
had a little space to spare.[23]

It was hard to recruit people who met the strict criteria for foster parents,
particularly where so much of the population lived anyway in overcrowded
settings, and the Board were compelled to contemplate the need to build or
buy a building away from the workhouse site to meet the demand for increasing
numbers of places for children.[24] The need for this course of action had,
however, not been resolved by the time that war broke out in 1914.

The Movement for Women's Suffrage

As identified earlier (p. 61), Daymond had told the WCG Conference in 1907
that 'she was not a Suffragette', probably using the term in the sense in which
it was used within the suffrage movement, meaning that she was not a member
of the militant wing.[25] It is possible, however, that she was already an individual
member of the National Union of Women's Suffrage Societies (NUWSS), the
largest of the pro-suffrage organizations and one that opposed the militant
action that the suffragettes endorsed. She was approached directly at the end
of 1908 by the NUWSS organizer, Margaret Robertson, with a view to
becoming the chair of a local branch, which Robertson had been sent down
to Devon to establish, and her name may already have been known to the
NUWSS.[26] Daymond agreed and was then provisionally elected chair of the
Three Towns and District branch in January 1909, a position confirmed at
the first public meeting in April.[27] The geographical scope of the branch
included initially not only surrounding areas in Devon such as Tavistock but
also Saltash, the town across the Tamar in Cornwall. Daymond addressed
meetings in both towns in the autumn of 1909.[28] She drew on her experience
as a Guardian to illustrate the kind of conditions which women's votes could

23. Ibid.
24. WMN, 9 July 1910, p. 8.
25. Gloucester Journal, 27 April 1907, p. 5.
26. Common Cause (CC), 29 April 1909, p. 42, though Robertson does not directly name Daymond.
27. WMN, 30 September 1909, p. 5, and as remembered by Dr Mabel Ramsay, Three Towns and
    District WSS secretary, in WMN, 15 January 1930, p. 3. The Three Towns were Devonport,
    Plymouth and Stonehouse.
28. CC, 4 November 1909, p. 393; 9 December 1909, p. 473.

be used to change and, while indicating her understanding of the militant position, emphasized the constitutional principles of the NUWSS. Whilst she was not one of the most active of speakers in the Plymouth branch, Daymond did give public addresses, for example during the General Election campaigns in 1910.[29] She was also one of those who addressed the crowds welcoming the 1913 Suffrage Pilgrimage in Victoria Park.[30] She regularly chaired public meetings such as that at Prince Rock and probably the one on her home territory of St Budeaux and the one attended by Helena Swanwick at the Welcome in Devonport in 1914.[31] She also played a role in the meetings of the South West Federation of NUWSS societies to plan the expansion of the movement in Devon and Cornwall.[32]

The 1920s: Service as a Borough Councillor

By the end of the 1910s Daymond was recognized as a woman who could be called upon in public service generally, not just as a Guardian. In 1912 Devonport set up its first National Insurance Committee and Daymond was elected to it by the Borough Council as one of only three women involved.[33] The start of the First World War saw the amalgamation of Devonport, Plymouth and Stonehouse into a single local authority, the county borough of Plymouth. George Daymond was transferred to become one of the new borough's councillors and was active in trying to ensure that the Devonport voice was not lost. The Devonport Guardians were vocal in their resistance to amalgamation with the Plymouth Guardians, and managed to continue to operate as an independent body. However, the Devonport workhouse was taken over for use as an additional military hospital and the Guardians had to manage with makeshift arrangements in collaboration with the Plymouth Board until 1919.

In 1917 when the food shortages of the First World War required drastic action, the borough set up a Food Control Committee, to which Daymond was nominated by the WCG. Her reputation became part of the debate in the Council when a member objected to over-representation from the Co-operative Society. Councillor Moses, himself a Devonport man, supported her nomination, saying that she had been suggested 'because of her keen interest in all

29. *CC*, 27 January 1910, p. 581.
30. *CC*, 4 July 1913, p. 213.
31. *WDM*, 19 October 1912, p. 8; *CC*, 1 December 1910, p. 17; *WDM*, 21 April 1914, p. 14.
32. *CC*, 4 May 1911, p. 63.
33. *WDM*, 26 June 1912, p. 6.

questions affecting womenkind and her prominent association with women's organizations'.[34] On this committee Daymond and her colleagues grappled with implementing the national policy on food distribution: issues of supply, demand, rationing and fair prices for what were seen as the staples of diet: potatoes, milk, butter, margarine and meat.[35]

The war interrupted NUWSS campaigning for the vote, but when the Representation of the People Act became law early in 1918, suffragists in Plymouth determined to set up a Plymouth Citizens' Association (PCA). Daymond made one of the speeches at the inaugural meeting in June 1918.[36] The organization was to be non-party, and open to men as well as women. As a speaker said at the meeting held before the General Election, its emphasis was to be more towards influencing women 'to use their vote, and record it for the candidate whom they thought would strive to make England a better and cleaner country' than to indicate which party should be supported.[37]

The following year, 1919, Daymond decided to stand for election to the Borough Council. This was something she would not have been able to do until just before the war, as regulations prohibited married women from standing for election in municipal boroughs until the County and Borough Qualifications Act of 1914 brought practice into line with what it already was for District Council seats. Although in national politics both George and Clara Daymond had hitherto worked for the Liberal Party, and George was also chair of the St Budeaux Liberal Association, in local politics he had always stood as an Independent, unwilling to accept nomination either from a political party or from the St Budeaux Ratepayers' Association. It was as an Independent, too, that Clara initially stood for St Budeaux Ward in the Borough Council elections, endorsed by the PCA. Dr Mabel Ramsay (subject of another chapter in this collection), who was the energetic PCA secretary, chaired a meeting in Daymond's support in St Budeaux, where Daymond advocated that women's wishes should influence the planning of new homes, and that women should be members of the Education and Maternity and Child Welfare Committees.[38] Two fellow candidates were also endorsed by the Citizens' Association: Mary Bayly in Mutley Ward and Annie Hambley in St Andrew's Ward. Daymond was elected on 1 November 1919, along with another woman and fellow suffragist Louie Simpson, who had stood as a Labour Party candidate in Stoke Ward. Daymond polled 477 votes, beating

---

34. *WMN*, 24 August 1917, p. 6.
35. E.g. *WEH*, 19 January, p. 4, 2 February 1918, p. 3.
36. *WMN*, 27 June 1918, p. 2.
37. *WMN*, 12 December 1918, p. 7.
38. *WMN*, 10 October 1919, p. 5.

off the Labour and Co-operative candidate, who polled 417 votes, and coming in well ahead of the retiring councillor, a Conservative, who polled 370 votes.[39] Although Mary Bayly lost in Mutley at that election, she did win a seat in the ward at the end of the month in a by-election caused by the election of one of the ward councillors as an alderman. There were thus three women councillors on Plymouth Town Council in 1919–1920. One of the Plymouth Parliamentary Divisions was also represented by a woman: Nancy, Lady Astor, was elected MP for Plymouth Sutton shortly after Daymond's election in November 1919. Daymond had lent her own support to Astor's candidature by making a public speech on her behalf, saying that Astor 'had high motives' and that she hoped that 'women would vote for the woman who would represent them in every sense of the word'.[40]

The idea that Citizens' Associations (or Societies for Equal Citizenship, as they were often called elsewhere) initially held was that there could be a new kind of politics, independent of political parties. This was not to survive the test of electioneering, however. There was an ambiguity about the appeal that women standing as independents with Citizen Association endorsement could make to the voter. Were they proposing themselves as specialists in 'women's issues', matters of health, housing, education and care in particular, whilst others elected in the ward dealt with issues such as transport? Or were they appealing on the basis of personality and values? Whilst appeals on these grounds continued to be made in many rural areas, party endorsement and access to party machinery to promote voting were becoming increasingly important in urban environments like that of Plymouth. This was driven by the rise of the Labour Party and the development of its electioneering activity. To be successful, women candidates increasingly needed the backing of a political party. Nonetheless, even when she formally became a Conservative, Daymond continued to support the PCA, initially as president and then as a member of the executive into the 1930s.[41] She lent her support as councillor to initiatives in which the PCA were interested, such as women police, and they in turn supported her candidature at election times.[42] She also continued to play an active role there in debates on the employment of women and on other issues important to the associations, equality of franchise equal pay, and an equal moral standard.[43]

39. *WMN*, 3 November 1919, p. 8.
40. *WMN*, 13 November 1919, p. 5.
41. *WMN*, 24 November 1919, p. 8; 5 February 1931, p. 4.
42. *WMN*, 5 October 1928, p. 7; 12 October 1934, p. 4.
43. *WMN*, 24 February 1922, p. 3; *CC*, 18 May 1923, p. 126.

Daymond also joined the Devon Council of Women on Public Authorities, an organization also initially sponsored by the National Union of Societies for Equal Citizenship. This had been set up in 1922 as a result of a Devon Conference on 'The Work of Women in Public Life' (for women magistrates, Guardians and councillors) prompted by the Women's Local Government Society. The aim was to provide a forum for women to learn together about topics of current interest, such as censorship and the cinema, using external speakers, both local and national; and to share experience and co-ordinate action, for example in support of the appointment of women police. Daymond seems to have valued the connections she made there: in 1937 she went all the way out to Torrington to speak at a public meeting in support of the candidature of Hilda Clifford, who was standing for re-election to the County Council, even though Clifford was a Liberal.[44] She also sent 'congratulations and love' by greetings telegram to fellow member Juanita Phillips of Honiton on her re-election as mayor that November.[45]

Contests between political parties were to dominate the landscape of Borough Council work in Plymouth during the 1920s, as the Labour Party sought to build a power base. They had increased the number of seats they held in 1919 from one to ten, and began gradually to build the numbers to challenge the Conservatives. By 1924 George and Clara Daymond had both concluded that they could no longer remain 'Independent' councillors on the Council. According to George this was because of the need to 'combat Socialism', which he abhorred.[46] They formally abandoned their old allegiance to the Liberal Party at Parliamentary elections and joined the Conservatives. They did, however, from time to time abstain on votes proposed by the Conservative leadership, objecting in 1934, for example, to the proposal for the Council to spend money on the 'Fyshing Feaste', a ceremonial event and outing for councillors, which they considered was a waste of money in a time of austerity.[47] The differences between the Conservatives and the Liberals on the Council had virtually vanished by that time, however, and during Daymond's election campaign that same year her candidature was endorsed by both Conservative and Liberal leaders.[48]

Pugh has described the environment faced by women in the House of Commons and elsewhere in political life: an assertive and adversarial style of debate; the

44. *Express and Echo*, 27 February 1937, p. 4.
45. Devon Heritage Centre Westcountry Studies Collection, Special Collections F6, *The Scrapbooks of Juanita Maxwell Phillips*, 9, p. 32, 9 November 1937.
46. *WEH*, 27 October 1927, p. 10, referring to 'three years ago'.
47. *WMN*, 6 March 1934, p. 3.
48. *WMN*, 17 October 1934, p. 4.

prizing of conformity above individualism; and colleagues who were patron-izing and hostile to feminism.[49] On the Plymouth Borough Council the growth in numbers of Labour councillors whose debating style had been honed by the Trade Union movement increased the level of acrimonious debate, though Daymond would on one occasion bravely assert that: 'You can laugh and you can shout … I don't shout you down, and we have a right to our opinions. I would like to see the man I was frightened of.'[50] The dominance of party politics in selecting committee membership emphasized the need for conformity. Daymond commented in the month she was elected that her reception in the Council Chamber had been very friendly, but 'not being a Party member I had very little choice of committees'.[51] Such discrimination contributed to the decision the Daymonds made to take on the party politics of the Conservatives in order to exercise influence on topics in which they were interested.

Patronizing and hostile views are less frequently reported, but the commit-tees for which Daymond was selected—Maternity and Child Welfare, Hoe and Parks, Sanitary (later Public Health), Allotments and Cemeteries, the Free Library—indicated the view of the parties about the position of women. It was not until much later in the 1920s that the first woman managed get a seat on the Finance Committee and it does not appear that women were ever appointed to committees such as the Works Committee or the Tramways Committee. This was not of particular concern to Daymond. 'We don't want to do men's work; we want to do our own work', she once told a conference, 'we must see that the things concerning women and girls are done by women themselves'.[52]

The committees on which she served nonetheless provided Daymond with an opportunity to take forward many of the practical projects she and the other suffrage activists had considered desirable: improving infant welfare clinics; creating more recreational space; building new houses to replace the worst of the slums; tackling tuberculosis. Committee work was at the heart of the Council's business: many committees had substantial delegated decision-making powers and though it was possible to challenge these in Council, it was hard to overturn a decision completely. The decision had to be referred back to the originating committee. The women councillors learned this the

---

49. M. Pugh, *Women and the Women's Movement in Britain* (Basingstoke: Macmillan, 1992), pp. 190–93.
50. *WMN*, 12 February 1930, p. 5.
51. *CC*, 28 November 1919, p. 429.
52. *WMN*, 12 October 1922, p. 3.

hard way over the issue of women police. Although the Watch Committee had in fact appointed two women police officers at the end of the First World War, the new requirements for pay and pensions led them to decide they needed to make economies, and the cuts they agreed included the women police. The PCA immediately organized a public protest meeting in the Guildhall, at which Daymond spoke, claiming that it was a question of 'purity, right and justice' that had brought them together.[53] In spite of the strength of feeling expressed there, the leader of the Council claimed that there was no point in a deputation of women's and other social organizations coming to the full Council, as that was not the decision-making body. Although he was over-ruled on this, discussion on the Watch Committee's decision was not permitted. The subject could only be ventilated by a resolution being put to the Council. Daymond's colleague Mary Bayly moved such a resolution, but this was defeated by a majority of two.[54]

What Daymond was able to do was to press the detailed case for local improvement, a task to which she was so committed that the *Western Evening Herald* described her in 1928 as the 'uncrowned Queen of St Budeaux', and her helpers as the 'St Budeaux Amazons'.[55] St Budeaux had grown from a village to a highly urbanized area without much attention being paid to planning the infrastructure that its expanding population would need. All councillors argued for local improvements for their own patch, especially just before they were due for re-election, but Daymond was recognized as being particularly assiduous. The battles which the reporter referred to as having been fought in 1928 were over the Devonport Camel's Head refuse tip, which stank; the perennial problems of inadequate public transport linking St Budeaux to the centre of Devonport; the high cost of travel; and the need for a supply of mains electricity. The reporter might also have mentioned the supply of gas and street lighting, the installation of fire alarms, and the provision of a park and tennis courts, all of which Daymond made it her business to press for.

In 1927 she was appointed vice-chairman of the Public Health Committee (PHC). This was proving to be one of the most dynamic of the Council's committees. Plymouth's public health commitment had been shaken up by the appointment of a new Medical Officer of Health in 1925. Dr Austen Nankivell was a distinguished academic and practical physician with a gift for

53. *WMN*, 8 April 1921, p. 7.
54. *WMN*, 12 April 1921, p. 8.
55. *WEH*, 19 October 1928, p. 6.

using 'propaganda' effectively to secure change. He seized on the opportunity offered by the initiation of local wireless broadcasting in the summer of 1925 to get across his messages to the public with a series of six talks tackling what he saw as the most profound of health problems.[56] Daymond invited him in April 1925, only a few weeks after his arrival, to address the St Budeaux District Nursing Association, for which he chose the topic of the importance of fresh food.[57]

Nankivell found a willing ally for his crusades in the new chair of the PHC, appointed in November 1926. As a result of an agreement between the political parties on sharing committee chair appointments, this was a Labour councillor, Bert Medland, who had been a Devonport Guardian with Daymond in the early 1920s. With the rest of the PHC she was soon committed to two major improvement schemes: one to provide hospital accommodation for infectious diseases rather than continue the use of the 'hospital ship', a redundant warship moored in the Sound providing isolation facilities; and the other to provide a comprehensive scheme for the prevention, treatment and after-care of tuberculosis, including an orthopaedic service.[58] Daymond had taken an interest in treatment for tuberculosis ever since she had argued in the Devonport Guardians more than fifteen years earlier for the women as well as the men to have fresh air balconies for the consumptives built on their wards.[59]

In addition to such civic work Daymond continued with other areas of her pre-war social service. She remained committed to her Methodist principles, and was in 1925 elected President of the Devon and Cornwall Federation of Brotherhoods and Sisterhoods.[60] She was also in demand to open or preside at Methodist events or to deliver a vote of thanks. She continued to support the temperance movement through the British Women's Temperance Association, as president and executive delegate for the Devon Union of Associations.[61] She stated even as late as 1925 her conviction that 'the day was coming when England, if it did not adopt prohibition, would at least have "local option"', the power for local authorities to determine whether to ban sales of liquor.[62] She also remained committed to the idea of medical services

56. WMN, 26 May 1926.
57. WMN, 25 April 1925.
58. The Box, Plymouth City Archive, PHC minutes, 19 May 1927.
59. WMN, 13 April 1911, p. 8.
60. WMN, 5 October 1925, p. 4.
61. WMN, 18 March 1922, p. 3.
62. WMN, 11 December 1925, p. 3.

provided for women by women doctors. The South Devon and East Cornwall Hospital pointed to their employment of women, but these were not in consultant posts with rights of admission to hospital beds. Daymond was mentioned as one of the influential people who signed a 1925 petition calling on them to reconsider their point of view.[63] The petition had no effect. She joined the committee set up to raise funds for women's medical services, ultimately for a Women's Hospital but in the meantime the maintenance of dedicated beds for women at the City Hospital and access to the Marie Curie Cancer Hospital for women in London.[64]

Daymond also remained one of the Devonport Guardians throughout the 1920s. In 1921 she had been elected vice-chairman, defeating the Labour Party nominee and in 1922 she was accorded the distinction of becoming the first, and in fact the only, woman to chair the Board.[65] That year the Guardians spent much of their time coping with the nationally imposed need for cuts to expenditure, taking decisions to cut the amount of relief offered to individuals and families.[66]

She also continued her role with children's services. The initial foster homes set up in 1910 had now been supplemented by 'Scattered Homes' run directly by the Guardians. The 'scattered' or 'cottage' homes movement had initially been based on the provision of small-scale units designed to provide children with a domestic rather than an institutional atmosphere. The Plymouth Guardians did develop homes along those lines. The Devonport Guardians, however, decided to lease two adjacent homes at Cotehele Villas, and used them to accommodate over thirty children. These were managed by one lady superintendent, Miss Holden, and two nurses and ancillary staff such as a cook, though the older girls did much of the domestic work. When the opportunity arose the Devonport Guardians decided to purchase a substantial house, with grounds around it (the Cotehele Villas had no recreation space) to convert as a home for up to fifty children. The home, Stoke House, was opened in December 1927 amidst a general tone of self-congratulation, including statements such as that this was 'a day of days in the work of the Board of Guardians'.[67] No doubt they all truly believed that they were providing a wonderful service for the children in their charge.

63. *WMN*, 21 November 1925, p. 3.
64. *WMN*, 21 May 1930, p. 5. This project is discussed further in the chapter on Dr Mabel Ramsay.
65. *WMN*, 20 April 1921, p. 8; *WMN*, 21 April 1922, p. 5.
66. *WMN*, 27 May 1922, p. 3; 2 September, p. 3.
67. *WMN*, 13 December 1927, p. 5.

There was, however, another view of Stoke House, that of its child occupants. Vicky Norman, herself once a child in the care of the Public Assistance Committee (successor to the Guardians), has collected and published a series of reminiscences of the Stoke House residents.[68] In this a picture emerges of Miss Holden's regime of drudgery, scolding, corporal punishment and very little joy.[69] This regime was initially invisible to visiting Guardians who saw the children only on their best behaviour.

The 1930s: Heyday of Municipal Activity

Major changes nationally took place as a result of the Local Government Act 1929, enacted by a Conservative government but implemented by a Labour one. Plymouth City Council (the borough had been granted city status in 1928) took on the work of the three former Boards of Guardians for Devonport, Plymouth and Stonehouse. These services were to be managed by a Public Assistance Committee (PAC). The local authority could mandate the PAC to administer the full range of Poor Law services, or to be confined to the provision of the core services of public assistance payments and some forms of residential care. Plymouth chose to remove the care of the sick poor to the remit of the PHC. The care of children and the management of Stoke House plus the former Plymouth scattered homes was henceforth to be a joint responsibility of the Education and Public Assistance Committees. Daymond's long years of experience as a Guardian were highly valued, and she was at once appointed as a member of PAC and became chair of its Management Sub-Committee.

This was a difficult time for the members of the PAC. In the wake of the Wall Street crash unemployment grew rapidly, and those whose national insurance coverage had ceased were compelled to turn to the PAC for the dole. One area of the Poor Law to undergo change as a result of the reforms was the service for homeless people, mainly men, who spent their lives on the road, known as 'vagrants' or 'casuals'. Under the earlier Poor Law the Guardians made provision to house them overnight in what were known as the 'casual wards' of the workhouses and to make them do a stint of manual labour the following day in lieu of payment. The new Public Assistance Committees took on these responsibilities, but, in the interests of making financial savings, were required to collaborate with neighbouring authorities to make the appropriate

---

68. V. Norman, *Scattered Homes, Broken Hearts* (Plymouth: Foxfield Publications, 2003).
69. Norman, *Scattered Homes*—for example Sybil Webb's chapter, 'Memories of Stoke House', pp. 147–51.

provision. Daymond was appointed as one of the six Plymouth members on the twenty-five-member Devon Joint Vagrancy Committee (JVC) which covered Devon County Council and the two county boroughs of Exeter and Plymouth. She and fellow woman councillor Jacquetta Marshall, a Labour alderman, served on the committee from its establishment in 1930 until its abolition in 1948.[70]

Krafchik has identified the 1930s as a period in which the old policy of 'deterrence' and the 'punitive' regulations applied to vagrants were being called into question. Another view, that vagrants only became so through misfortunes such as unemployment and required assistance to find work and settle down, was gaining wider acceptance.[71] Daymond was one of those who held the latter view. The number of annual nightly admissions in the county rose, fell during the First World War, and then rose again to record levels. In 1915 there had been 23,000 admissions (over sixty per night). From then onwards the numbers fell rapidly to 1,600 (just over four per night) in 1919. They then rose steeply throughout the 1920s to 78,000 (over 200 per night) in 1930 and continued to rise in the recession until 1934.[72] Daymond pointed out to the JVC the link between the increase in admissions and the rise in unemployment.[73] She tried to prevent a restructuring which meant that the vagrants might have to walk more than twenty miles from one casual ward to the next. That failed, but she was able to support the successful resolution of a fellow member who argued that if men were to walk such distances they should at least be given a ration of bacon with their breakfast of bread and margarine.[74]

The views of Devon members on the JVC were less liberal than those of Plymouth Public Assistance Committee, and Daymond and her fellow Plymouth representatives on the JVC sometimes found themselves under criticism by their own PAC colleagues over issues of joint policy such as when the 'casuals' should be permitted to smoke, or whether they could be given a food ticket to buy their own lunch on the road rather than be issued with a pack of bread and cheese.[75]

---

70. *WMN*, 21 February 1931, p. 6. The papers of the Devon Joint Vagrancy Committee do not seem to have survived.

71. M. Krafchik, 'Unemployment and Vagrancy in the 1930s: Deterrence, Rehabilitation and the Depression', *Journal of Social Policy*, 12 (1983), 195–213.

72. *WMN*, 3 October 1931, p. 3.

73. *WMN*, 29 April 1933, p. 6.

74. *WMN*, 20 February 1932, p. 8.

75. *WMN*, 20 February 1934, p. 5; 22 April, p. 10; 1 June, p. 5; 30 July 1935, p. 4; 6 May 1939, p. 5.

It was perhaps not surprising, therefore, that it was the Plymouth PAC that agreed to take forward the most significant local development during the 1930s: the creation of a hostel with a work training programme attached, for the 'reclamation of casuals'.[76] Here vagrants who signed an undertaking would be instructed in carpentry and boot and shoe repairing and helped to obtain a job. Clarence House opened in Stonehouse in 1938.[77] It was apparently one of only six local authority training hostels in England before the Second World War.[78] In most areas such training hostels were run by voluntary organizations, if they existed at all.

The Second World War saw a decrease in vagrancy, as men were able to enlist, and Clarence House became a general hostel when so much of Plymouth's housing was destroyed in the Blitz in 1941. After the war the management of the hostel was handed over to the new Social Welfare Committee, of which Daymond was a member.[79] She also continued to serve on the JVC until it was wound down in 1948, and was elected vice-chairman in 1945.[80]

Children's services also came under scrutiny during the 1930s. Norman records that in 1931 a member of the grounds maintenance staff was convicted of the sexual abuse of some of the girls, although the case was heard 'in camera' and kept out of the public eye.[81] Complaints about Stoke House continued. One PAC member mentioned at a meeting in January 1933 that 'complaint had been made to her only this week of the manner in which things were conducted there', and another said, 'These little tots are not being cared for as they should be. I have seen them running about without any slippers on their feet and no one to look after them.' The committee agreed to appoint an extra trained member of staff for children aged between three and five.[82] In November, however, the subject of the rumours was raised again. This time Daymond herself said she was rung up one day with an allegation about the state of the children. She at once investigated and found it to be 'utterly without foundation'. A Guardian who had recently visited expressed satisfaction about the state of the young ones in particular.[83] There must, however, have been some lingering unease, and this was probably added to by two episodes in 1934 that offered

76. *WMN*, 1 July 1938, p. 8.
77. Ibid.
78. *WMN*, 4 May 1940, p. 2.
79. *WMN*, 24 February 1948, p. 6; 4 June 1948, p. 2.
80. *WMN*, 3 November 1945, p. 6.
81. Norman, *Scattered Homes*, p. 43.
82. *WMN*, 6 January 1933, p. 5.
83. *WMN*, 11 November 1933, p. 4.

cause for concern. The first of these was when the Guardians discovered that their instruction that children should not wear headgear that distinguished them from other children had been ignored.[84] The second was when two boys absconded after their August holiday in camp at Maker in Cornwall.[85] The problems with the staff and with the regime continued on into the evacuation of the home to Clovelly during the Second World War.

The work of the PHC, where Daymond remained vice-chairman, was also affected by change following the Local Government Act 1929. Dr Nankivell put together a scheme to use this opportunity to transform one of the former workhouse infirmaries, Greenbank, into a municipal hospital providing acute medical and surgical care.[86] This was renamed the 'City Hospital', and new doctors were appointed to transform the service.[87] The next scheme was to acquire some 'municipal radium' for cancer treatment; Daymond was involved in local discussions with doctors (including Dr Mabel Ramsay) and voluntary hospital representatives about plans for the scheme.[88] 'The people of Plymouth will soon see that real economy is the saving of life and not necessarily the saving of pounds,' argued the PHC chair, Bert Medland.[89]

'Citizen', the *Western Evening Herald*'s columnist, characterized the PHC at that period as operating like a 'motor car with two accelerators [Medland and Nankivell] and no brake'.[90] Daymond, however, seems to have seen no reason to criticize the plans they were making. In 1931 the Ministry of Health gave Plymouth a glowing report during their national inspection of authorities.[91]

That same year, precipitated by the economic crisis that gripped the nation, this expansion came to an abrupt end. The Conservatives, now back again with the majority on the Council that they had lost to Labour the year before, determined to make economies and Daymond followed the party line by supporting the move for a cut in the rates for the financial year 1931–1932.[92] Public Health was the first area the Council targeted for additional scrutiny. Councillor Baxter,

84. *WMN*, 22 March 1934, p. 7.
85. Norman, *Scattered Homes*, pp. 18 and 136–37.
86. The Box, Plymouth City Archive, Special Purposes Committee minutes, 7 March 1930.
87. J. Neville, 'Explaining Variations in Municipal Hospital Provision in the 1930s: a study of councils in the far south west' (unpublished doctoral thesis, University of Exeter, 2009), pp. 60–68.
88. *WMN*, 29 April 1930, p. 5; 3 September 1930, p. 5.
89. *WEH*, 22 August 1931, p. 3.
90. *WEH*, 27 February 1932, p. 5.
91. The National Archives, MH 66–618, Local Government Surveys: Report for the City of Plymouth, November 1930.
92. *WMN*, 10 March 1931, p. 4.

who chaired the committee undertaking this work, showed that Public Health expenditure had risen from £55,000 in 1925–1926 to £69,000 in 1930, an increase of over 25%.[93] Medland lost his chairmanship of the PHC in the autumn of 1932, but rather than being replaced by Daymond, who was his vice-chair and a Conservative, it was Baxter who took over, with a remit to prepare a scheme for economies which was presented and agreed in April 1933.[94]

While this was under way Dr Nankivell was suspended from duty and dismissed as a result of being charged for 'attempting to procure the commission by a young man of acts of indecency'.[95] Nankivell's successor was a man of more cautious temperament, and public health development in Plymouth stalled. This is demonstrated in the Ministry of Health's review of Plymouth's arrangements to tackle the problem of maternal mortality in 1935.[96] The report showed that the city had failed to tackle arrangements for specialist obstetrician support and for better in-patient accommodation at the City Hospital, and the numbers of health visitors had been reduced rather than increased. The PHC were charged to take action, and they did, though in a limited way. Later that year, however, the PHC refused to make a grant to the Plymouth Branch of the National Birth Control Association.[97] Similar grants, recognizing the benefits of such work for maternal health, had long been made by Devon County and Exeter City Council. This set-back may have been discouraging for Daymond and was possibly one reason why she chose to withdraw from the vice-chairmanship of the PHC. In November 1936, Mrs Brock took over as vice-chair.[98]

Daymond continued to foster the development of services for women and children, and for the vulnerable. She became a member of the committees dealing with the Care of the Mentally Defective and of the Mental Hospital Visiting Committee. She continued to support the committee raising funds for a Women's Hospital.[99] She chaired the Plymouth and District branch of the Electrical Association for Women, saying that she 'would not rest content until every household in the city had its own supply of electricity'.[100] In 1937 she attended the International Women's Week conference in Budapest where she spoke on

93. *WMN*, 10 May 1932, p. 5.
94. The Box, PCA, PHC minutes, 20 April 1933.
95. The Box, PCA, PHC minutes, 13 July 1932 and 22 September 1932; *WMN*, 11 July 1932, p. 4.
96. The Box, PCA, PHC minutes, 20 June 1935.
97. The Box, PCA, PHC minutes, 21 November 1935.
98. The Box, PCA, PHC minutes, 19 November 1936.
99. *WMN*, 21 May 1930, p. 5.
100. *WMN*, 21 October 1930, p. 4.

behalf of the Devon Federation of the Women's Electrical Association.[101] She made common cause with other women councillors to try to persuade the Tramways Committee to provide for free travel for nurses employed by local voluntary nursing organizations, though without success.[102] She supported the establishment of Townswomen's Guilds in Plymouth, which she saw as a recruiting ground for women to serve on the Council, offering 'the skilled knowledge which only a woman could give'.[103] She argued against injustice to women employees of the City Council on discovering that if they resigned in order to get married they lost access to refund of their superannuation contributions, whereas, if they had waited to be dismissed, this would automatically have been paid.[104]

Later Years

In 1938 George Daymond was elected by his fellow councillors to an aldermanic seat.[105] He was not, however, to enjoy his well-deserved honour for long. In March 1939, just after attending a Council meeting, he had a stroke and died within a couple of days. His funeral service was held in the St Budeaux Methodist chapel, with an interment afterwards in the parish churchyard, accompanied by a masonic oration.[106] Both George and Clara had long been involved with the Masonic Brotherhood. George left about £4,000, the equivalent of £280,000 in 2019. A month later Clara Daymond was unanimously elected alderman in his place, the first woman Conservative alderman on the Council.[107]

Daymond continued to pursue her life of public service, both through her statutory positions and, less formally, with the Plymouth Guild of Social Service, or organizations such as the National Spinsters' Pension Association, which she supported, recognizing the financial problems women not covered by the National Insurance Scheme experienced.[108] She remained a member of the WCG and was Secretary to their Executive Council.[109] When war broke out in September 1939 she was involved in the evacuation of Ford House, and later with the Wartime Nurseries and Child Welfare Scheme.

101. *WMN*, 23 August 1937, p. 5 and 1 September, p. 3.
102. *WMN*, 10 October 1933, p. 4.
103. *WMN*, 18 September 1934, p. 5.
104. *WEH*, 25 October 1935, p. 5.
105. *WMN*, 8 January 1938, p. 10.
106. *WMN*, 17 March 1939, p. 11 and 21 March, p. 3.
107. *WMN*, 18 April 1939, p. 8.
108. *WMN*, 8 November 1938, p. 5.
109. *WMN*, 24 February 1939, p. 7.

After the Second World War, Plymouth City Council decided to hold an 'all out' election and aldermen as well as councillors resigned their seats. Daymond led the fight for the Conservative candidates in St Budeaux Ward. They lost to the three Labour nominees, though not by as much as Conservatives did in some other wards. The newly elected City Council then met to choose its new aldermen. Almost all nominations were of sitting councillors. Daymond, uniquely, was appointed from outside the Council; a recognition of the value of her contribution and of her long service. She returned to the Council for a final stint as alderman and vice-chairman of the PHC, now led by her Labour colleague Alderman Mrs Marshall.[110] Gradually she retired from public life. She died at home in St Budeaux on 11 February 1957, leaving an estate of over £20,000, the equivalent of £140,000 in 2019.

Conclusion

Clara Daymond devoted her life to public service, initially in support of her husband's work as a councillor, but later on in her own right. She and her husband had both come from working-class backgrounds and by dint of hard work, non-conformist discipline and masonic support made their way to the upper echelons of civic society.

It was probably her religious background that taught her to stand for 'goodness and high ideals', as she said in 1919, 'purity, right and justice', which she thought were the particular standards women held to.[111] It may have been the Salvation Army that gave Daymond her first experience of being trusted to take on tasks side by side with men.[112] It was undoubtedly the WCG that brought her, like other working women with 'only limited schooling and uneven political experience, into an "active life"', as Scott described its aims.[113] She lived all her life in Devonport, imbued with what Hilson has called the 'dockyard culture' among the population, one which was 'associated with equality, mutual support, self-reliance and independence'.[114] Yet she recognized that there were times when people needed help. They were not all 'spongers', but people who had 'sickness and difficulties' to cope with.[115] Thus in 1937, despite being

110. *WMN*, 24 May 1949, p. 3.
111. *WMN*, 13 November 1919, p. 5.
112. *WDM*, 2 September 1912, p. 10.
113. Scott, *Feminism and the Politics of Working Women*, p. 6.
114. M. Hilson, 'Consumers and Politics: The Co-operative Movement in Plymouth, 1890–1920', *Labour History Review*, 67.1 (2002), p. 10.
115. *WMN*, 5 July 1935, p. 7.

committed to keeping the rates down, she voted against the attempt to reduce the rate of out-relief and risked the surcharge being applied to councillors. In weighing up the 'three pence off the rates' that she would personally like she decided that this could not be done 'at the expense of things that are essential to the welfare of the citizens'.[116] Although she chose to join the Conservative Party during the 1920s, while the WCG forged closer links to the Labour Party, she continued to support its work. Her association with the Guild had led her to the suffrage movement and to stand successfully for election as a Poor Law Guardian and as a councillor. She fought throughout her career for improvement on many fronts to the way women were treated and the services they received.

---

116. *WMN*, 30 April 1937, p. 5.

CHAPTER THREE

Mabel Lieda (Lida) Ramsay (1878–1954)

ANN ROBERTS

Mabel Ramsay, portrait cropped from a photograph taken at graduation from
University of Edinburgh in 1906, ©University of Edinburgh Archives. EUA CA1/
Female MBChB graduates, 1906, with signatures. Reuse not permitted

By the time Mabel Ramsay was able to cast her first parliamentary vote she
was already successful in her vocation.[1] And yet there was still much more
that she wanted to achieve. Although the path she had chosen was not an easy
one for a woman, in many ways she had been lucky. Her chosen profession
of doctor had already been opened up to women, albeit in limited numbers.
She does not herself explain why she was so determined on a career in medicine but it is clear that this was a course she had set for herself from a very
early age. Moreover she was encouraged by her parents, neither of whom

---

1. Mabel Ramsay wrote a memoir entitled *A Doctor's Zig-Zag Road*, which is unpublished. A copy
   is held by the Royal College of Physicians Archive referenced MS87. It is dated 1952 with hand-
   written updates to 1954.

Ann Roberts, 'Chapter Three: Mabel Lieda (Lida) Ramsay (1878–1954)' in: *Devon Women in Public
and Professional Life 1900–1950: Votes, Voices and Vocations.* University of Exeter Press (2021).
© Ann Roberts DOI: 10.47788/MTUG2347

suggested that such a route was not suitable for a woman. Even so, her turn to begin medical training had to wait until the family finances permitted, the medical education of her brother taking priority.

Born in Wandsworth, London on 14 November 1878 whilst her mother was staying with a family friend, she was the daughter of Andrew John Ramsay, a naval officer, and his wife Annie Catherine (née Thiele). Known to her family as 'Mabs', Ramsay was the middle child of the family, having an elder brother, Palmer, and a younger sister, Hilda. She described growing up in a close and loving family and having a happy childhood. Both her parents were a great influence, but especially her mother.

Ramsay's early childhood was spent in a variety of locations as her father was posted to naval establishments including Bermuda and Malta. Her mother was exceptionally well educated for a woman of her time and whilst the family were living abroad Mrs Ramsay herself undertook much of the education of her children. Later naval postings in Plymouth, Portsmouth and Scotland provided the opportunities that the young Mabel needed for a more structured education. Private schooling for six years at the Misses Lane's Ladies' School in Tavistock Road, Plymouth provided the grounding in subjects such as Latin and chemistry which were to become so important for her. Her obituary in the *British Medical Journal* records that after leaving school she trained as a gymnast as she had the idea that such training would help her in the orthopaedic work in which she hoped to specialize.[2] Her own account of her time as a pupil assistant at a gymnasium in Exeter suggests that it was a post she undertook reluctantly. It was thought that it might lead to permanent work and she felt she had to contribute to the family's finances. At that time it was by no means certain that her family would ever be in a position to fund her medical training. Her time as a pupil assistant at the gymnasium was not a success as she did not enjoy the work. She left after a year, feeling that she had failed.[3]

Fortunately, the family finances then improved as the result of an inheritance, so Ramsay joined her father who was stationed at Cobh, Ireland (then known as Queenstown) where, already over 20 years old, she enrolled at Cork High School for Girls. With the extra tuition she received at Cork she was able to pass the entrance examination, which enabled her to matriculate as a medical student at Edinburgh University, which she did on 1 October 1900, studying at the Medical College for Women. At that time most medical

---

2. *British Medical Journal (BMJ)*, 22 May 1954, p. 1212.
3. London, Royal College of Physicians Archive (RCP), autobiographical memoirs entitled 'A doctor's zig-zag road', MS87, pp. 21–22.

education for women was conducted separately from that for their male colleagues as mixed classes were deemed immodest and indelicate. Ramsay herself relates that she was so unsophisticated that when she became a medical student she had much to learn as she knew very little of the facts of life.[4] During her time at Edinburgh the undergraduates annually petitioned the Senate to ask that all of the University's medical educational facilities should be equally available to men and to women students.[5]

Whilst she was at Edinburgh, Ramsay met and was befriended by Dr Elsie Inglis[6] whom she described as 'a good and stalwart friend during the six years I spent at Edinburgh'.[7] Inglis was lecturer in gynaecology at the Medical College for Women and Ramsay regarded her as a particular mentor, both as a doctor and as the person who first awakened her political interests. She recounts in her memoir how her political education began when Inglis asked her to act as a 'teller of votes' at a Women's Liberal Conference in Edinburgh. Later, during the suffrage campaigns, Ramsay acted as understudy for Inglis at an open-air meeting in Dundee, addressing the crowd from the back of a flat-bed lorry.[8] Inglis was one of a small group of friends invited by Ramsay's parents to a postgraduation dinner held to celebrate her successful qualification.

Immediately after the graduation ceremony her father gave her £5 to cover the cost of the fees for registration with the General Medical Council (GMC) saying to her that as she was now qualified to earn her own livelihood, her brother was a naval surgeon, and her sister married with a family, that his life's work was done. He died unexpectedly three weeks later.

After graduation and qualification as a doctor and a few weeks providing locum cover for friends, Ramsay's first appointment was as house surgeon at the Glasgow Maternity Hospital. She accepted this post on the recommendation of Dr Rosa Bale, the first woman doctor in Plymouth, who advised her that 'a woman doctor should always be well trained in midwifery'.[9] It was in this role in Glasgow that she experienced the extent of the overcrowding and poor living conditions of the tenement blocks and common lodging houses, where she was

---

4. RCP, MS87, p. 19.
5. RCP, MS87, p. 33.
6. Dr Elsie Inglis was an innovative Scottish doctor and suffragist. She was joint founder, with her father, of the Edinburgh Medical College for Women and founder of the Scottish Women's Hospitals. For more information see L. Leneman, 'Inglis, Elsie Maud (1864–1917), physician and surgeon' in *Oxford Dictionary of National Biography*.
7. RCP, MS87, p. 29.
8. RCP, MS87, p. 43.
9. RCP, MS87, p. 48.

required to deliver babies in insanitary conditions. Many of her patients suffered from pelvic deformities as a result of rickets, making childbirth particularly difficult, and she frequently carried back with her the bodies of stillborn babies.[10] Ramsay describes how her patients were grateful for her to do this as it saved on funeral costs, which was a significant cost for poor families. At this time stillbirths did not have to be registered and so no formal funeral was required. Registration of stillbirths did not become a legal requirement in England until 1927 and in Scotland until 1939.[11] It was, however, not uncommon for the stillborn baby's body to be used for research purposes. Ramsay had been asked to send any of which she took possession to Professor William Macewen of the Glasgow Western Infirmary for his research in to bone development.[12] Later, whilst expressing her hopes that she had made some small contribution to Professor Macewen's research, Ramsay refers to the stillborn babies as 'foetuses' rather than as babies, perhaps in an attempt to distance herself from the process and signifying a degree of unease about the practice.[13]

Ramsay's next position was that of Assistant Medical Officer of Health at Huddersfield under the direction of the Medical Officer of Health, Dr Samson George Moore. Her time at Huddersfield coincided with the pioneering work being undertaken by Moore under the chairman of the Public Health Committee, Alderman Benjamin Broadbent. Huddersfield is recognized as a pioneer of the infant welfare movement, by introducing a comprehensive system of notification of births and health visiting.[14] Ramsay became one of the women doctors recruited by Moore to carry out a systematic programme of visiting newly delivered mothers and their babies in an attempt to reduce the high infant mortality rates then prevailing. The scheme was predicated on a local Act which required the notification of all live births within two days of the delivery taking place. This Act was to lead to the passing of adoptive national legislation, the Notification of Births Act 1907, which became compulsory in 1915. Although it is not clear that the Huddersfield Scheme produced any greater reduction in infant mortality rates than occurred elsewhere, it was certainly regarded at the time as a success

10. RCP, MS87, p. 49.

11. Research by the University of Glasgow, *The Scottish Way of Birth and Death*, has demonstrated how the introduction of legislation concerning birth and death registrations in Scotland frequently lagged behind that in England.

12. For more information about Professor Sir William Macewen and his research into bone development and particularly into rickets see I.F. Russell, 'Macewen, Sir William (1848–1924)' in the *Oxford Dictionary of National Biography*.

13. RCP, MS87, p. 50.

14. H. Marland, 'A Pioneer in Infant Welfare: the Huddersfield Scheme 1903–1920', *Social History of Medicine* 6.1 (April 1993), pp. 25–50.

and was the foundation of the English infant welfare movement.[15] Ramsay believed that the scheme was not just successful on its own terms of reducing infant mortality, but also in the provision of child welfare and maternity clinics across the country and even internationally.[16] Ramsay spent eighteen months in Huddersfield, travelling around the district visiting mothers and babies and attempting to counter some of the lingering superstitions regarding childbirth such as a belief that a lying-in woman needed to remain confined to bed for ten days with a roaring fire, no open windows, no cold drinks and not permitted to wash, even in the hottest of summer weather.

It was during her time at Huddersfield that Ramsay studied for, and successfully obtained, her Diploma in Public Health (DPH), although other women doctors involved in the Huddersfield Scheme did not do so. On two afternoons each week she travelled to Manchester to attend the Public Health Diploma lectures at Owens College. After six months' study she entered for the Victoria DPH exam and although she 'passed brilliantly in bacteriology' she failed the chemistry exam.[17] Unwilling to be deterred by this setback, or to wait for a further six months to re-sit the exam, she took extra coaching in chemistry with a lecturer at Huddersfield Technical School and registered for the DPH chemistry exam at Cambridge, which was due to take place a fortnight later. This time she passed, and was just in time to register for the second part of the diploma at Cambridge. Throughout her career, she continually strived to learn more and to become a better clinician.

Huddersfield was also to provide her with an introduction to medico-politics, an area which was to become a major factor in her working life and which was to benefit from her prodigious energy. The women doctors at Huddersfield had been appointed on a reduced salary of 100 guineas (£105), after the members of the Public Health Committee several times reduced the budget they were willing to invest in the scheme.[18] In part this was a consequence of Dr Moore's insistence on the necessity of employing medically qualified women in the role, believing them to be best able to dispense advice, and presumably more likely to have their advice followed.[19] However, the salary was significantly less than any male doctor, even one newly qualified, would have accepted. Hilary Marland suggests that as a result there was a rapid turnover of the assistant Medical

---

15. H. Marland, p. 25.
16. RCP, MS87, pp. 52–53.
17. RCP, MS87, p. 57.
18. H. Marland, p. 36.
19. H. Marland, p. 35.

Officers of Health.[20] Dr Ramsay appears to have remained in this post for longer than many others who were appointed in order to make the most of the opportunity to obtain her public health qualification.

However, the low salaries had not gone unnoticed. The Association of Registered Medical Women (ARMW)[21] had already passed a resolution to the effect that women practitioners should under no circumstances accept a lower salary than that which had been agreed by the profession.[22] It had already been noted that where local Education Boards were advertising posts for medical inspectors of schools as required by the 1907 Education Act as being suitable for medical women, the salaries offered were lower than those offered to men. Fearing that this practice was now spreading to the first women being appointed to public health roles, Dr May Thorne, president of the ARMW, addressed a meeting of the Northern Association where Dr Ramsay was in attendance, deploring the practice. Ramsay recalled that she told Dr Thorne that she was staying in Huddersfield for a short time only so that she could do postgraduate work and achieve her DPH qualification. She explained that she had no intention of staying in the post permanently and so she was not censured.[23]

Although she appeared to have enjoyed her time in Huddersfield, and to have been able to use the experience to further her professional development, Ramsay's heart was not in public health work and she was keen to return to a more clinical role. However, it is likely that her experiences in Glasgow and Huddersfield informed her passionate support of maternal and child welfare services, for which she was to campaign so eloquently through her later work with the Plymouth Citizens' Association.

A further appointment as senior house surgeon at the Women's and Children's Hospital, Leeds followed.[24] It was here that she began work on her thesis to Edinburgh University for the MD based on 'Three-hundred cases of Bacillus Coli Infection', a study of the bacteria now generally referred to as E. coli, and its effects on a range of organs in the body. She completed and submitted her thesis during her early years in Plymouth. In order to obtain the necessary case studies Ramsay needed to obtain the support of house

---

20. H. Marland, p. 36.
21. The Association of Registered Medical Women was founded in London in 1879 with only nine members, representing most of the qualified medical women then in existence in the United Kingdom. A number of provincial associations were set up as more and more women qualified in medicine. It later became reformed as the Medical Women's Federation.
22. *London Daily News*, 10 January 1908, p. 9.
23. RCP, MS87, p. 56.
24. *BMJ*, 22 May 1954, p. 1212.

physicians to examine cases in their wards. As house physicians were almost all male doctors, many of whom resented the intrusion of women into their profession, this support was not always forthcoming. During one six-month period she was unable to progress her research, but eventually two doctors, an ophthalmic surgeon and an ear and throat specialist, enabled her to attend outpatients' clinics to carry out examinations and collect sufficient material to complete her thesis.[25]

She had returned in 1908 to Plymouth, where her widowed mother was living. It was here that she set up her medical practice and was to spend the rest of her life. Her mother took the lease on a property in Wentworth Villas, Tavistock Road, and mother and daughter moved together. On her way to Wentworth Villas on the day that she and her mother were moving in, as she passed the building site of the new civic museum and library, Ramsay came across an accident where a workman had fallen from scaffolding and she stopped to provide assistance. The workman therefore became the first of Ramsay's very many patients in Plymouth.

Ramsay later bought the Wentworth Villas premises when the landlord, a German musician, decided to sell up and return to Germany in 1913. By this time she was sufficiently well established to consider such an investment. Initially she cycled around the town on her calls but soon adopted a more modern mode of transport, being, she suggested, the first woman to ride a motor bicycle in the town.[26] An accident on her motorcycle in 1913 was reported in the local newspaper with a degree of interest.[27] She purchased her first car in 1916.

Ramsay had set up her medical practice in Plymouth at the suggestion of her mother and encouraged by the first woman to work as a doctor in the town, Dr Rosa Bale. Dr Bale had set up her own practice in 1895 and so Ramsay found she already had a natural ally. She was to describe Bale as 'one of the finest women doctors with whom I ever had the happiness to be associated'.[28] Even so, and with a precedent already set, Ramsay did not find that the medical establishment welcomed her presence unequivocally. Despite repeated attempts she was unsuccessful in obtaining posts within the hospitals and public dispensary. In fact, after one application she was sent a letter saying that the committee of the Plymouth Public Dispensary had resolved that 'No

---

25. RCP, MS87, p. 65.
26. RCP, MS87, p. 64.
27. *Western Evening Herald (WEH)*, 1 September 1913.
28. RCP, MS87, p. 60.

woman doctor would ever be considered as eligible for appointment on the medical staff', although no such resolution had been passed.[29]

It was during the early years of her career that Ramsay was to develop her lifelong interest in promoting the interests of women. Alongside her medical work, much of her life was spent in campaigning for the rights of women. She was to say much later that one third of her life was given to her medical practice; one third to her social and political work—medical and otherwise; and one third in sleep and play.[30] She was also an ardent supporter of the next generation of women doctors who came along after her, as she had been supported by those who preceded her. Dr Annie Bryce was to write in an obituary to Ramsay which was printed in the *British Medical Journal* (BMJ) in 1954 that she was a 'steadfast friend to the young and newly qualified'.[31]

Ramsay was already aware of the difficulties that many women such as she faced. Her own ambition of becoming a surgeon was still denied to women doctors. She was also acutely aware that despite her status as a taxpayer and as a professional woman with a university degree she was not entitled to vote in parliamentary elections. But it was not until she was approached by Margaret Robertson, one of the organizers for the National Union of Women's Suffrage Societies (NUWSS), that she became an active campaigner. Robertson had suggested that Ramsay help form a Plymouth branch of the NUWSS. This prompted her to read a book she had been given some years earlier but had not so far read. *The Subjection of Women* by John Stuart Mill convinced her to assist in the formation of a NUWSS branch, of which she became secretary. The branch office was established at 4 Wentworth Villas, Plymouth, the address of her home and surgery. Both Ramsay and her mother Mrs Annie Catherine Ramsay became active in the suffrage campaign. As branch secretary Dr Ramsay tirelessly organized meetings, wrote letters to the press advocating the cause of female suffrage, and quizzed prospective parliamentary candidates on their attitude to women's enfranchisement. She brought national figures, such as Millicent Fawcett, Eleanor Rathbone and Viscountess Snowden to speak at Plymouth, inviting them to stay at her home. In the early days of her involvement with the suffrage movement, though, she did not seem to have advocated universal suffrage, saying at one meeting that 'We would give the vote to a woman who possesses the same qualification as a man.'[32]

---

29. RCP, MS87, p. 62.
30. RCP, MS87, p. 121.
31. BMJ, 22 May 1954, p. 1212.
32. *Devon and Exeter Gazette (DEG)*, 14 October 1909.

Ramsay was much in demand as a speaker at suffrage meetings and rallies throughout the region, speaking at meetings across Devon, Cornwall and Somerset as well as at the meetings organized in Plymouth itself.[33] She also attended the national conferences and annual meetings of the NUWSS in London, where she processed wearing her cap and gown.[34] In the summer of 1911 a series of meetings in Cornwall and Devon was organized by Rev. Hattie Baker.[35] A horse caravan was hired and relays of suffragists carried out open-air meetings at various towns throughout the two counties. Ramsay spent two weeks of her summer holiday taking part in the caravan tour, speaking at rallies and sleeping in the caravan.[36]

Such high exposure in the cause of women's suffrage was difficult for women doctors, who needed to maintain a professional status and not risk their reputations through active campaigning. It has been suggested that it was problematic for professional women to take an active role in the suffrage movement.[37] For most professional women, and especially for women doctors, it was important that they maintained their reputations and did nothing that could lead to allegations of impropriety. Many thought that open support for women's suffrage, even through the constitutional suffrage organizations, might well harm their newfound status. One exception to this was women teachers, probably through sheer weight of their numbers. By 1911 there were over 50,000 women members of the National Union of Teachers, more than half of the membership, and 180,000 women who called themselves teachers. By contrast the number of women doctors was still just a tiny proportion of the profession. Fewer than 2% of medical practitioners were women, around 1,000 women in total. So although some women doctors were supporters of the movement this was usually in the guise of making financial donations and sometimes taking part in the great processions.

Doctors, both men and women, needed to avoid any activities which could be considered as against the law. Acquiring a criminal conviction could result in any doctor being struck off the medical register. But women doctors also

---

33. For example *Exeter and Plymouth Gazette*, 14 October 1909; *West Briton and Cornish Advertiser*, 21 November 191; *Western Times (WT)*, 8 February 1913.
34. RCP, MS87, p. 104.
35. *Common Cause (CC)*, 7 September 1911. More information about Rev. Baker can be found here: Devon History Society, *Lives of Devon Women Suffrage Activists, 1866–1918* <https://www.devonhistorysociety.org.uk/baker-rev-harriet-hatty>.
36. In her memoir Ramsay records the event as taking place in the summer of 1912, although reports in *CC* confirm that the tour took place in the July and August of 1911.
37. J.F. Geddes, 'The Doctors' Dilemma: medical woman and the British suffrage movement', *Women's History Review*, 18.2 (2009), pp. 203–18.

needed to protect their reputations and decorum in a way that men did not. That so few women doctors became involved in the suffrage movement is therefore hardly surprising but is also testimony to their reluctance to risk bringing their profession into disrepute, particularly in view of the opposition that many faced from their male colleagues over becoming doctors in the first place. Much later in her life, Ramsay was shocked to discover that the GMC had recorded some motoring fines she had received against her name.

The boycott of the 1911 census was a matter of debate for the NUWSS—a debate conducted largely through the correspondence pages of the *Common Cause*, the weekly newspaper of the National Union. Correspondents to the paper were concerned not just about the law-breaking that would be entailed by a refusal to complete census returns but also that statistics relating to motherhood and women's share in the industrial life of the country would be of benefit to women and should therefore be collected. Ramsay joined in the debate. In her view census resistance was an immediate way of making a protest against the continued disenfranchisement of women. More significantly, though, she argued that the new questions to be asked of married women concerning fertility rates and childhood mortality required a special protest. She was concerned that such statistics would be misused as a way of restricting women's employment by arguing that high infant mortality rates were caused by women's factory work. She personally had no fear that statistics, when correctly used, could form a reason for restricting married women's employment, but was concerned that evidence was being sought to formulate legislation seriously affecting the interests of women, who had no say in the formulation of such legislation.[38]

The committee of the NUWSS decided to take no part in a boycott of the census, arguing that such 'anti-social' acts were only justified when all else has been tried and that that point had not been reached and also that to do so would impair the validity of data affecting the interests of women for the next ten years.[39]

Ramsay and her mother did take part in the census boycott, and in fact hosted a 'census resistance party' at their home, where around twenty women gathered to evade the enumerators. The following morning Mrs Ramsay stayed at home to await the enumerator, whilst Dr Ramsay went about her clinical activities. Mrs Ramsay refused to provide any information, leaving the enumerator to gather such information as he could from neighbours. The census form

---

38. *CC*, 16 March 1911.
39. *CC*, 16 March 1911.

was eventually completed and signed by the enumerator. It recorded the names of Annie Ramsay, Mabel Ramsay and their lodger Nora Christine Bridges, with their approximate ages. Three other residents are listed with their names as 'unknown' and described as a maternity nurse, a cook and a domestic servant. The census form is further inscribed 'Suffragettes'. There is, though, no mention of the remainder of the twenty or so women who had spent the night there. One of those other women was almost certainly Dr Ramsay's sister, Mrs Hilda Andrew, for whom no census return appears to exist.

Dr Ramsay later described how she spent several months worrying about whether a summons would arrive taking her to court.[40] No summons was issued, though, and she was able to avoid a court appearance, although she could not have known at the time that that would be the outcome. She was to say that she later understood that there had been so many resisters that the authorities had considered it would be unwise to take proceedings. Ramsay's census resistance was undoubtedly a brave decision to have taken, which could have had significant consequences, and was clearly one she did not take lightly. Her concern for women's rights sometimes outweighed personal considerations. The *Common Cause* later congratulated Mrs and Dr Ramsay and described a rather jolly party with much laughter.[41]

Both Dr and Mrs Ramsay also participated in the 1913 suffrage pilgrimage, which was probably, along with the census boycott, the most high profile of the suffragist activities.[42] When the 'pilgrims' arrived in Plymouth she joined her mother who, at the age of 60, travelled the whole way from Land's End to Hyde Park, and the rest of the pilgrims at their rally at the Corn Exchange. After their weekend in Plymouth, Dr Ramsay marched with the pilgrims as they continued their journey as far as Plympton. After a meeting there, she left them to continue on their way, whilst she returned to her medical duties in Plymouth. But each evening until they reached Taunton, she caught the train to their overnight stop to see that all was well with her mother and to take part in the meetings, returning to Plymouth by train early the next morning.

In March 1923, whilst visiting Bermuda at the invitation of Gladys Misick Morrell, Ramsay addressed a public meeting at the Mechanics Hall in Hamilton about how best to achieve women's suffrage there. Morrell was a leading light of the Bermudan women's suffrage movement. She had been involved in the suffrage movement in England, where she had been attending university and

40. RCP, MS87, p. 105.
41. *CC*, 27 April 1911.
42. RCP, MS87, pp. 102–15.

it may be that this is how the two women met, or possibly they had been childhood friends since Ramsay's mother had been born in Bermuda and it is where she herself spent part of her young life. Morrell clearly regarded Ramsay very highly and admired her campaigning tactics. Ramsay urged the Bermudan women to start a properly organized suffrage society. As a result the meeting concluded with a resolution to establish the Bermuda Woman Suffrage Society (BWSS), of which Morrell became secretary. The campaign by the women of Bermuda was not ultimately successful until 1944.[43] When she was writing her memoirs in 1952, Ramsay commented that matters had progressed quickly since that time and there were by then three women MPs in Bermuda. When visiting the island in 1950 Ramsay renewed contact with some of the original members of the BWSS and expressed a great sense of satisfaction in their achievements.[44]

The suffrage movement gave Ramsay her first experience of public speaking and it was where she honed the skills which were to prove invaluable to the many roles she was to take on in the interwar period.

Ramsay was continuing to pursue her medical ambitions and within her practice she took every opportunity that came her way to undertake minor surgical procedures in the hope of one day being able to become a surgeon.[45] It was the First World War, though, that gave her the greatest exposure to surgical work. In September 1914, Ramsay served under the Women's National Service Unit at Antwerp with the Belgian Red Cross and was in Antwerp during the bombardment and the retreat to Ostend. There she served in an entirely female unit, staffed by seven women doctors, twelve nurses, six VADs and a female transport officer. She then worked with the French Red Cross at Cherbourg before returning to Plymouth in May 1915. Later service as a civilian medical practitioner with the Southern General Territorial Hospital followed.[46] The experiences of her time serving in Belgium and France were to stand her in good stead after the war, when she was admitted to the Royal College of Surgeons, Edinburgh. Ramsay herself said: 'I would not have it thought that I was filled only with the desire to help wounded soldiers. It seemed to me a useful way of getting the experience I wanted in order to become a surgeon.'[47] During her time in Belgium and France, Ramsay carried

43. *Bermuda Bios*, 'Gladys Misick Morrell' <http://www.bermudabiographies.bm/Biographies/Biography-Gladys%20Morrell.html> [accessed 16 March 2017].
44. RCP, MS87, pp. 111–12.
45. RCP, MS87, p. 66.
46. Plymouth, The Box, 1670/20, Plymouth Medical Society papers.
47. RCP, MS87 pp. 68–69.

out many surgical procedures, including amputations, of which it would have been impossible for her to gain experience under normal circumstances.

Back in Plymouth she worked to rebuild her practice, which had lost patients during her absence, and was also appointed as Anaesthetist and temporary Outpatient Surgeon to the South Devon and East Cornwall Hospital. She also took on the role of civilian medical practitioner at the Territorial Hospital in Salisbury Road. When it became clear that it would be necessary to recruit women for auxiliary military services she was asked by the BMA, along with Dr Christine Murrell, to attend a conference to advise on how medical examination of mobilized women should be carried out. She went on to carry out medical examinations of the women recruits in Plymouth herself. In charge of seventy-eight surgical beds at Salisbury Road, she undertook both medical and surgical work. The surgical work again reinforced her determination to specialize in this area. She took full advantage of these appointments, which in peacetime had been denied to her. She also participated as lecturer in a programme of talks about her experiences in Belgium and France given for the purpose of raising funds for the Scottish Women's Hospitals in France and Serbia and the Belgian Soldiers Fund.[48]

At the end of the summer of 1918 the influenza epidemic arrived in Plymouth. Already working long hours providing medical care to her own patients, those of another general practitioner who was on war service, and her patients at the Territorial Hospital, during the epidemic Ramsay frequently had to work eighteen hours a day. She was not infected herself, having had a mild bout of influenza earlier in the summer. She describes the situation in the town as being one of terror which she compared to that of the cholera outbreaks of former times. The sight of a doctor's car in a street brought crowds asking for help and people attempted to press money into her hands to obtain treatment for their relatives. For a time no funerals were able to take place.[49]

Amongst the patients in her hospital wards, no cases of influenza occurred. This she attributed in part to having given instructions that every soldier was to gargle every night and morning, but also to having given permission for convalescent patients to continue taking daily exercise in the parks proving that they undertook not to go into public houses, private homes or public vehicles. She believed that her patients had kept their promises as in other wards within the hospital there were many cases of blue pneumonia and a

---

48. See for example *DEG*, 23 April 1915; *WT*, 28 September 1915.
49. RCP, MS87, p. 95.

very high mortality.[50] For her war service, Dr Mabel Ramsay was awarded the Mons Star, the General Services Medal, and the Victory Medal.

Towards the end of the war the passing of the Representation of the People Act 1918 enabled some women to vote for the first time, although not on equal terms with men. The Sex Disqualification (Removal) Act was passed in 1919 following which the Council of the Royal College of Surgeons, Edinburgh, decided to admit women doctors for examination. The first two women were admitted in June 1920. The RCS Edinburgh was not the first of the Royal Colleges to admit women to its membership. The Royal College of Surgeons, London, had admitted its first woman fellow, Eleanor Davies-Colley, in 1911, although by 1919 there were still only four women fellows.[51] During 1913, Ramsay gave up her practice for six months and went to the Royal Free Hospital School of Medicine in London to undertake postgraduate work for the Primary FRCS England under the tuition of the first two women professors in England, Mary Lucas Keene, Professor of Anatomy, and Winifred Cullis, Professor of Physiology. She did not sit the examination at that time, though, as the war intervened and when she did sit the examination in 1918 she failed in both subjects.[52] After her mother's death in 1920, Ramsay decided that she would study once more in order to again sit for the examination but this time in Edinburgh, studying every night for four hours. In January 1921 she went to Edinburgh for the examination. She was one of only two women amongst the fifty-seven candidates. Both women were successful so she became the joint third woman to gain admission,[53] specializing in Obstetrics and Gynaecology. As is the convention, on being admitted as a surgeon, Ramsay ceased to use the title of Doctor in medical settings and reverted to being Miss Ramsay. In due course she became consulting gynaecologist to the City Hospital, Plymouth and to the Infirmary; consulting obstetrician to the Three Towns Maternity Home, to the Salvation Army Maternity Home and to the counties of Devon and Cornwall; and consulting surgeon to the Plymouth Public Dispensary. She also lectured to midwives in the district and examined for the Royal College of Nursing.[54] In 1929 she was admitted, by invitation, as a foundation member of the British (later Royal) College of Obstetricians and Gynaecologists. She was a regular contributor of papers on clinical topics

50. RCP, MS87, pp. 94–95.
51. Royal College of Surgeons in England, *History of Women in Surgery* <https://www.rcseng.ac.uk/careers-in-surgery/women-in-surgery/history>.
52. RCP, MS87, p. 66.
53. RCP, MS87, p. 98.
54. BMJ, 22 May 1954, p. 1212.

to medical journals such as *The Lancet*, the *BMJ*, the *British Journal of Obstetrics and Gynaecology*, and the *Journal of State Medicine*.

After the franchise was gained, the Plymouth branch of the NUWSS was reconstituted as the Plymouth Citizens' Association, of which Ramsay was elected Hon. Secretary.[55] The Citizens' Association was non-party political, its aims being to foster an impartial study of the wider social and political questions, and to stimulate interest and participation in municipal affairs. Whilst continuing to campaign for women's enfranchisement to be on equal terms with that of men, it also helped to promote the candidature of women for the town council. Its chairman, Mrs Clara Daymond, was one of the first to be elected and others followed crossing the political spectrum. When Viscountess Astor stood in the parliamentary by-election of 1919 the Citizens' Association promoted her candidature, too, Ramsay speaking for her at many meetings. Ramsay's own political affiliations are unclear. She supported women candidates regardless of the political party they represented or whether they were standing as independent candidates. There were, however, rumours circulating in 1924 that Ramsay might stand as a Labour candidate herself for Tavistock.[56] No such candidature came about.

One long-running campaign of the Citizens' Association was that to have women officers appointed to the police service. Ramsay and Lady Astor were both passionate about the need for policewomen to be appointed, seeing it as a moral issue. In their view women officers were necessary to deal with cases of child assaults, and questioning and taking evidence from women prisoners. Women officers were also thought to be vital for patrolling the parks and preventing unseemly or immoral behaviour.[57] The Citizens' Association joined forces with other local organizations including the women's division of the Labour Party, the Women's Co-operative Guilds, social workers, and religious groups, in lobbying the Watch Committee and the Town Council on the issue. Two women were appointed in 1919 but the women officers' division was disbanded and the policewomen dismissed two years later on the grounds of cost. Ramsay and Astor continued to lobby especially at election times, writing letters and sending deputations throughout the 1920s and 1930s but without success. It took until 1945 for the campaigning to gain success, with the appointment of women police constables with the powers of arrest, although some auxiliary officers were taken on a little earlier.

---

55. RCP, MS87, p. 109.
56. *WT*, 17 October 1924.
57. *Western Morning News*, 19 November 1925.

The Plymouth Citizens' Association concerned itself with a wide range of issues, especially those of concern to women, including the control of alcohol.[58] This is hardly surprising given Astor's famous teetotalism. Ramsay herself was not an abstainer, although she was concerned about the effects of excessive alcohol consumption, in particular as a cause of domestic abuse and child cruelty. She came across many examples of the latter when she was asked, shortly after the end of the war, to act for the NSPCC in visiting cases of child cruelty and acting as expert witness at subsequent court proceedings.[59]

Her previous experiences in Glasgow and Huddersfield meant that Ramsay was a passionate supporter of the introduction and expansion of mother and child welfare services. Even before the 1914–1918 war, efforts were under way to persuade both Plymouth and Devonport Councils to adopt health and welfare schemes for mothers and children. A national conference held in Plymouth in 1912, at which Ramsay spoke, proposed the setting up of school medical and dental clinics. When an infant welfare clinic was finally established in Plymouth she became the first medical officer, drawing on her Huddersfield experience to good effect. Baby shows soon followed, in conjunction with National Baby Weeks and although she judged many baby shows she soon realized that such shows always lead to disappointment for most of the mothers, and she refused to take part in any more.[60] Speaking in support of Waldorf Astor during his election campaign in 1918, she endorsed Astor's statement that children deserved better than was currently provided.

Other issues embraced by the Citizens' Association, and endorsed by Ramsay, included the provision of family planning services, adult education, and the abolition of private slaughterhouses. In 1920 the Citizens' Association provided a list of women to be recommended for appointment as magistrates.[61] Ramsay also spoke out against suggestions that the Contagious Diseases Acts should be reintroduced as a way of controlling the spread of sexually transmitted infections. She was to say, 'I am entirely opposed to anything in the way of compulsory legislation,' arguing instead that boys as well as girls should be taught to revere their bodies and understand the sanctity of marriage and parenthood.[62] Her unstinting support for the provision of family planning services was perhaps unsurprising. Many women obstetricians were particularly passionate about the provision of information on birth control, in view of the

---

58. *WMN*, 23 June 1920.
59. RCP, MS87, pp. 131–32.
60. RCP, MS87, pp. 52–53.
61. *WMN*, 30 June 1920.
62. *WMN*, 21 February 1921.

number of patients they had to treat as a result of botched illegal abortions. Ramsay certainly saw her share.

One of the issues that crossed Ramsay's medical and social interests concerned the lack of women doctors being successful in gaining hospital appointments. Although a few women's hospitals had been established, such as those in London and Edinburgh, women patients who needed hospital care were rarely able to be treated by a woman doctor unless they could afford private nursing home fees. Although a petition was signed by 3,500 Plymouth women calling for the appointment of a woman surgeon, the committee of the local hospital refused to see the deputation bearing it.[63] As a result, in November 1925 an appeal was launched for funds for the upkeep of two beds so that women patients who preferred the services of a woman doctor could obtain them.[64] The fundraising was so successful that this was later increased to three beds. Non-fee paying patients could then, with the consent of the Guardians, be admitted to Greenbank Nursing Home under the care of a woman doctor of their choice, as if they were private patients. By the time of the Committee's first annual meeting in February 1928, the committee, chaired by Ramsay, consisted of twenty-five women and included six women doctors.[65] The Women's Hospital Fund continued its work until 1946, when the National Health Service Act showed that it would no longer be necessary. The Fund had never been in debt and its surplus funds were handed over to Plymouth charities. Much of the surgical work carried out under the Fund's auspices was carried out by Ramsay.[66]

Ramsay's medico-political activities ran alongside her medical practice and her social work. Her early introduction to the work of the ARMW during her time in Huddersfield was to foreshadow her involvement with many of the associations and societies which represented the interests of doctors, and some which were particularly concerned with the interests of medical women.

Almost as soon as she set up her practice in Plymouth she became aware that the local medical establishment was unwelcoming to women doctors. Dr Bale, who had been in practice in Plymouth for thirteen years when Ramsay arrived, had not been invited to join the Plymouth Medical Society (PMS). The PMS, one of the longest established societies of its kind in the country, had been founded in 1794. Membership was by the proposal and seconding of existing

---

63. RCP, MS87, p. 128.
64. The Box, 1670/20.
65. *WMN*, 24 February 1928.
66. RCP, MS87, p. 128

members followed by election by ballot, but if one in five of the membership blackballed the nominee they would be excluded.[67] Bale had not been proposed for membership, nor initially was Ramsay invited to join. However, Ramsay did not wait for an invitation and applied for membership as she wanted to be able to use the Society's library resources to help in her writing of her MD thesis.[68] After some discussion, in October 1909 the Society decided to elect members without a ballot on the nomination of two members, unless a ballot was specifically called for.[69] In 1911 a further amendment to the constitution allowed for membership to be extended at the invitation of the Council. In February 1910 the first 'Lady Member', Dr Mabel Ramsay, was admitted. It was not until 1919 that Dr Bale became a member. By this time several women doctors were practising in the town and more were to become members during the 1920s. The timing of the change in the rules, coming as it did shortly after Ramsay's arrival and the fact that Ramsay and not Bale was the first to be nominated, does suggest that Ramsay was already less willing to settle for the status quo than perhaps Bale had been. In 1930–1931 Ramsay became the first medical woman to serve as President of the Society.

With the commencement of the National Health Insurance Act of 1911, the BMA formed its National Insurance Act Committee in order to give panel doctors an independent voice. Panel doctors were those doctors who provided medical services for the members of the population who were covered by the Insurance Act. The work of this committee continued until the formation of the NHS. In 1916, Ramsay was appointed by the Plymouth Panel Committee as their representative to attend the annual National Health Insurance Act Conferences, the only medical woman to attend. She was subsequently invited to become a member of the BMA's Insurance Act Committee, in which capacity she served from 1919 until 1938.[70] She also served on the Additional Benefits Sub-committee from 1928 to 1938 and a number of other BMA committees including the Disciplinary Procedure Committee and one concerned with the causes of puerperal morbidity and mortality. When the BMA held its Annual Meeting in Plymouth in 1938, she acted as vice-president of the Obstetrics and Gynaecology Section. During the week of the conference, the South Western Association of the Medical Women's Federation (MWF) held a luncheon for one hundred

---

67. The Box, 1670/18 Plymouth Medical Society Rules and Regulations 1904.
68. RCP, MS87, p. 125.
69. The Box, 1670/19, Plymouth Medical Society Rules and Regulations 1913.
70. RCP, MS87, p. 116; 22 May 1954, p. 1212.

women members of the BMA who were attending the meeting, including Dr Rosa Bale. As the first woman doctor in the south west of England, Bale received a standing ovation.[71]

Ramsay became a founder member of the MWF, the successor organization to the ARMW, on its creation in 1917. When a South Western Association was formed two years later, Ramsay was appointed as representative to the national council.[72] She later became honorary secretary of the MWF and from 1932 to 1934 served a two-year term as president. Her association with the MWF was the longest lasting of her career, extending from the Federation's inauguration beyond her retirement and until her death in 1954. It was also the organization whose work took the most of her non-clinical time and was closest to her heart. At the MWF she met and worked with many of the most significant and influential medical women of the 1920s and 1930s including Lady Florence Barrett, Louisa Martindale, Catherine Chisholm and Louisa Aldrich-Blake.

The MWF's aims were to 'obtain equal treatment for women doctors within the profession and to promote the education, study and practice of medicine among women and to advance medical research'.[73] In the 1920s, a number of medical schools which admitted women during the First World War began to return to a policy of exclusion, and the principle of medical co-education came under threat again. This would have resonated with Ramsay in light of her own participation in petitioning at Edinburgh during her time as a student. Although the Sex Disqualification (Removal) Act had apparently opened professions to women, local authorities and other employing bodies frequently instituted their own regulations imposing marriage bars. Such regulations had a significant impact because of the increasing employment of women doctors within expanding public health services. A Standing Committee on Public Health was eventually set up to deal with the issues affecting the numerous women in the public health service, which had already been of concern when Ramsay herself was working as an Assistant Medical Officer of Health in Huddersfield.

The MWF was also concerned with wider issues of women's health. Committees were appointed to address the question of nutrition, lunacy law reform, assaults on young persons, the registration of nursing homes, adequate provision of birth control information, and the menopause. A leaflet on advice

71. RCP, MS87, p. 129.
72. RCP, MS87, p. 116.
73. Quoted in J. M. Scott, 'Women and the GMC: the struggle for representation', *Journal of the Royal Society of Medicine*, 81 (1988), 164–66 (p. 164).

regarding the hygiene of menstruation was published and sold 10,000 copies within a year.[74] These were all subjects with which Ramsay was concerned and were causes that frequently had direct relevance to the causes she was involved with through the Plymouth Citizen's Association.

The MWF had to be constantly vigilant that the views of women doctors were represented in matters affecting the medical profession and that their particular expertise was drawn upon where they may be able to contribute a gendered perspective. A case in point occurred in 1924 when the Home Office set up a committee to 'Enquire into Sexual Offences Against Young Persons'. It came to the attention of the MWF that although representatives of the medical profession had been asked to serve on the committee, no medical woman was appointed. The MWF wrote to the Secretary of State welcoming the formation of the committee, but expressing regret that no woman doctor was included. As they pointed out: 'The medical condition of the child and the offender plays such an important part in these cases.'[75] No reply was received other than a formal acknowledgement, and no woman doctor was appointed to the committee, but in February of 1925 the Home Office wrote asking if the Federation could provide any evidence or suggestions for their committee to consider. The Federation decided to form a small committee to be chaired by Miss Louisa Martindale to prepare evidence and recommendations for the Home Office Committee. Because of her experience in working with the NSPCC in Plymouth, Ramsay was asked to serve on the committee and to provide evidence and suggestions drawing on her own knowledge.

As well as providing anonymised information of some of the distressing cases with which she had been involved, Ramsay made suggestions for improvements to the judicial system which subsequently formed part of the evidence provided to the Home Office Committee by the Federation as a whole. One issue which was of concern to her was that young girls who had been subject to an assault which had resulted in a pregnancy were often taken to a rescue home pending the outcome of judicial proceedings—a situation that she thought to be most unsuitable. Her recommendation was that unless the assault was a case of incest the girl should be cared for by her family. In any court proceedings she was concerned that cases were not always held in camera and that the victims were not granted anonymity, particularly in cases where the

---

74. Medical Women's Federation, *Our History* <https://www.medicalwomensfederation.org.uk/about/our-history> [accessed 25 March 2017].

75. London, Wellcome Library (WL), SA/MWF/D/7, 7 August 1924.

child had turned 16 by the time the case came to court, resulting in young people being named in news reports.

Another concern was that there were no women accompanying female victims. As she reported, 'I am struck with the fact that at magistrates' courts the child gives evidence before men and undergoes a very severe cross-examination. A policeman stands beside her. It should be a police-woman! She often does not understand the questions put. The atmosphere is always antagonistic and difficult.'[76] Although much of the campaigning by Citizens' Associations around the appointment of women as police officers related to the policing of public spaces and the imposition of a moral standard, it is clear that Ramsay had far wider concerns about the issue borne of her direct experience from her work with the NSPCC. As she pointed out, if there were no women police officers, female victims had of necessity to be questioned by policemen.

In addition to the lack of women police, a major concern for Ramsay, and the MWF as a whole, was the fact that there were no women police surgeons and so victims were usually medically examined by male doctors, causing much distress to already traumatized girls. The recommendation to the Home Office Committee was that in all cases where a medical examination was required the examining doctor should be of the same sex as the child. The issue of the lack of women police surgeons was one which exercised the MWF for many years. The first woman police surgeon to be appointed was Dr Nesta Wells, who was appointed in Manchester in 1927. Ten years later, when she wrote an article for the MWF quarterly newsletter, Dr Wells recorded that she was still the only woman police surgeon in the country.[77]

In 1924, a meeting of the MWF Council was held in Plymouth when a motion was passed that steps should be taken to have a woman doctor nominated for the next election to the GMC, the statutory council of the medical profession. Nothing came of it, but four years later, Ramsay wrote to the MWF Council, raising the matter once more. Jean Scott has described the lengthy campaign that followed for women's representation on the GMC.[78] There were many false starts and missed opportunities, but eventually in 1933, supported by the BMA, Dr Christine Murrell was elected. However, Murrell never took up her place as she died before she could do so. Ramsay, who knew her well and considered her a friend, would often call on her at her home in Porchester Terrace after overnight train journeys to London, where

---

76. WL, SA/MWF/D/7.
77. WL, SA/MWF/B.2/9, The Medical Women's Federation Quarterly Review, October 1937.
78. J. M. Scott, pp. 164–66.

they would share breakfast. It fell on Ramsay to call on her and notify her of her election to the GMC, but she 'came away from her home sad at heart' knowing she would never take her seat.[79]

At the next GMC election in 1934, Ramsey herself was nominated by the MWF. However, this meant standing against a popular sitting member who was seeking re-election and who was supported by the BMA. Fighting as an independent against a BMA nominated candidate was a difficult call. In her election leaflet she stressed her extensive experience as a clinician and in the area of medical politics. She highlighted that there were by then in excess of 5,000 women practitioners on the register and that she believed the time had come for the election of a woman Councillor.[80] She was unsuccessful, but polled a respectable 2,346 votes against 9,317 and 2,665 respectively for the other two candidates. However, as *The Lancet* pointed out, 'The astonishing thing is that … the other candidate [Ramsay] should have polled so many votes, and the voting is evidence of the strong desire of the constituency to have a woman among its five representatives.'[81] It was not until 1955 that an elected woman was to take a seat on the GMC, although two women doctors sat as nominees. A campaign almost certainly begun by Ramsay herself when the MWF met in Plymouth took over thirty years, so did not bear fruit during her own lifetime. She was to reflect that 'the lesson learned, I think, that one must continue an agitation once a policy has been decided on as the right one. The Women's Suffrage Campaign taught many of us a good lesson in sticking to a path.'[82]

Ramsay supported women in all walks of life, championing many causes which improved the lives of working class women. She supported business and professional women through the Soroptomist movement. She was the first president of the Plymouth Venture Club, founded along the lines of the Rotarians and which merged shortly after with the Soroptomist Clubs.[83] She personally supported women's businesses and services. When she completed her term of office as President of the PMS she presented a presidential chair for the use of future presidents which is still in use today for ceremonial occasions. The chair was proudly commissioned from 'a lady woodcarver', Miss Violet Pinwill of Rashleigh, Pinwill and Co. Amongst the symbolism the chair is carved with bull's heads, the symbol of St Luke, 'the beloved physician', and on the back of the chair the Latin motto *Audi Alteram Partem* (let

79. RCP, MS87, p. 121.
80. The Box, 1670/30, Plymouth Medical Society Newspaper Cutting Book p. 23.
81. Quoted in *The Medical Women's Federation Quarterly Review*, January 1935, WL, SA/MWF/B.2/8.
82. RCP, MS87, p. 122.
83. RCP, MS87, p. 119.

the other side be heard).[84] In choosing the motto Ramsay only refers to it only as being something that she took from the back of a chair made by her great uncle, and yet it seems to sum up her philosophy of support for the underdog in many of the causes she supported.

Ramsay was also a fierce supporter of internationalism, making links and attending international conferences, particularly of women doctors of other nations. In 1922 the first international meeting of the Medical Women's International Association (MWIA) was held in Geneva, Ramsay being one of the five-strong British delegation.[85] Other delegations attended from the United States, Canada, Australia, Mexico, many European nations and Turkey. The meeting agreed on the constitution and subsequently held regular council meetings and congresses around the world. The meeting in Geneva coincided with a gathering of the League of Nations. Such was Ramsay's support for internationalism that she confessed to gate-crashing the League of Nations opening session because although a few tickets for the session had been provided to the MWIA she had not been successful in obtaining one.[86] The MWIA was another organization with which her association was to last for many years, with her final attendance at the international meeting held in Philadelphia, USA in 1950.

By the 1930s, Ramsay had become sufficiently well established in her practice that she was able to take on a partner. Planning ahead for her future, Ramsay had a house built for herself on the outskirts of the town overlooking the Laira, whilst her partner lived in her practice premises at Wentworth Villas. She continued to practise from Wentworth Villas, although no longer resident herself.

The Second World War brought new challenges. Already aged 61 at the start of the war, Ramsay continued to work full time in circumstances she herself described with a degree of understatement as 'strenuous'. When taking refuge during air raids she, on several occasions, attended to the needs of women who suffered miscarriages, sometimes even driving them to hospital in her own car whilst the raid continued around her. On other occasions she had to attend patients further afield in farmhouses or more remote villages, always travelling alone and sometimes having to drive without any lights. She wrote a short article for the *Medical Women's Federation Quarterly Review* entitled 'A Morning's Medical Work after a Blitz':

84. RCP, MS87, p. 125; Wilson, Helen, *The Pinwill Woodcarving Catalogue: Plymouth Medical Society* <http://www.pinwillwoodcarving.org.uk/catalogue.htm#_Toc32766374>.

85. Medical Women's International Association, *History* <https://mwia.net/about/history>; RCP, MS87, pp. 117–18.

86. RCP, MS87, p. 118.

After a night spent in part in a cupboard under the staircase and in part running around the house to see if any incendiaries had fallen, I watched from the veranda many hundreds of flares dropping in the estuary facing my house—an awesome and wonderful fireworks display; then we retired to bed after three hours of nerve-wracking noise. Next morning I went to the hospital at which I work and found it was in the process of partial evacuation, for three large unexploded bombs were in the vicinity.

My admiration must be expressed for the calm and lack of fear shown by all the nursing staff and the women ambulance drivers who were carrying away to a place of safety, mothers and babes. No one seemed to bother that at any moment part of the building might come hurtling down on her. Luckily those three bombs were safely removed within five days, and once more the hospital resumed its normal work.

Having given what help I could I left the hospital and went to visit an old lady of 94 years. She was somewhat upset by the previous night's blitz. But after a weep upon my shoulder she gradually calmed down. Satisfied that she was all right, and it being Sunday morning, I decided to go to church. But I was not to remain there for very long for a lady 'large with child' began to faint and I deemed it advisable to escort her out of the church lest I should be faced with a delivery in church.

However some 'air and water' revived her and I then, having my car, took her to her home. Satisfied that she could now call upon her own doctor I left her. As I came through her gateway I was met by two women who stopped me and demanded whether I could tell them how to get a house or rooms as they had nowhere to sleep. I directed them to the Y.W.C.A. nearby. Another woman asked me if I could tell her where she could get a doctor as she had a friend at her house in need of immediate medical attention. I replied that I could help her as I was a doctor. 'Jump into the car and direct me.' Within a few minutes I was taken to a cellar dwelling and found her friend in bed and obviously ill. After a few questions and a rapid examination I diagnosed a ruptured ectopic.

Then I was faced with the problem where to send her. So once more the friend got into the car with me to bring back information which hospital would take her.

I telephoned my hospital and in spite of the danger was able to secure a bed in a comparatively safe place.

Then the problem of getting an ambulance faced me, for I could not drag the patient up twelve steps with the inefficient help available and lift her into my car. No information was at first available where an ambulance could be obtained so I drove all over the city to find one. No one could tell me the evacuation place for the said three bombs had caused their removal to an unknown destination. Finally I returned to my own telephone and proceeded to do some heavy swearing at the telephone operator until, at last, the needed number was obtained. An immediate promise of an ambulance followed. This had taken me about one and a half hours. Within another hour I received word from the hospital that the patient had arrived and was 'in extremis'. I ordered the theatre to be got ready and that she should be immediately transfused with plasma. One hour later I began to operate on the patient with a scarcely feelable pulse. But just before she went under the anaesthetic I asked her if she had done anything to bring on an abortion. Her reply was 'Not this time'.

My diagnosis was correct and there was free blood up to umbilicus and there was a bleeding isthmial end of fallopian tube. This was excised and blood mopped out. She was stitched up and blood now feelable; plasma transfusion had continued during the operation.[87]

After the war Ramsay retired from general practice, although she continued to maintain a few private patients. She never gave up her medico-political and social work, though. The foundation of the NHS set her new opportunities and challenges. New organizations were established to oversee the workings of the NHS known as Local Executive Councils, which were concerned with the administrative work and the supervision of the General Practitioner Services, functioning through two committees, the Financial, and the General Purposes Committees. She became a member of the Plymouth Local Executive Council and was elected Chairman of the General Purposes Committee.[88]

87. In RCP, MS87, pp. 154–55.
88. RCP, MS87, p. 125.

Mabel Ramsay MD, FRCS(Ed), MRCOG, DPH died unexpectedly on 9 May 1954 in Sheffield whilst attending a council meeting of the MWF. As her friend and colleague Dr Annie Bryce wrote, 'she herself would be delighted to know that she ended her days still in harness and at a council meeting of the Medical Women's Federation ... She never lost her energy and drive, and was always fighting for some minority cause.'[89]

In her will she left a bequest to the Royal Free Hospital School of Medicine of the sum of £1,000—approximately £28,000 in today's value. This was to be used to set up a fund with the income generated to be used for the benefit of any woman medical student, but with special consideration being given to older students who were not eligible for ordinary grants. The scholarship was to be known as the Annie Catherine Ramsay Fund, named for her mother whom she had described as 'my inspiration and source of encouragement in my work'.[90]

As the *BMJ* wrote in its obituary, 'Mabel Ramsay's life was spent in one long fight for the rights of women.'[91] She reflected towards the end of her life on the changed position of women, commenting: 'The former conventions and taboos have mostly wilted; the legal and political status of men and women is nearly equal, and there are now open to women fields of activity undreamed of before the shattering impulse of two world wars forced the tardy pace of social evolution.'[92] In relation to the position of women as doctors she expressed the hope that medical women now had a well-organized and well-trodden path to follow which would help them to attain their ambitions explaining that she had chosen the title of her memoir *A Doctor's Zig-Zag Road* as for her it had been neither a straight nor an easy road to follow.[93]

> If one stops for a moment and recalls the past one must realise that advances have been made in 83 years. In 1869 Dr Sophia Jex-Blake began her campaign for the medical education of women ... Today we have over 10,000 women on the British Register, many of them occupying high positions in medicine, surgery and public health. A fine record.[94]

89. BMJ 22 May 1954, p. 1212.
90. RCP, MS87, p. 98.
91. BMJ 22 May 1954, p. 1212.
92. RCP, MS87, p. 115.
93. RCP, MS87, p. i.
94. RCP, MS87, pp. 126–27.

However, she was well aware that there were still battles in the world of medicine and elsewhere which had so far been unsuccessful, including the campaign for a woman to be elected to the GMC and that women were still unable to sit in the House of Lords.

In order to achieve her ambitions both for herself and for the causes she fought for, by her own admission she could be seen as having a hard core of ruthlessness. But by doing so she attained 'a great deal of what [she] wanted but not all'.[95] She was also a woman of bravery, of compassion, of vigour, of intellect and of humour.

She recounted the achievements of many of her friends and colleagues and the honours bestowed on them with generosity and pride, listing many who had been awarded DBEs and other honours.[96] It is hard to see why such honours did not also come her way as she was surely as deserving as those for whom she expressed such satisfaction.

---

95. RCP, MS87, p. 164.
96. RCP, MS87, p. 126.

CHAPTER FOUR

Jessie Headridge (1871–1946)

JULIA NEVILLE

Jessie Headridge, photograph printed in Bishop Blackall School
Commemorative Magazine, 1983.

In July 1901 Miss Jessie Headridge came to Exeter to be interviewed for the
post of headmistress at the Exeter Episcopal Middle School for Girls. She left
an account of her interview. It is how she opens her memoir *Labuntur Anni*,
published in 1932. Characteristically, as she always took a great interest in dress,
it describes her costume in great detail. There was a hat, 'a severe and plain one
specially chosen for its severity', a 'coffee-coloured hard panama with a round
turned-up brim and black taffeta silk-gathered trimming'. There was a dress, 'a
navy blue and white-patterned silk dress, which was in its second year ... a pair
of clean white kid gloves, and black cashmere stockings with black kid shoes'.[1]

---

1. J. Headridge, *Labuntur Anni* (Exeter: A. Wheaton, 1932), p. 3. Jessie Headridge wrote this memoir
just after she retired, providing 'more personal details' to complement the 'many official records'.
The title, a quotation from the Roman poet Horace, means 'the years slip by'.

Julia Neville, 'Chapter Four: Jessie Headridge (1871–1946)' in: *Devon Women in Public and
Professional Life 1900–1950: Votes, Voices and Vocations*. University of Exeter Press (2021).
© Julia Neville DOI: 10.47788/IGCG9296

Headridge had never been west of Bristol before, and enjoyed her train journey down to Exeter. However, when she was shown round the school 'it was so very different from anything that she had imagined, and it seemed old-fashioned and strange'. She decided overnight that she did not want the job. The next morning she was interviewed by the Governors, an all-male panel of fifteen or sixteen. Despite her nervousness, since this was the first headship she had applied for, she must have impressed them, for she was offered the job. Her reservations of the night before vanished. She decided that it had been 'ordained', and that she should 'make the best of it'.[2] So she did for thirty years, guiding the fortunes of more than 2,000 girls from the city and county, and becoming a respected member of Exeter society.

Jessie Headridge was born on 1 November 1871 in Manchester, the daughter of Peter Headridge, a dentist, and Annie, formerly Parsons.[3] Peter Headridge was in practice in Chorlton, a village on the edge of Manchester increasingly popular amongst middle-class Mancunians as a place to live because of its charming rural setting. Jessie was the third child in a family of six. The family were sufficiently well off to employ three resident servants.

Jessie and two of her sisters, Marion and Amy, were fortunate enough to benefit from the actions taken by pioneering women in the 1860s and 1870s to improve education for girls. The 1867 report of the Schools Inquiry Commission (the Taunton Commission) had been scathing in its findings about girls' secondary education, which they stated showed:

> Want of thoroughness and foundation; want of system; slovenliness and showy superficiality; inattention to rudiments; undue time given to accomplishments, and those not taught intelligently or in any scientific manner; want of organization—these may sufficiently indicate the character of the complaints we have received, in their most general aspect.[4]

One of the results of criticisms such as this was that a group of Mancunians resolved 'to provide for Manchester's daughters what had been provided without stint to Manchester's sons', and founded the Manchester High School

---

2. J. Headridge, *Labuntur*, pp. 4–5.
3. Family and census information from <www.ancestry.com>.
4. Schools Inquiry Commission, *Report of the Commissioners* (London: HMSO, 1868), Vol. I, pp. 548–49.

for Girls in 1874.[5] The school was itself based initially in Chorlton, so would have been familiar to the Headridges. By the mid-1880s, however, when they sent their daughters there, it had moved into central Manchester.

Headridge seems to have thrived at school, where she wrote for the school magazine and spoke at the debating society. After success in the Cambridge Local examinations, she was awarded an exhibition at the Women's Department of Owens College which provided classes to prepare women for admission to degree courses.[6] She then obtained a scholarship to Newnham College, Cambridge, where she read for the Mathematical Tripos, taking the equivalent of a BA degree in 1894 as a Senior Optime.[7] After Cambridge she became a mathematics teacher. At the time of the census in 1901 Headridge was working as an Assistant School Teacher at the Orme Girls' Endowed School, Newcastle-under-Lyme, another school for girls founded in the 1870s. She and three other teachers were resident in a boarding house headed by the headmistress.

It was at the end of the summer term in 1901 that Headridge travelled down to Exeter for her interview. Exeter's Middle School for Girls had been founded in the wake of the Endowed Schools Act of 1869 which permitted reform of historic endowments under the oversight of an Endowed Schools Commission. The funds of the Exeter Episcopal Charity Schools foundation, established in 1709, were reorganized and an endowment created for a new girls' school to complement the older foundation of the Blue Maids' School, then known as Exeter High School for Girls. The distinction between a 'High School', modelled along public school lines and offering a more academic curriculum with a focus on university entrance, and a 'Middle School', offering a more 'popular' form of secondary education, was characteristic of the period, and the Taunton Commission's work had focused on the development of the latter function.

The new school opened in 1876 and within ten years it had outgrown its first premises and a new school was built which opened in 1889.[8] This provided the 'fine solid buildings', as Headridge described them, that formed

---

5. Quoted on the Manchester High School for Girls Archive website <http://www.mhsgarchive. org> [accessed 21 December 2018].

6. Ibid.

7. Cambridge University did not formally award degrees to women until 1948. 'Senior Optime' is the term used in the Mathematical Tripos for a Class II degree; Headridge's class is recorded in *The Davis Historical Archive: Mathematical Women in the British Isles, 1878–1940* <https:// mathshistory.st-andrews.ac.uk/Davis/Names/Headridge_Jessie.html> [accessed 12 October 2020].

8. Taken from *Bishop Blackall School Commemorative Magazine* (Exeter: Bishop Blackall School Old Girls' Society, 1983), p. 3; the new buildings were opened in 1889 (*Evening Post*, 10 September 1889, p. 1) and not as the *Commemorative Magazine* states (p. 4) as early as 1884–1885.

the location for her interview and became her charge.[9] By 1900 the school took girls from 9 to 18 plus, with a preparatory department or Kindergarten for younger pupils, both girls and boys. The Episcopal Schools Charity and other local charities offered scholarships for girls who passed an entrance examination, but the majority of girls at the Exeter Middle School were fee-paying pupils. Numbers fluctuated, rising on occasion to more than 300.

1901–1910: The Exeter Middle School for Girls

Exeter was a very traditional city, but one at least where girls' secondary education, thanks to Bishop Temple who had overseen the reformation of the endowments, already had a secure place. The question for its citizens was not whether girls should be able to access post-elementary education, but what its purpose and content should be. Headridge recalled that at her interview she was asked by the Archdeacon whether English or Mathematics developed a child's mind more. Her precise answer she did not recall, but she remembered her interrogator and the Bishop laughing and exclaiming 'Well, she won't give up her mathematics!'[10] They were not deterred from giving her the appointment.

It was a requirement of the foundation that the headmistress should be a practising Anglican, and Headridge remained so all her life. Her beliefs shaped her approach to the education of the girls in her care. Her views on educating children about God were that, important as the teaching of faith and of morality was, it was also important to inculcate in children's minds the true conception of God as a Person.[11] She did indeed consider it important to teach morality, and to do this by example. She argued against an attempt to prohibit the taking of charity collections in Exeter schools, for example, saying she considered it essential to teach children generosity.[12] The school provided support for charities such as the Church of England Waifs and Strays Association, through bazaars and dramatic performances, and also for the Mayor's Relief Fund and the Police Court Poor Box.[13] She also promoted the support of missionary work overseas, encouraging the establishment of

9. *Western Times (WT)*, 26 February 1932, p. 12.
10. J. Headridge, *Labuntur*, p. 5.
11. *Devon and Exeter Gazette (DEG)*, 25 June 1931, p. 7, in an address to the Aylesbeare Sunday School Teachers' Union.
12. *Western Times (WT)*, 21 December 1921, p. 2.
13. *Express and Echo (E&E)*, 30 May 1910, p. 5; DEG, 29 May 1912, p. 3; 14 February 1925, p. 7; 23 December 1930, p. 5.

the youth movement of the Society for the Propagation of the Gospel within the school.[14]

The early years at the school must have been challenging. Under a 'weird arrangement', as Headridge described it, the handover took place mid-term.[15] She arrived when lessons were under way and was ushered into the headmistress's room. Miss Pemberton (whom she was succeeding) summoned the staff one by one to meet her, and then took her 'to see the girls and to hear a Scripture lesson and a catechism lesson'.[16] The catechism lesson took place in the main hall, with about eighty juniors assembled together.

When Headridge looked back in 1932 on the school in 1901, she recalled that it was one where girls 'were trained to be good citizens, but both as regarded accommodation and curriculum the limits were narrow. English, French, arithmetic, history, geography, botany, a little drawing and fine needlework formed the whole curriculum.' There were no mathematics, Latin, general science, domestic science, proper gymnastics or organized games.[17] 'Boys', as the Schools Inquiry Commission had found in 1867, 'were educated for the world, and girls for the drawing room', and though much had improved since that time, there was still a gap to be tackled.[18] Headridge's intention was to educate girls for 'the world'. In her first decade she worked to modify the curriculum; secure the right staff to teach it; and persuade the Governors and other authorities to pay for additional accommodation.

Headridge says nothing about these challenges in Labuntur Anni, which she wrote primarily for the amusement of former pupils. Her comments on her early years are confined to her reorganization of the school dinners and the introduction of a school uniform. For girls who stayed at school for dinner Headridge stopped the practice of allowing senior girls (together with their younger siblings) to eat their lunches at their desks, which she considered made the rooms stuffy. All lunches were instead to be eaten in the main hall. She also stopped the primitive arrangement under which the cook would brew up cocoa or boil eggs in the 'stoke-hole' for the girls to purchase, and established a proper buttery with a service counter.[19]

---

14. *WT*, 1 December 1916, p. 8.
15. J. Headridge, *Labuntur*, p. 6.
16. Ibid.
17. *WT*, 26 February 1932, p. 12.
18. Quoted in Carol Dyhouse, *Girls Growing up in Late Victorian and Edwardian England* (London: Routledge & Kegan Paul, 1981), p. 44.
19. J. Headridge, *Labuntur*, pp. 8–9.

Advertisements for the school illustrate the tone she was trying to create. It is clear from the style used at this period that Headridge's emphasis, despite the fact that this might have seemed to be the prerogative of the High School, was on academic performance.

This can be seen in the following extract from the 1902 advertisement for the Exeter Middle School:

> Exeter Middle School for Girls.
> Head Mistress Miss Headridge (late Scholar of Newnham
> College, Cambridge, Mathematical Tripos)
> The summer term commenced Tuesday May 6
> Fees 4 guineas to £6 per annum
> At the last Cambridge Local Examinations Thirty
> Certificates were gained, Nine in Honours with Ten
> Distinctions in Religious Knowledge, English, French and
> Science. Scholarships of the aggregate value of £100 are
> awarded annually, and four County Council scholarships
> (£80 each) have been gained.[20]

The successes recorded in the advertisement were amplified in the local paper with the claim that this was 'the greatest number of certificates obtained in any girls' school in Devon'.[21] Headridge sought to create a school rather different from the High School which was a much smaller school (137 pupils in 1904), and one at which there were no 'free places' obtainable through a scholarship examination. The majority of girls there, unlike those at the Episcopal Middle School, did not expect to earn their own living after school and many were admitted there only after the age of 14, partly because of its reputation for the teaching of modern languages.[22]

The climate nationally was encouraging for secondary education. The rise of the school leaving age to 12 in 1899 meant that there were more pupils in the public educational system. Demand for post-elementary education grew. The Education Act of 1902 gave new powers in the organization of schools to county and county borough councils. (Exeter was a county borough.) The new education authorities, in addition to managing public elementary schools,

---

20. *DEG*, 9 May 1902, p. 5.
21. *DEG*, 4 March 1902, p. 6.
22. Devon Heritage Centre (DHC) 4110Z/27/9/5/8/3, Michael Sadler, *Report on Secondary and Higher Education in Exeter*, 1905, pp. 13–14.

were to have powers to 'consider the educational needs of their area' and 'supply or aid the supply of education other than elementary'.[23] At the end of 1903 Exeter's Education Committee, considering how to implement these responsibilities, commissioned Professor Michael Sadler to 'undertake an educational inquiry in Exeter and to report to the Education Committee on the best manner of co-ordinating and developing the work of both primary and secondary schools, so as to avoid waste of effort, money etc'.[24]

Sadler was an academic with a distinguished record in the promotion of secondary education.[25] He had worked with Sir Thomas Acland (of Killerton) as Director of the Office of Special Inquiries and Reports to the national Board of Education. He was by the early 1900s Professor of the History and Administration of Education at the University of Manchester, an appointment that allowed him time to undertake special commissions like the Exeter one. He spent the spring term of 1904 there visiting schools and interviewing headteachers. He was surprised to find that the proportion of girls receiving secondary education was higher than at towns he had studied elsewhere. In Exeter the proportion was 13.73 per 1,000 population, whilst in Liverpool and Huddersfield it had only been 3.7 and 3.46 respectively.[26] His report on the High School for Girls is brief, and the headmistress subsequently commented that he had spent no more than a day there. He evidently spent more time at the Exeter Middle School for Girls and it is possible to recreate some of the changes Headridge had been making from his report.[27]

Sadler's overall verdict was that the school was 'well organized and well managed. The classes are kept within reasonable limits, only two exceeding thirty. The discipline is excellent; the moving of the classes from room to room is effected rapidly and quietly. The timetable is well arranged'.[28] Headridge, he added, was doing 'great work in the teeth of great difficulties'.[29] His principal criticism was that the school was under-resourced. This applied both to the lack of capital investment in additional accommodation and to the inadequacy of the annual revenue allocation for the recruitment of better qualified teachers.

23. Quoted in Derek Gillard, *Education in England* (2018), ch. 7 'Secondary Education for Some', available at http://www.educationengland.org.uk [accessed 31 May 2019].
24. *WT*, 13 January 1904, p. 1.
25. D. Phillips, 'Michael Sadler and Comparative Education', *Oxford Review of Education*, 32.1 (2006), pp. 39–54.
26. Sadler Report, p. 2.
27. Sadler Report, pp. 19–25.
28. Sadler Report, p. 23.
29. Sadler Report, p. 22.

It seems from Sadler's report that Headridge had tried to tackle the problem of large classes. His table of class sizes, reproduced in Figure 4.2, shows that classes ranged from ten in the sixth form to thirty-two in Form IVA. (It also shows how pupils were grouped by ability rather than by age.) The need to accommodate eleven classes put extreme pressure on classroom space. The main hall was divided by curtains so that four separate classes could work there, and the headmistress's room and even the corridors were sometimes used for class teaching.

Headridge had obtained permission to appoint the first graduate teachers, although Sadler feared that she would lose them because she was unable to pay them at a professional rate. The staff that she had inherited comprised assistant mistresses, who might at best hold the title of LLA, and student teachers, of whom there were three in 1904.[30] The student teachers were former pupils whose practical and academic education as teachers took place entirely within the school, including a weekly lecture from Headridge. After a two-year period they might stay on as assistant mistresses. Sadler was critical of such training, which meant that the students had no outside experience. This was, however, the background of most mistresses at the school.[31]

After Sadler's visit there was a long delay. Pressure of business meant that he did not finally report to the Exeter Education Committee until the middle of 1905, and the full City Council only agreed their secondary education scheme in 1906.[32] These must have been anxious times for Headridge, and she was evidently keen to make sure her qualifications appeared to best effect. She decided to take her Master of Arts degree at the University of Dublin so that she was able to include the letters 'MA' after her name and this she did in 1905.[33]

When the report was published in 1905 it entirely vindicated Headridge's approach. Sadler's recommendations were unambiguous. The school was doing good work but it urgently needed more space, perhaps three additional

---

30. LLA (Ladies Licensed in the Arts) was a qualification offered to women by the University of St Andrews, which was obtainable by examination but did not require residence.

31. Sadler Report, p. 22.

32. DHC 4110Z/27/9/5/8/3.

33. Manchester High School Annual Report, 1905 <http://www.mhsgarchive.org/article_307.php> [accessed 21 February 2019]. Headridge had been careful to describe herself in school advertisements not as 'BA' but as Senior Optime'. She was able to change this clumsy description by taking an 'ad eundem' MA degree at the more enlightened Trinity College, Dublin, which did admit women to degrees and extended that offer to those who had studied to degree level at Cambridge and Oxford Universities; see S.M. Parkes, 'Steamboat Ladies', *Oxford Dictionary of National Biography* <https://www.oxforddnb.com/view/10.1093/ref:odnb/9780198614128.001.0001/odnb-9780198614128-e-61643> [accessed 26 July 2020].

Figure 4.2: V.—Number of Pupils in each of the public secondary Schools for Girls in Exeter, on 1 March 1904, classified according to Ages and Forms.

Episcopal Middle School

Name of Form	Under 8	8 and under 9	9 and under 10	10 and under 11	11 and under 12	12 and under 13	13 and under 14	14 and under 15	15 and under 16	16 and under 17	17 and under 18	Over 18	No. in Form	Average Age of Form
Kindergarten	34	2	—	—	—	—	—	—	—	—	—	—	36	5 yrs. 3 m.
First	15	1	1	—	—	—	—	—	—	—	—	—	17	7 " 7 "
Lower Second	2	12	4	1	—	—	—	—	—	—	—	—	19	8 " 9 "
Upper Second	—	5	9	6	1	—	—	—	—	—	—	—	21	9 " 6 "
Lower Third	—	—	4	7	6	7	1	—	—	—	—	—	25	10 " 5 "
Upper Third	—	—	1	5	16	7	1	—	—	—	—	—	30	11 " 1 "
IV C.	—	—	—	—	1	6	7	5	—	—	—	—	20	13 "
IV B.	—	—	—	—	3	10	7	10	1	—	—	—	31	13 " 6 "
IV A.	—	—	—	—	—	3	6	18	3	2	—	—	32	13 " 10 "
Fifth	—	—	—	—	—	—	1	9	8	2	2	—	22	14 " 9 "
Sixth	—	—	—	—	—	—	—	—	1	6	3	—	10	16 " 7 "
TOTALS	51	20	19	19	26	33	23	42	15	10	5	—	263	

Michael Sadler, *Report on Secondary and Higher Education in Devon*, 1905. Appendix A.

classrooms and a laboratory. It also needed to employ teachers with higher qualifications, and more scholarships should be offered.[34] The cost of implementation for this school alone was calculated by Sadler as requiring an extra two pence on the rates, not an easy recommendation for the Council to accept. In the end, however, they and the Governors did agree a final scheme.

Meanwhile the implications of the 1902 Act were still unfolding. In 1904 the Board of Education set up a branch of its inspectorate to cover secondary schools and set out requirements for a curriculum. This would cover English language and literature, geography, history, a foreign language, mathematics, science, drawing, physical training, manual work, and, for girls, housewifery. Study in these subjects would lead to a certificate. Conformity with this curriculum was required to secure the full education grant. The new inspectorate made a visit to the Episcopal Middle School for Girls and approved its provisions, although the Governors were required to develop a domestic science strand.[35]

The question of grants was also reviewed. There was a long-standing concern about the appropriateness of state funding for denominational schools. The new regulations provided that grants could not be made to denominational schools unless they had already received them. Headridge recalled: 'I had read that paragraph over and over, but as we had earned several small grants for science and mathematics I hoped we were safe'. However, the Board of Education initially refused to endorse their grant. The Inspector came to tell Headridge the bad news in person. She 'at once went down to Mr John Stocker, the Vice-Chairman of the Governors and explained how desperate our case was'.[36] He approached the Bishop, and the Bishop, a member of the House of Lords, arranged for the Minister to receive a deputation at Westminster.

The Bishop, the Vice-Chairman (Mr Stocker) and the clerk to the Governors, together with Headridge, formed the deputation. Headridge recalled the unexpected difficulty she faced in gaining access to the Houses of Parliament:

> It was the time of suffragettes ... the deputation had assembled, all but Bishop Robertson, who was in the House of Lords. We proceeded to the glass door dividing the hall from the House proper. The way was barred by a policeman.
>
> 'The lady cannot go in! She must sit down', he said. In vain did

34. Sadler Report, pp. 49–51, p. 70.
35. WT, 30 November 1907.
36. J. Headridge, Labuntur, pp. 9–10.

Mr Stocker explain, 'She has an appointment with Mr McKenna'. 'Mr McKenna must come and fetch her, if he wants her,' was the rejoinder. This was an impasse, and for a moment we stood nonplussed; but then on the other side of the door appeared the Bishop, who greeted me. Again the policeman barred the way, and said to the Bishop, 'The lady cannot go in' ... The Bishop calmly said, 'I am a member of this House, and I can take the lady in.' He held his arm out for me and I sailed past the policeman.[37]

The matter was quickly settled. The Bishop explained the position. McKenna asked whether the Governors had spent money since the Board's inspection in expectation of grants. Stocker and Headridge explained they had begun to prepare plans for new accommodation, and had appointed an additional French teacher. '"Very well", was the answer, "that settles it; you are entitled to the grant."' That was it. Headridge recalled they all 'got out into the corridor as quickly as we could in case the sentence might be reversed'.

Back in Exeter all was not quite so straightforward, for a new constitution was required, and Devon County Council (also a provider of scholarships) initially objected to the cost, but once that was settled the future of the school was assured. By the end of 1907 the Governors were able to announce a new scheme under which the public authorities would be represented on the Board of Governors, the episcopal foundation of the school would be recognized by maintaining the links with the Church of England (with a clause permitting parents to withdraw their daughters from prayers and religious instruction) and the local authorities would provide additional core funding and scholarships.[38] In recognition of the changes the name of the school would change, and it would become the 'Episcopal Modern School for Girls'.

Work on the new building began in 1908. There are some minor differences of record about the content and the timing of the extensions in earlier accounts of the school's development but the contemporaneous record in the *Devon and Exeter Gazette* refers to the opening of this first phase of new building on 11 February 1909.[39] It provided five additional classrooms, an art room, dining room and kitchens, chemical and physical laboratory, balance-room and new staff rooms, store rooms and a library. This was a more generous provision than Sadler had suggested and Headridge could

---

37. J. Headridge, *Labuntur*, pp. 10–11.
38. *WT*, 30 November 1907, p. 2.
39. *DEG*, 12 February 1909, p. 11.

now hope to implement more of her plans. 'Good work had been done, in spite of difficulties and some discouragement' was the verdict of the chairman of Devon Education Committee on the first seven years of Headridge's tenure as headmistress.[40]

1910–1919: Episcopal Modern School for Girls—Peace and War

In 1910 the new scheme came into force. The Governors comprised eight members of the Episcopal Charity Schools Trust, six members of Exeter City Council and two members of Devon County Council. In view of the fact that there was only one woman among the nominees, four Exeter women were co-opted directly onto the governing body. These were the daughter of the Exeter MP and three wives of city councillors.[41]

The minutes of the Governors' meetings survive from the first meeting in October 1910 until well beyond Headridge's retirement in 1931. An early requirement was that the headmistress should produce a report each autumn, and these were incorporated within the minutes from 1911 to 1919, and again from 1925. Those for the missing years appear to have been produced in printed form and have not survived in the archive. Their absence is partly compensated for by the headmistress's report at the annual prize-giving, but there were some items that Headridge told the Governors, chiefly issues about the staff, which would not have been appropriate to mention in public and which did not appear.

The advertisements for the school went through a transitional period in 1910 when both the old and the new titles were used. By 1911, advertisements appeared as shown below in this extract from the 1911 advertisement for the Episcopal Modern School:

> Episcopal Modern School for Girls
> Headmistress,
> Miss J. Headridge, MA
> (Camb. Mathematical Tripos)
> Assisted by a large and well-qualified staff
>
> This school provides at very moderate fees an excellent education for girls. The curriculum includes courses in Housewifery, Cookery,

---

40. *WT*, 29 June 1908, p. 4.
41. DHC 3169C/EFG 1, *Governors' Meeting minutes*, 7 October 1910.

Handwork, Gardening, Commercial Training, Physical Training, as well as the ordinary school subjects. Girls are prepared for the Cambridge Local Examinations and London Matriculation. There were many honours and distinctions, and NO failures in the July examinations.

The School has large and airy buildings on Pennsylvania Hill, and extensive hockey and tennis grounds. There is a Kindergarten Class (Mistress, Miss Gillett, Higher Froebel Certificate) for little boys and girls.[42]

School numbers were regularly reported throughout the decade, showing an increase from 295 in 1911 to 372 in 1918. There does not seem to have been any external pressure to increase numbers, presumably because the participation rate was still high by national standards. In 1911 there were seventy free places amongst the 296 (23%): thirty-eight were funded by Governors' scholarships; and thirty-two by local education authorities or charities.[43]

Headridge used the total number of girls passing examinations as a regular performance measure, and also the numbers of admissions to university. At this time girls were entered for the Cambridge Senior and Junior Local Examinations. Headridge explained the policy at the annual prize-giving in 1910:

All the girls in the two highest forms were prepared every year for the Senior and Junior Examinations, and all received the same teaching. But it was not advisable in the case of girls to insist upon all taking the examinations, and therefore their entrance was decided by the wishes of their parents. It would thus be seen that the girls were not sent in for examinations merely as an advertisement, and that in the attainment of 'no failures' the girls had gained what was far more valuable than any certificate—the habit of steady work.[44]

The emphasis on academic successes, so much a feature of the early years, was now balanced by the details of other subjects the school was required to

42. *DEG*, 3 Jan 1911, p. 1.
43. Governors' Meetings, General Purposes Committee, 12 October 1911.
44. *WT*, 15 December 1910, p. 4.

provide under the regulations. The intention was to fit girls for 'professional, commercial or home life'.[45]

Reports to the Governors always covered staff numbers, qualifications, performance and salaries, and demonstrated the progress being made on increasing numbers and improving the level of qualifications. By 1912, in addition to Headridge, there were fourteen assistant mistresses rather than the original nine, with visiting male staff providing classes in drawing and singing. Three of the assistant mistresses had BA or BSc degrees. The new scales of pay allowed for a higher maximum to be paid to the graduate teachers. Headridge herself elected initially to stay on a low annual salary supplemented by a capitation payment of £1 per pupil. This would have brought her in a salary of just over £300 per annum. Three more graduates were appointed in 1913 and more as time went on.

The accommodation was still not adequate for all the functions of the school and was supplemented by the tarmacking of a piece of the grounds for games, a games field with a pavilion, and by a further extension which provided a purpose-built art room and additional cloak room accommodation.[46] This was opened on the annual prize-giving day in 1912, at which point Headridge must have felt that there was now nothing to limit the school's progress. She decided to ask the Governors for permission to take a long unpaid break and visit South Africa, where her sister Amy was teaching. The Governors gave their consent and Headridge went away as soon as the prize-giving was over. She recalled:

> As soon as the visitors had gone I put on my things to go up to my house … To my amazement and pleasure, when I came out of my room I found the whole school drawn up on both sides of the stairs and corridors and stretching right down to the gate to say good-bye. 'Good-bye, good-bye', sounded all along the lines, and many pocket handkerchiefs appeared to wave me on, though to be used surreptitiously for other purposes. I was almost in tears myself before I reached the gate, and I was glad it was dark.[47]

The staff en bloc saw her off at the station and she was away for 'five months of sunshine and warmth and freedom from care'.[48] She received weekly reports

45. *E&E*, 12 January 1910, p. 2.
46. *Governors' Meeting minutes*, Report to the Governors, 5 October 1913.
47. J. Headridge, *Labuntur*, p. 14.
48. Ibid.

about the school, none of which gave her any cause for concern, and returned
to take up her duties again towards the end of the summer term of 1913.
Five of the staff resigned at this point, for reasons, she noted, not connected
with the school. This enabled her to appoint more graduate staff and prepare
for a solid performance for 1913–1914.

Exeter was a small enough city for the Headmistress of the Episcopal Modern
School to be a well-known figure in local society, invited to formal city events
such as the 'At Home' for the visit of the conference of the British Medical
Association, and the Mayoral reception for clergy attending the summer course
of lectures.[49] Headridge also contributed to wider civic and professional life
throughout her tenure, for example becoming a member of the Executive
Committee of the Devon County Arts and Crafts Association, the Exeter branch
of the Educational Society of the South West, and supporting the Exeter branch
of the League of Nations.[50]

Early in her time in Exeter, Headridge met Miss Jessie Montgomery, who
was a member of Exeter's School Board and a driving force in the development of the University College of the South West. Headridge invited her to
present the prizes at her first annual prize-giving in 1902.[51] Montgomery
later founded the Exeter and District branch of the National Union of Women's
Suffrage Societies, of which Headridge became a member. In an address to
the branch Headridge spoke about the importance of experts such as 'the
woman doctor, the woman teacher and the members of other women's
professions' being able to vote for 'the reforms their experience had taught
them were necessary'.[52] After the first stage of women's enfranchisement was
achieved in 1918, Headridge became a member of the Exeter Citizens'
Association, which aimed to encourage women and men to take a more active
part in political life.[53]

Headridge recalled that the news of the assassination of the Archduke of
Austria arrived at the school on the day the school was performing, for the
first time, a play in French.[54] She immediately wondered what the future
might hold for them. She guessed that the buildings of the Episcopal Modern
Girls' School would be 'sequestered', as she put it, to become a Red Cross
Hospital for the treatment of sick and wounded soldiers. This had been

49. *DEG*, 30 July 1907, p. 6; *WT*, 27 July 1910, p. 2.
50. *DEG*, 18 April 1912, p. 3; 14 February 1919, p. 6; 19 October 1923, p. 16.
51. *DEG*, 16 December 1902, p. 6.
52. *E&E*, 27 April 1910, p. 3.
53. *WT*, 1 October 1921, p. 4.
54. J. Headridge, *Labuntur*, pp. 16–17.

mooted after a Devon Red Cross exercise in May 1914 and was implemented that August.[55]

The Governors met urgently at the school to confirm the loan to the Red Cross and to agree what should be done to accommodate the classes. The City Council agreed to lend the school Rougemont House, a historic and virtually empty building. This accommodated the youngest (Kindergarten to the second forms) and the oldest (the fifth and sixth forms). The accommodation did not easily meet the needs of the school. The sixth form was housed in a bathroom complete with an old-fashioned bath covered with a wooden top which served as a table, and two of the classrooms had large windows looking out over the public gardens through which the public could peer at the girls. Overall, however, supported by the City Council's excellent caretaker couple, their stay was a 'happy and comfortable' one.[56]

The middle forms were not so fortunate. The Governors' brainstorming about possible premises in Exeter produced as the only realistic option 11 Higher Summerlands, a large fourteen-room house at the lower end of the Heavitree Road. This had been leased to Exeter High School, but they had vacated the property and, following Headridge's inspection, she concluded that they could manage within the building, although it was in rather poor condition. The house, though large, proved inadequate for the numbers of girls involved within a year, and the Governors soon leased 10 Higher Summerlands as well.

Headridge had to make arrangements to move the school's equipment and furniture out to these alternative buildings. Girls came in from their holidays to lend a hand; the Red Cross adopted some of the furniture; and some items were stored by Headridge and her colleagues in their own homes. Their work must have been completed at speed, for by 25 August the school had not only been emptied but recommissioned as a hospital, and Miss Buller, the Exeter Divisional Red Cross Commander (subject of another chapter in this collection), reported to the Press that 'We are now quite ready'.[57]

Although Headridge would not have been able to predict this, the evacuation was to last five years. For those five years the staff shuttled between one site and the other for their teaching duties, organized on a master timetable which ensured that their moves across town, usually on foot, were undertaken during break periods rather than between lessons. The girls too had to walk

55. *WT*, 18 May 1914, p. 2.
56. J. Headridge, *Labuntur*, pp. 17–18.
57. *WT*, 25 August 1914, p. 3.

between sites, and from 1915 to an independent gymnasium for drill. Laboratory space was rented from the Royal Albert Memorial College.[58] 'How great this upheaval was', Headridge wrote, 'only I and those who went through those difficult years with me shall ever realize'.[59] The Governors recognized the staff's dedication with a 'war bonus', awarded at the end of 1918.[60]

The Summerlands properties were less satisfactory than Rougemont House. 'Number 11', Headridge reported to the Governors, 'is particularly cold and draughty, and it is almost impossible to keep the girls free from colds', and she reported in other years the bad colds and influenza in the winter months.[61] The girls' feet shook the dilapidated stairs, and fire drills to evacuate almost 200 girls from the twenty-six rooms in the two houses had to be carefully practised.[62]

Despite all this the numbers of girls (and Kindergarten boys) rose to 342 In September 1917 and 372 in September 1918.[63] Numbers entered for examinations remained steady, and a few students took scholarships and places at University of London colleges and teacher-training establishments. Headridge noted successes of past students in obtaining their degrees and certificates, and also their war work. One former student was appointed as a woman teacher at Exeter's Hele's School for boys; others were working as nurses and cooks in hospitals, one was doing research in chemistry for the Board of Trade, and another had 'taken a man's place in the Westinghouse Engineering firm in Manchester'.[64]

Although the Armistice was signed in November 1918, the Exeter War Hospitals continued to care for soldiers for the first six months of 1919. Stocker, as Deputy Chair of the Governors and a City Alderman, raised the question of the continuing occupation of the school buildings at a Council meeting in February 1919 and secured a Council resolution pressing the War Office to release them urgently.[65] The Council received the assurance that this would be done as soon as possible. The buildings were not released until the summer. Headridge was insistent that the school should return for the start of the autumn term, but the builders were still undertaking repairs, and it

58. DHC, *Governors' Meeting minutes*, 10 January 1917.
59. J. Headridge, *Labuntur*, p. 15.
60. DHC, *Report to Governors*, 9 October 1918; *Governors' Meeting minutes*, 9 July 1919.
61. DHC, *Report to Governors*, 10 October 1917.
62. J. Headridge, *Labuntur*, p. 21.
63. DHC, *Report to Governors*, 9 October 1918.
64. DHC, *Report to Governors*, 11 October 1916.
65. *WT*, 12 February 1919, p. 3.

was a rather uncomfortable first term. In addition, now that numbers were approaching 400, the buildings were not large enough for the whole school. The junior forms stayed on at Rougemont House for six months, then moved into unsatisfactory temporary accommodation, and the Governors agreed in 1921 to close the Kindergarten temporarily. It reopened as a preparatory department in a new building in 1923.[66]

The Episcopal Modern School for Girls, 1920–1931: Education in a Changing World

The builders were still at work when four Board of Education inspectors arrived at the end of 1919. They had been preceded by specialist inspectors for drill and games, music, art and domestic science. Attention nationally was focused on education as never before. In laying plans for life after the war the Ministry of Reconstruction had recognized the significance of education to its broader plans for social and industrial reconstruction. 'Upon the extent to which the country develops and makes use of the innate abilities of its citizens its future prosperity and happiness depend', the popular pamphlet, *Aims of Reconstruction*, loftily announced in 1918.[67] That same year a new Education Act was passed. This set out a National System of Public Education to be implemented by local education authorities. Most of its provisions dealt with local authority responsibilities for public elementary education, but it acknowledged that one of the consequences of the raising of the school leaving age to 14 would be to increase the demand for places for the 11–14-year-olds, and it therefore sought to encourage local authorities to transfer more students to secondary schools. As Mandler suggests, there was a spirit abroad which linked education with the development of citizenship, and, at a time when the first women were being enfranchised, this was seen as just as significant for girls as it was for boys.[68]

In practice the changes were tempered by economic problems, and thus slower and less radical than had been foreseen in 1918. At the time of this first postwar visit, however, the inspectors of the Board of Education were still fired with zeal for a radical increase in opportunities for teenagers. Headridge commented that the inspectors were surprised to find that the standards of the school had been maintained during their enforced stay in

66. *DEG*, 17 December 1923, p. 5.
67. Ministry of Reconstruction, *The Aims of Reconstruction* (London: HMSO, 1918), p. 14.
68. P. Mandler, 'Secondary Education and Social Change in the United Kingdom since 1945' <https://sesc.hist.cam.ac.uk/2018/06/20/the-centenary-of-the-fisher-act-1918> [accessed 2 August 2019].

temporary accommodation.[69] The school produced a dazzling set of examination results in 1919, with six of the thirty-six girls who sat the Senior Cambridge Examinations obtaining First Class Honours. No other girls' school in the country achieved so many, Headridge reported.[70]

The future of educational trusts like the Exeter Episcopal Charity in the National System of Public Education must initially have seemed precarious. Its foundation was specifically Anglican, and the national trend was towards the lessening of the influence of religion on education. Its endowment was far too small to maintain the school and the school had become dependent on the system of national grants and local authority grants, and on scholarship fees from other charities. A committee was established nationally to examine the question of scholarships and free places in secondary schools. Its report (the Young Report) placed the responsibility for increasing free places for children between 11 and 16 firmly on local education authorities. This was initially reassuring, as it meant the school would receive more pupils in its middle forms funded by local councils. As the 1920s went on, however, Devon County Council built more secondary schools, and their scholarships went increasingly to pupils taking up places in these rather than at the Episcopal Modern. Headridge noted in 1923 the impact of the opening of secondary schools in Exmouth and Teignmouth and hoped that now this was complete their own numbers would have reached their lowest level.[71]

Debates over what the local education authorities would do were a continuing preoccupation of the Governors' meetings. So was the question of teachers' pay. The Burnham Committee, established in 1919, set out a scale of pay for teachers. The Governors were not, of course, obliged to pay it, but they did need to keep salaries competitive, and to set their own pay scale. The Governors noted in 1919 a letter sent by teacher Clarissa Saunders thanking them for the 'just and fair settlement' they had arrived at.[72] What the staff felt when, in 1922, they were asked to forego 5% of their salaries following a national scheme to cut the costs of superannuation is not recorded, but all bar one did so.[73]

Changes also occurred in the curriculum. The examination system had been reformed in 1917, with School Certificates and Higher School Certificates the recognized two stages of public examinations. As Headridge explained to

---

69. J. Headridge, *Labuntur*, p. 22.
70. DHC, *Report to the Governors*, 8 October 1919.
71. *DEG*, 17 December 1923, p. 5.
72. DHC, *Governors' Meeting minutes*, 9 July 1919.
73. DHC, *Governors' Meeting minutes*, 11 April 1922.

parents, the intention was that no girl should leave before she had taken the School Certificate, and 'a fair percentage' should take the Higher Certificate. Studies for the Higher Certificate had now begun.[74] In 1921 an advanced course in modern studies, English, French and history, for which the Board made an additional grant, was approved, although girls were still able to study mathematics and science to Higher School Certificate level.[75] By October 1922 the Board of Education confirmed that the school was now included in the list of those complying fully with the grant conditions.[76] The school advertisement was recast in September 1922 as shown below. The advertisement was briefer than earlier ones, used the new title, was explicit about the fees (instead of referring to them as 'very moderate'), mentioned Board of Education recognition, and continued the emphasis on public and university entrance examinations.

Extract from the 1922 advertisement for the Episcopal Modern School for Girls:

Exeter Episcopal Modern School for Girls
Headmistress Miss J. Headridge, MA

The school provides a thorough education for girls at Moderate Fees (£4 per term) and is recognised by the Board of Education for an Advanced Course in Modern Studies.

Girls prepared for Cambridge Locals, Matriculation, Higher Certificate and University Scholarship examinations.

Young children can now be received in the Preparatory Department, fees £3 per term.[77]

In her speech at the annual prize-giving in 1922, Headridge noted that in 1901 the number of girls taking the Cambridge Senior Examination was six, whilst in 1922 there had been forty-seven. There had also been six girls taking the Higher Examination and nine who were admitted to universities. She was gratified by the large numbers of girls staying on beyond the age of 16 and

---

74. *DEG*, 3 November 1920, p. 3.
75. DEG, 17 December 1921, p. 1.
76. *Report to the Governors,* 11 October 1922.
77. *DEG*, 15 Sep 1922, p. 13.

noted the opportunities that now existed for them to go on after their Higher
Certificate to study in Exeter at the University College of the South West for
a degree.[78] In 1924 the school decided to switch over from the Cambridge
Local examinations they had taken since the early years of the school to those
of the University of London, to which most students for university entrance
applied and to which the University College of the South West was affiliated.[79]

Headridge did not write much about the 1920s in her memoir. After her
description of the end of the war she turned back further into the past,
with accounts of the parties and plays that she recalled. Her reports to the
Governors for 1921–1924 were not transcribed so her insights about the
early years of the 1920s are lacking. This was another difficult period financially. It was a time of national austerity. The Geddes Committee, set up in
1921, recommended a 12% cut to the education budget, and though this
was not immediately implemented in full, cuts went on for several years.
In 1922 the Board of Education decided that they would reduce direct grants
to non-maintained schools, and the local education authorities would be
expected to replace the grants. Though the local education authorities
accepted the responsibility it was unclear for some time whether this would
mean a lower income for the Episcopal Modern School. The 'trying financial
position' required Headridge to keep costs down to the minimum, which
she seems to have done to the Governors' satisfaction as in 1924 they
recorded their congratulations to her for 'carrying on the school as econom-
ically as possible so far as is consistent with efficiency'.[80] Nonetheless the
school ran for several years at a deficit from which it was only rescued by
the Exeter Education Committee's decision in 1925 to raise the grant per
city pupil by more than a third.[81]

The twenty-first anniversary of Headridge's appointment occurred in 1922
and was marked by a presentation from the Governors of a gold wristlet watch
and books on architecture. Lady Owen, one of the Governors, said that 'Miss
Headridge has not given the Governors a moment's anxiety or trouble. We
have never had a single complaint from the parents nor from the teaching
staff, in whose welfare she takes a keen interest.'[82] Past and present teachers
and pupils clubbed together to fund a portrait to be hung in the school.[83]

78. *DEG*, 13 December 1922, p. 7.
79. *Governors' Meeting minutes*, 9 April 1924.
80. *Governors' Meeting minutes*, 25 June 1924.
81. *DEG*, 2 February 1925, p. 3. The grant per pupil went up from £3 to £4 6s.
82. *WT*, 18 May 1923, p. 12.
83. *DEG*, 19 July 1923, p. 5.

New developments in school life between 1920 and 1925 included the 'house' system, intended to foster team spirit, with the houses named after female saints: St Catherine, St Margaret, St Monica and St Ursula. A number of after-school groups were established: the Literary Society, French Society, Missionary Study circle, Political Debating Society and Girl Guide Patrols.[84] The school had electric light installed in 1926; Headridge promised that no substantial contribution would be sought from the Governors to the installation. The girls put on a concert to raise the funds required.[85]

The economic situation had an effect not only on public expenditure, but also on wages and unemployment which in turn had an impact on girls' education. Whilst in 1922 Headridge had been enthusiastic about the numbers of girls staying on beyond the age of 16 and the opportunity that the newly chartered University College of the South West presented to them to undertake degree courses after Higher Certificate, by 1925 she was expressing her concern about the low numbers of girls continuing their education after the age of 14.[86] There were so few that the school only needed a single form of twenty-four covering the two years preparing for the General School Certificate. As a whole form had to be entered for examination, this showed up as an unusually high set of failures (seven out of twenty-four girls).[87]

Headridge blamed commercial organizations: 'They like to have girls from secondary schools but they also like to have cheap labour and so lengthen their years of apprenticeship'. She recognized the need for action, though, and planned to 'restart the commercial classes in the hope that I may keep the girls at the school just during those years when they most need school discipline and school life'.[88] She recruited a teacher with a diploma in 'economic subjects' to run the course, and was able subsequently to report that it was 'popular' and 'the girls are working well at it'.[89] The course, which contained classes in shorthand, book-keeping and typewriting, was targeted at sixth-form girls who had already taken their School Certificate.[90]

---

84. *DEG*, 3 November 1920; *DEG*, 13 December 1922.
85. *Governors' Meeting minutes*, 8 April 1925; *Report to Governors*, 28 October 1925.
86. *DEG*, 13 December 1922, p. 7; 17 December 1925, p. 4.
87. *Report to the Governors*, 28 October 1925. The regulation about entering a whole form was generally considered to be a nonsense and was subsequently abolished.
88. Ibid.
89. *Report to the Governors*, 10 October 1928; 23 October 1929.
90. *DEG*, 30 November 1929, p. 4.

As a further gesture to encourage girls to stay on, and to help the balance-sheet, the school began to run dancing classes as an extra. Headridge's view was that it did 'fairly well', attracting those whose parents would not normally have been able to afford such tuition. She was disappointed, though, that parents wanted their daughters to learn 'the Charleston and some ballroom dances, and do not care for the classical dancing to good music'.[91]

Although there was a bright moment in 1927 with the school's Golden Jubilee, marked by many celebrations and gifts to the school, the exodus of girls after the age of 14 continued. Headridge reported in 1929 that twenty-three girls had left that year between the ages of 14 and 16 and were not known to have gone to another school. The inspectors had considered that this was too high a percentage and advised Headridge that their grant for running the Higher Course in Modern Studies might be in jeopardy if the numbers taking the course did not grow.[92] Headridge considered that this was chiefly an economic issue. 'As soon as the girls approach fifteen', she wrote, 'the parents are anxiously waiting for the moment the girl can earn and begin to look out for work for them.'[93]

At the annual prize-giving in 1929 Headridge gave her overview of the school's progress, partly perhaps aimed at impressing the former teacher whom she had recruited to award the prizes, Nancy Webb-Johnson, who after leaving Exeter had served with distinction as a nurse in the First World War and was now Headmistress of the Collegiate School in Pietermaritzburg, Natal. Headridge mentioned the first full report for ten years by the Board of Education inspectors, which she said contained 'nothing to hide and much to be proud of'. She referred in addition to academic successes, to the commercial course and the opportunities for advanced training in domestic science. Beyond the curriculum she mentioned the thriving Brownie pack and Guide Company, school societies in literature, history, geography, science; a League of Nations branch; the orchestra and choir.[94] In 1930 she was also able to mention the formation of a swimming club, where medals for life-saving were being awarded for the first time.[95]

In 1931 Headridge reached the age of sixty and tendered her resignation. She left the school at Easter 1932, having guided its development for over

---

91. *Report to the Governors*, 12 October 1927.
92. *Report to the Governors*, 24 October 1929.
93. *Report to the Governors*, 3 October 1930.
94. *DEG*, 30 November 1929, p. 4.
95. *DEG*, 18 December 1930, p. 5.

thirty years. The annual prize-giving was deferred to February that year to allow the occasion to become a formal farewell, and the Governors to pay tribute to her work.[96] She herself recalled the transformation there had been from the time when

> there were no mathematics, Latin, general science, domestic science, proper gymnastics or organized games. All those things, however, now found their place in the timetable, while the building was twice as large and had a gymnasium, an art room, a kitchen, science room, library, as well as four more classrooms.[97]

It is noticeable, however, that what Headridge referred to with pride had all been achieved by the time of the First World War. Her impetus to be at the forefront of change had lessened by the 1920s. Some pupils who were admitted to the school in the late 1920s recall her both as 'a very lovable person', but also as someone slightly archaic, 'a very upright Victorian lady' who 'instilled ... discipline in her pupils'.[98] Nancy Stratford, who transferred in 1927 at the age of 14 to the Episcopal Modern School from the King's High School at Warwick, which was run by the inspirational Miss Doorly, considered the school much inferior to the Warwick one.[99] It is difficult not to feel that some of the optimism and acuity that had guided Headridge for so long had now been lost. In what was to be her final report to the Governors in 1930, reflecting again on the high numbers of girls leaving before School Certificate, she confessed that 'this is a great problem, and I do not know how best to meet it'. Her one tentative solution, to concentrate on the 11–14-year-olds, would have been the negation of all her efforts for thirty years to support girls in taking higher examinations and progressing towards further education or degree courses.[100]

After her retirement Headridge took a second trip to South Africa and penned her little book of memories, *Labuntur Anni*, for the amusement of her former pupils. 'Some of those who are now mothers or fulfilling other important duties would', she wrote, 'be surprised perhaps to know how much

96. *WT*, 26 February 1932, p. 12.
97. Ibid.
98. M.L.E. Hadden, *Bishop Blackall School, Exeter, 1877–1983* (Exeter: the author, 1983), p. 22.
99. Personal communication by Margaret Stratford, the author's mother, of what her sister Nancy had said.
100. *Report to the Governors*, 5 October 1930.

I knew and remember about their doings at school'.[101] She retired to her home in Exton, where she continued to play a leading role in parish and community life until her death there on 2 January 1946.[102]

Conclusion

Jessie Headridge was one of a number of headmistresses who, during the first quarter of the twentieth century, took forward post-elementary education for girls, striving to open up and to consolidate opportunities for women to assume an equal place in society alongside men. She seems to have been able to win the respect and affection of the staff who worked for her and the pupils whom she taught, and she had the continuing confidence of the School Governors and of Exeter's Higher Education Sub-Committee, which she regularly attended as a co-opted member. After substantial early success in raising standards, she came to face difficulties in the mid-1920s. This was partly, as her own analysis suggests, because the economic situation meant that poorer parents, even when assisted by a scholarship, looked for their daughters to begin earning. Headridge referred in her final report to the ease at which a girl from Episcopal Modern could leave at 14 and get a job at Boot's the Chemist, earning 14 shillings a week.[103]

The decline in numbers was also affected by the general attitude of society in the 1920s towards secondary education for girls. Dyhouse has described the climate of strongly held beliefs about education for adolescent girls that continued to prevail.[104] These views were given credence by a Board of Education Report in 1923.[105] The report, on the *Differentiation of the Curriculum for Boys and Girls Respectively in Secondary Schools*, suggested that the pursuit of equality of the sexes in education had perhaps gone too far and that the 'old and delicate graces' had been sacrificed on the 'altar of equality'.[106] A range of medical evidence about girls' physiological and psychological development was presented, and greater differentiation between educational expectations for boys and girls was proposed. Whilst the Governors of the

---

101. J. Headridge, *Labuntur*, p. 30.
102. *DEG*, 11 January 1946, p. 8.
103. *Report to the Governors*, 5 October 1930.
104. Dyhouse, *Girls Growing up*, pp. 115–48.
105. Board of Education, *Report of Consultative Committee on the Differentiation of the Curriculum for Boys and Girls Respectively in Secondary Schools* (London: HMSO, 1923).
106. Dyhouse, *Girls Growing up*, pp. 132–33. The quotation is from the Consultative Committee Report.

Episcopal Modern School did not require Headridge to follow this path, the debate would have been known to many parents and may have affected the numbers of girls staying on beyond 14. At the end of her career Headridge must have felt she needed to fight all her battles again. Her discouragement in the last few years she was headmistress should, however, in no way lessen appreciation of the real achievement she secured in the first twenty years of her headship.

CHAPTER FIVE

Florence Gascoyne-Cecil (1863–1944)

JULIA NEVILLE AND HELEN TURNBULL

Florence Cecil, photographed by Lafayette in 1926

In the autumn of 1916, people in Devon said farewell to their much-respected bishop and his wife, and awaited news of the new episcopal appointment to the Church of England Diocese of Exeter. The appointment of all bishops lay ultimately in the hands of the Prime Minister, who was not at the time required to take account of local views before making a final nomination to the monarch. In October the new bishop was announced: it was to be William Gascoyne-Cecil, Rector of Bishop's Hatfield. 'Amiable, earnest and unconventional to the point of eccentricity, he might', observed the *Church Times*, 'have died a simple rural dean if he had been plain John Smith'.[1] However, he was not.

---

1. *Church Times*, 20 October 1916 <https://www.churchtimes.co.uk/archive> [accessed 30 September 2019].

Julia Neville and Helen Turnbull, 'Chapter Five: Florence Gascoyne-Cecil (1863–1944)' in: *Devon Women in Public and Professional Life 1900–1950: Votes, Voices and Vocations*. University of Exeter Press (2021). © Julia Neville and Helen Turnbull DOI: 10.47788/OFEM9606

He was the brother of the Marquess of Salisbury, a senior figure in Conservative politics, and Asquith, then Liberal Prime Minister of a coalition government, needed all the friends he could get. Power was ebbing away from him and, he probably felt, he might secure support by the appropriate exercise of patronage in the making of appointments.

The bishop-designate, as the *Church Times* also pointed out, 'took his degree—apparently a pass degree—at one of the less distinguished Oxford colleges, was ordained to the curacy of Great Yarmouth and after two years there went to Bishop's Hatfield (a living in the gift of the Marquess of Salisbury) where he remained.' He was notable for his interest in mission work abroad, principally in the Far East,[2] and it was only in that capacity that he was known to the Diocese of Exeter, where he had addressed mission conferences.

Lady Florence Cecil, his wife, was the second daughter of the Earl of Lathom, another Conservative peer and politician. Born in 1863, she grew up in the same political circles as her husband. The 1881 census records Florence (aged 17) as a 'scholar', but Cecil's own view was that she was 'a rather badly educated woman', though 'she did not blame her parents for that'. Education, she felt, was not then taken so seriously as it was now (she was addressing the girls of Crediton High School in 1921).[3] 'The groundwork', she thought, 'had been good, but it was not thought out and developed, and was very much more dull.'

From somewhere, however, she had gained a love for literature, and in the same speech she advocated the reading of classical works of fiction which helped develop 'the gift of perception'. She would thus, probably, have been familiar with Anthony Trollope's *Barchester Towers*, and the towering figure of the bishop's wife in that novel, Mrs Proudie, a masterful woman who dominated her husband and interfered in diocesan business. It was a caricature, but also an awful warning. William's absent-mindedness was well known, and Florence provided a backbone to the marriage, so the temptation to interfere would have been great.

---

2. The Cecils had visited China, Korea and Japan in 1907, and visited China again in 1909 to explore the possibility of founding a Christian University there. Lady Florence conducted research on women's lives there, including the work of female missionaries. They wrote a book about their experiences: Lord William Gascoyne-Cecil, 'assisted by Lady Florence Cecil', *Changing China* (London: James Nisbet, 1911).

3. *Devon and Exeter Gazette (DEG)*, 1 December 1921, p. 1.

Family Background

The Cecils had been married in 1887, and had brought up seven children, with Anne, the youngest, only ten at the time of her father's appointment to Exeter. On their first visit, in the week following his appointment, the Cecils saw over the Bishop's Palace and resolved that they would not live there. On the bishop's death, newspapers claimed that this had been because the Cecils felt that it was inappropriate to live in a 'palace', but the house they ultimately chose as an alternative, Barton Place, was itself a substantial mansion. Exeter's Bishop's Palace had been rebuilt in 1845–1846, and was scathingly described in the 1930s as 'the most uncomfortable and badly planned house that ever man conceived, utterly devoid of any decent sanitary arrangements'.[4] It may therefore have been for purely practical reasons that they chose only to retain a couple of rooms there for diocesan business and to live on the edge of the city. Cecil's home was 'very precious to her' and she worked to make Barton Place 'a house of great hospitality, delightful entertainment and rich in sympathetic interest'.[5] The bishop became a well-known feature of the Exeter landscape, cycling in along the Cowley Road; but, though Cecil had been a cyclist in her youth (an unconventional practice for a clergy wife), there is no reference to her using anything but a car in Exeter.

In total the Cecils had nine children, including two sets of twins. One set of twins did not survive, but four boys and three girls grew to adulthood. By the time the Cecils moved to Exeter in 1917 all the boys were serving in the army, and Rupert, the youngest boy, had already been killed in action. Their daughter Molly became an agricultural worker, responding to the call for women to take on jobs and release men for military service.[6] Over the next two years their eldest and third sons were also killed: Randle in December 1917 and Jack in August 1918. Nancy Astor, at that time the wife of Plymouth MP Waldorf Astor, later recalled how she and Cecil had arranged to host a party in Plymouth for American sailors on war service. The day of the party was the day after the news had come of Jack's death. Although Astor begged Cecil to cancel the arrangements, she refused, saying, 'But Nancy, they too are far away from home, and we must do all we can.'[7] The bishop was later to remember how 'seven times they received a yellow envelope containing a telegram, with news that a

---

4. J.F. Chanter, *The Bishop's Palace, Exeter, and Its Story* (London: SPCK, 1932), pp. 118–19.
5. *Western Times (WT)*, 26 May 1944, p. 4.
6. *WT*, 13 March 1918, p. 4.
7. *DEG*, 1 May 1922, p. 3.

son had either been wounded or killed'. Both he and his wife became strong supporters of the League of Nations and other peace movements.[8]

After the war Cecil became an advocate for the right of families to choose the style of the memorial to be placed on the graves of their relatives in the war cemeteries. The War Graves Commission wished to have a standard head-stone on which, if required, a cross could be carved, rather than to permit families to choose different monuments such as a sculpted cross or an angel. Cecil became Vice-President of the British War Graves Association, founded to oppose the policies of the Commission, and personally organized one of the petitions to the Prince of Wales, who was President of the War Graves Commission. The text of the petition, probably drafted by Cecil, ran:

> It is only through the hope of the Cross that most of us are able to carry on the life from which all the sunshine seems to have gone, and to deny us the emblem of that strength and hope adds heavily to the burden of our sorrow ... Is it too much to ask that the present wooden crosses may be replaced at our own expense, by more durable ones of stone?[9]

She obtained 8,000 signatures, and her husband's influential brothers lobbied on her behalf, but the members of the Commission were not to be swayed from their decision about the importance of uniformity, no differentiation being made between rich and poor, officer and private.[10]

The family tragedies were not to end there. On a holiday abroad in 1924 Anne and her sister Eve both contracted typhoid. They were admitted to a nursing home in Plymouth on their return and, though Eve recovered, Anne died a fortnight later. The Cecils' experience of parenthood helped shape some of the arguments they later made about what they regarded as the inappropriate availability of contraceptives. To their religious conviction that one of the purposes of marriage was the procreation of children, and therefore no action should be taken to inhibit that purpose, they added arguments designed

---

8. Lady Florence lent her name to the support of the Peacemakers' Pilgrimage in 1926 (*The Vote*, 26 March 1926, p. 101); the bishop spoke, with Lady Florence beside him at an Exeter League of Nations rally, reported in *DEG*, 31 July 1928, p. 8.

9. Commonwealth War Graves Commission, *Shaping our Sorrow* <https://shapingoursorrow.cwgc. org/news-and-events/collection-item/petition-to-the-prince-of-wales-from-lady-florence-cecil-wife-of-the-bishop-of-exeter-presented-in-1919> [accessed 22 September 2020].

10. P. Longworth, *The Unending Vigil: A History of the Commonwealth Graves Commission* (London: Leo Cooper, 1985 edition), pp. 49–55.

to appeal to a wider audience.[11]Cecil wrote in 1933, following letters the bishop had received after his pronouncement on birth control, of the comfort she had derived from her large family. 'As in time we were to be bereaved of three of our sons in the Great War, and also later of our youngest girl, while others were lost at birth, it is easy to understand how thankful we are that we did not limit our family.'[12]

Cecil had spent almost thirty years as a parson's wife before coming to Exeter, and summarized the role as that of her husband's 'best curate'. (He also had four male curates.) She described how, in addition to attendance at parish functions and church services,

> her morning would be spent in housewifely duties—kitchen,
> garden, nursery and schoolroom ... Probably, while teaching the
> children she is interrupted again and again by callers from among
> her humbler friends to ask for a hospital letter, to give advice for
> a sick baby, to ventilate a grievance against a neighbour, or a school
> teacher, or the doctor, or even against herself. Or someone wants
> a character or a place, or needs a letter written. In the afternoon
> perhaps she takes a woman's meeting of sorts, or else she visits,
> particularly where she knows there is sorrow or sickness.[13]

This experience had given her a very practical grounding in social work and a sense of 'definite usefulness'. Her privileged background, however, had given her a sense of entitlement to advise, which meant that she ventured sometimes beyond 'help' towards 'interference'. No doubt Devonians were surprised when, only a few months after their arrival, Cecil, or rather her husband, since at that date the law regarded husband and wife as one person, featured as defendant in a case heard in the King's Bench Division. This concerned a letter which Cecil had written from Hatfield in 1914, which, the plaintiff claimed, was libellous. The letter was written to the mother of a girl employed as a housekeeper by the plaintiff, who was separated from his wife. It alleged that the plaintiff was 'deceiving your daughter ... and making love to her'.[14] Cecil was compelled to acknowledge in court that she had entirely taken the side of the wife. She

---

11. As described in the introduction of the service for the Solemnization of Matrimony according to the 1662 Book of Common Prayer.

12. Letter in the *Exeter Diocesan Gazette*, quoted in the *Taunton Courier*, 21 June 1933, p. 4.

13. *Western Morning News (WMN)*, 8 January 1923, p. 3.

14. *WT*, 4 May 1917, p. 5.

believed that the statements in the letter were 'fair and true' but had not made enquiries to confirm them. Her defence was that the information was privileged, and she had honestly believed it was true. The judge ruled that the information was indeed privileged, and the jury acquitted her.[15] Nevertheless it must have been a humiliating experience.

As the bishop's wife, however, she no longer had much scope for individual casework. She became drawn into committee work and was invited to join a good many local diocesan, county or city organizations involved in welfare or public service work. Some of these organizations, such as those concerned with temperance and mission work, were related to interests she shared with her husband, but her own principal interests lay in work with women and children.

Early Years in Exeter

Cecil was a strong supporter of what was generally described as 'training, preventive and rescue work' among girls who had been, or were at risk of being, sexually exploited. This work was led in and around Exeter by the Exeter Diocesan Association for the Care of Friendless Girls (EDACFG), an organization 'set up by women on behalf of women' in the second half of the nineteenth century.[16] By the time Cecil joined its committee, which she was later to chair, it ran a range of establishments. It provided training, primarily for domestic service, a refuge to which workers could refer girls or to which girls could come direct; a maternity home; and a small hospital for girls and women with sexually transmitted diseases. During her time in office a separate building, St Elizabeth's, was opened in 1920 for refuge work, and national and county grants were successfully secured for its maternity services.[17]

Over time the very strait-laced approach of the founders shifted a little, as societal attitudes changed. The elderly Mrs Knight-Bruce gave her 1922 talk to the Annual General Meeting the title of 'A Less Defiled Heritage', and referred to the 'fallen girl' and her 'fallen brothers'.[18] Even in 1920, however, Sir Robert Newman, Exeter MP and social reformer, told the Association:

---

15. *DEG*, 5 May 1917, p. 3.
16. E.D. Irvine, 'A Century of Voluntary Service: The Exeter Diocesan Association for the Care of Girls', *Transactions of the Devonshire Association for the Advancement of Science*, 113 (1981), p. 143.
17. In October 1919, reported in *DEG*, 21 February 1920, p. 1.
18. *WT*, 27 April 1922, p. 3.

When an unfortunate girl made a false step there were some people who looked at her as being almost contaminating in herself. People as a rule, however, were getting more Christian in their outlook. Most people had faults, but some took a form which did not get so much publicity as others. A helping hand might very well mean to an unfortunate girl the difference between a respectable life in the future and one going from bad to worse.[19]

Cecil herself felt strongly that it was important to form public opinion on the subject of 'impurity', of which she held a broad definition. She said that it was as disgraceful to get drunk as to 'fall morally'—in other words participate in sexual activity outside marriage. She was also clear that a double standard was wrong: men who 'sinned against the laws of purity' should be regarded just as much as an 'unfortunate' or a 'fallen character' as women.[20]

In a practical way EDACFG shifted its provision in line with the times, moving away from a regime based entirely on training the girls who came to them for domestic service. By 1934 the Dean of Exeter rephrased the organization's responsibilities as 'prevention, medical care and rescue work'. The training home, Melbourne House, was remodelled as a home for children with learning disabilities (the 'feeble-minded' in the terminology of the day). The Home of the Holy Innocents at Franklyn House was opened in 1927 for 'mentally defective helpless children'.[21] For both these services EDACFG received some financial support from statutory grants, a joint voluntary-statutory sector partnership that proved increasingly popular between the wars.[22] Attempts were being made during the 1920s to lessen the stigma of entering the workhouse as an alternative place of refuge. While some argued that the EDACFG provision was therefore unnecessary, Cecil herself deplored the attitude of such 'hard-hearted' people, firmly believing that the voluntary sector homes that EDACFG provided were 'more beneficial' than the workhouse.[23]

By the time that Cecil arrived in Exeter, the prospect of parliamentary votes for women was a real one. It has not proved possible to ascertain whether

19. *DEG*, 21 February 1920, p. 1.
20. *DEG*, 20 March 1920, p. 3.
21. *DEG*, 11 June 1931.
22. As discussed by Elizabeth Macadam in *The New Philanthropy* (London: G. Allen and Unwin, 1934).
23. *DEG*, 27 July 1929, p. 8.

Cecil supported the cause of women's suffrage before the First World War. Her brother-in-law, Lord Robert Cecil, and his wife were certainly strong supporters of the Church League for Women's Suffrage. By 1917 Cecil anticipated a more significant role for women in the future, referring at the Annual General Meeting of the EDACFG to the need for the 'co-operation and help of young women ... because each generation had special influence on its own generation'.[24] The responsibilities of younger women was a theme she returned to in her addresses on the speech days of girls' secondary schools where she was asked to distribute the prizes. As she told Exeter's Episcopal Modern School for Girls (where Jessie Headridge, subject of another essay in this collection, was headmistress) in 1919:

> The main purpose of education was to make good citizens, to teach girls and boys how to behave in the world, and to do good in their generation and not evil. In these days, undoubtedly the scope for girls and women was widening in such a manner that it was necessary girls should think of the vistas which lay before them.[25]

Similarly she told the Crediton Girls' High School that 'all education was intended to form character, to fit scholars ... to become good citizens' and St Hilda's School, Exeter, that: '[t]he main purpose of education was to make good citizens, to teach girls and boys how to behave in the world, and to do good in their generation and not evil'.[26] Although she had a traditional belief that 'boys and men cared about things, girls and women cared about people', she felt that this would fit women to deal with 'all questions relating to the welfare of women and children, the health question, and many other subjects which were so prominently before them just now'.[27]

Her interest in the growth of equal opportunities was perhaps what led her to support the foundation of the Exeter and District Society for Equal Citizenship, which grew out of the local National Union of Women Workers branch and the former women's suffrage organizations. She had been a member of the Executive Committee of the Exeter branch of the National Council of Women (NCW), which was later subsumed into the Equal Citizenship Association.[28] She was one of the hosts of a conference

---

24. *WT*, 17 February 1917, p. 2.
25. *DEG*, 15 December 1919, p. 1.
26. *DEG*, 1 December 1921, p. 1; 30 November 1928, p. 16.
27. *DEG*, 1 December 1921, p. 1; 15 December 1919, p. 1.
28. *DEG*, 1 April 1919, p. 3.

promoted by the Women's Local Government Society in Exeter in 1922 for women councillors, guardians and magistrates, where social issues of the day were explored and the need for more women to work in public life advocated.[29]

Cecil accepted a number of other committee positions during her first three years in Exeter, principally related to her interest in women and children. These received less of a share of her time than EDACFG, but even her name was of use to the organizations concerned in attracting other support. She became President of the Exeter Branch of the Girls' Friendly Society; a governor of the Maynard School; a committee member on the Devonshire Nursing Association and also the Exeter and District Nursing Association; President of the Alexandra Rose Day Committee; patron of the Exeter Lying-in Charity; Vice-President of the Ladies' Branch of the RSPCA; a Council member of the Devon County Commission of the Women's Section of the Comrades of the Great War; a Committee member of the Exeter Save the Children Fund branch; and a committee member of the Royal West of England Institution for Deaf and Dumb Children.[30]

She was also available to open missionary exhibitions, sales of work and bazaars organized by parishes and societies all over the diocese, often including the need to make 'one of those characteristically happy little speeches which have endeared her to the hearts of Church people throughout the diocese'.[31] This was a task to which she only gradually reconciled herself, saying in 1932:

> Sales of work are not things to be looked down upon … They help to promote better feeling in the parish. My family organised an anti-bazaar league at one time and when I came to Exeter I announced that I was not going to open bazaars and sales of work. I gave in, however, and today I am more and more convinced that they are excellent institutions. They collect money in a marvellous way; they promote so much kindly church feeling and unity, and they bring out many good characteristics in the workers.[32]

---

29. *WT*, 13 October 1922, p. 7
30. *WT*, 12 January 1917, p. 8; *DEG*, 31 January 1917, p. 3 (she resigned from this role in 1922); *WT*, 17 February 1917, p. 2; 22 March 1917, p. 3; *WT*, 22 June 1917, p. 5; *WT*, 26 January 1918, p. 3 (she resigned from this role in 1921); *DEG*, 26 January 1918, p. 3; *WT*, 10 July 1919, p. 2; *WT*, 27 September 1919, p. 4; *DEG*, 18 May 1926, p. 2 (the note of her resignation from the committee notes that she had served since 1917).
31. *DEG*, 16 October 1923, p. 5.
32. *DEG*, 29 January 1932, p. 12.

Raising funds was indeed a huge task in all the charitable organizations linked to the church. The EDACFG often found it had made a loss over a year, or had been required by Ministry of Health inspectors to put urgent repairs in hand, and special efforts were necessary to return to balance or meet the unexpected bills.[33] Cecil also led special appeals in which the bishop was involved, such as the 1925–1927 Devon Church Schools Appeal for a £20,000 repair fund. She also worked with her husband on the Devon League of Workfinders, as they were both interested in the plight of the young men on the tramp from place to place seeking work at the peak of the depression in the 1930s.[34] That led to a major fundraising effort for the training home they helped establish at Blackborough, of which the principal feature was a garden fete at which pride of place was given to items Cecil had secured from Queen Mary herself.[35]

If the world of charitable and welfare organizations was familiar to her from her childhood, the world of church administration at diocesan level was probably less so. However, just as she had been her husband's 'best curate' in Hatfield, now she turned to help him in other ways. The bishop once said, reviewing women's roles in the church, that women could become more involved in church business, citing as an example Cecil who, he said, 'in addition to her own personal correspondence ... often writes thirty or forty letters a day on the bishop's behalf'.[36] When the clergyman editor of the *Exeter Diocesan Gazette* retired at the end of 1918 it was announced that he was to be succeeded by 'two ladies'.[37] Cecil was one, and the other was the wife of the Rector of St Paul's, Exeter, Mary Thompson, already known to Cecil through her work for the Mothers' Union. Thompson had some experience of editing a newsletter as assistant to her clergyman father in New Zealand. The 'two ladies' announced a new approach to the *Diocesan Gazette*, seeking a different range of contributions. Its principal feature remained the bishop's letter, which addressed issues of current concern to him, but on occasion Cecil would put in an item over her own initials, for example commenting on the debate in Parliament over the War Graves Commission, or responding to the correspondence the bishop had received after a pronouncement on birth control.[38]

33. *DEG*, 19 May 1933, p. 15; 21 February 1920, p. 1.
34. *DEG*, 20 January 1933, p. 14; *WT*, 27 January 1933, p. 9.
35. *WMN*, 14 June 1935, p. 8.
36. *WMN*, 25 June 1932, p. 5.
37. *Church Times*, 20 December 1918 <https://www.churchtimes.co.uk/archive> [accessed 30 September 2019].
38. *WT*, 7 January 1920, p. 2; *Taunton Courier*, 21 June 1933, p. 4.

Cecil also took advantage of the new opportunities that opened up for women in church governance. Reforms in 1919 enabled women to stand for election not only to Parochial Church Councils, but also to the Diocesan Conference. She was first elected to the Diocesan Conference in 1919 and re-elected triennially, either the only woman, or one of only two women among the nine lay representatives, until she left the diocese. Immediately following her election she was also voted onto the Conference's Standing Committee, and in the review of the constitution proposed and secured representation both for the Mothers' Union and for the Girls' Friendly Society.[39] She successfully used her position to press for her priorities; for example, she argued successfully in 1921 that parochial budgets should make provision for rescue and preventive work.[40]

Her diocesan role led her into a wider geographical connection with preventive and rescue work amongst 'friendless girls' as there were separate organizations in North Devon, in Plymouth and in Torquay, working independently though along the same lines as the EDACFG. It was her responsibility to bring reports from the Preventive and Rescue Work Committee to the Diocesan Conference and encourage support for its work, and in 1934 she secured agreement to rename it the Moral Welfare Work Committee.[41] As a diocesan worker said at a conference in 1935, 'their three principles were respect for the individual in their care, unconquerable hope, and individual responsibility'.[42] They had to respond to new challenges: diocesan discussions covered the way in which motors and cinemas and dances with 'bad music', not to mention ignorance about how to educate the young, falling standards in the 'big houses', and overcrowding in the cottages made it more difficult to provide a 'sure foundation … with regard to questions of morality'.[43]

When in 1920 Diocesan representatives to the House of Laity in the national Church Assembly were elected for the first time, Cecil was one of those elected, and again she remained a member until she left the diocese.[44] As well as general participation in the business of the church, for example over the 1928 reform of the Prayer Book, one of the pieces of work in which she became involved for the Church Assembly was a review of the provision of

39. *WT*, 12 March 1919, p. 2; *DEG*, 5 February 1920, p. 3.
40. *DEG*, 1 June 1921, p. 3.
41. *WT*, 8 June 1934, p. 9.
42. *DEG*, 21 June 1935, p. 8.
43. From a discussion at the Diocesan Committee for Preventive and Rescue Work Conference, *DEG*, 21 November 1928, p. 5.
44. *DEG*, 3 June 1920, p. 1.

the Church of England's Pensions Board. Cecil was appointed to the Widows and Orphans' Committee, as one of four women out of a total of eighteen members.[45] She worked on this with one of the Exeter clergy representatives, Prebendary Hay. It seems to have been a frustrating experience, as Hay was led to declare: 'The Assembly does not do its work properly; it gets sick to death of the word "widows" and does not care what is done ... as long as something is done.'[46] Cecil had earlier referred to the lack of pensions for widows as 'one of the scandals of the church' and on this occasion made a speech about the need for increased pensions for older widows who could rarely earn their own living. The proposals were finally accepted in 1933.[47]

The Mothers' Union

One of the first responsibilities that Cecil took on in the diocese was the Presidency of the Exeter Diocesan Mothers' Union (MU). She embraced the MU in Devon from the start, and she took an extremely active role in its work, both locally and nationally. Her first letter to members was sent shortly after her election, which the Council had agreed even before she arrived in Exeter. 'My dear fellow members', it began, 'we are as yet strangers to one another', and she went on to explain that the MU was 'very near to her heart'.[48] Nineteen years later, after her husband's death and her own move to London, she closed her final note to them mentioning 'dear Devon, that Devonshire which my husband and I learnt to love so dearly—Devon, and the Devon people, not least the Devon Mothers. God bless you all!'[49] During Cecil's presidency the numbers of members of the MU in Devon expanded from 11,000 in 1918 to 13,000 in 1926, and by 1931 to 15,500, making it the largest women's organization in the county.[50] Member numbers were not overtaken by those of the Women's Institute until after the Second World War.

The MU, founded in a Hampshire parish in 1876 to teach and support women in the fulfilment of their roles as wives and mothers, had become a national organization in the Church of England. By the time of the First World War it had a very formal structure. The organization was parish-based, each branch requiring the approval of the parish priest to operate. (Not all parishes

45. *Church Militant*, 15 July 1925, p. 52; *Nottingham Journal*, 25 March 1933, p. 5.
46. *WMN*, 16 June 1933, p. 4.
47. *Western Daily Press*, 4 February 1932, p. 9; *WMN*, 16 June 1933, p. 4.
48. Devon Heritage Centre (DHC) 7137G, *MU Newsletter*, 1916–1917.
49. DHC 7137G, *MU Newsletter*, December 1936.
50. *WT*, 22 February 1918, p. 8; *WMN*, 4 June 1926, p. 3; *DEG*, 20 October 1931, p. 8.

supported a branch.) Branches, each with an Enrolling Member as the lead, were set within a hierarchy that mirrored the organization of the Church of England. Branches were overseen by a Deanery Committee, with a Presiding Member; Deanery Committees by an Archdeaconry Committee; and the whole by a Diocesan Council with delegates from these geographically based organizations together with the 'departmental heads' such as the Diocesan Secretary or the social service worker. As President, Cecil chaired the Diocesan Council. The Diocesan Secretary to the Mothers' Union was Cecil's adjutant in all MU matters, and Cecil was fortunate that, following the retirement of the original secretary in 1918, the able and energetic Mary Thompson, mentioned above as her co-editor on the *Diocesan Gazette*, took on the position, which she held throughout Cecil's term of office and indeed afterwards.

The objects of the MU were threefold.[51] The first, referred to as 'Object One', was '[t]o uphold the sanctity of marriage'. The second was '[t]o waken in all mothers a sense of their great responsibility in the training of their boys and girls (the fathers and mothers of the future).' The third was '[t]o organize in every place a band of mothers who will unite in prayer and will seek by their own example to lead their families in purity and holiness of life.' This final object, related to spirituality, was especially dear to Cecil, who described the MU as 'a body of praying women'.[52]

From time to time when the Diocesan Council was debating its priorities and reviewing the challenging social and educational agenda of the day, she would remind members that 'we must not forget the spiritual side', or desired 'that the spiritual side of the society should be fully explored this winter'.[53] She ensured that the Devon MU supported national initiatives such as the 'Deepening of Spiritual Life' campaign in 1919, and where she emphasized that 'the leading notes would be those of prayer and the effort to inculcate order, discipline and obedience to God'.[54] In 1929 she promoted the diocese's contribution to the Wave of Prayer.[55] She also worked energetically to establish a small chapel within the cathedral for the use of MU members, which was finally dedicated by the Dean in 1930.[56]

---

51. See discussion in C. Moyse, *A History of the Mothers' Union: Women, Anglicanism and Globalisation, 1876–2008* (London: Boydell and Brewer, 2009), ch. 1, 'Launching the Mothers' Union', pp. 26–32.

52. DHC 7137G, *MU Newsletter* 1927.

53. DHC 7137G, *Exeter Diocesan Mothers' Union (EDMU) Council*, 31 May 1919; 14 October 1921.

54. DHC 7137G, *EDMU Council*, 31 May 1919; *DEG*, 11 October 1919.

55. DHC 7137G, *Minutes of the MU Executive Committee*, 25 January 1929.

56. *DEG*, 15 February 1930, p. 3.

In pursuit of the second object, the education of children, the MU followed two linked pathways. The first was about supporting mothers to bring up their children in a Christian way, an important topic which was regularly featured by approved MU speakers. This was an area in which Cecil offered her own services as a speaker.[57] The second was about 'faith teaching', the provision of religious education not only in church schools but also through the curriculum of state schools. As the Hon. Lady Acland,[58] who was a MU diocesan vice-president, explained to the Council in 1917, the MU agreed that it was important 'to get members to understand that parents must ask in all grades of school for religious teaching'.[59] Cecil later acknowledged that they were fortunate in the diocese to have 'a County Council who not only encouraged a very definite scheme of religious education but also encouraged the admirable Diocesan Church inspectors to inspect their schools'.[60] She warned Honiton MU of the dangers of assuming that because the battle about religious education had been won 'there is an end of the business. As a result vigilance is slackened and one day they are shocked to find the battle has to be fought all over again.'[61]

It was over Object One, the sanctity of marriage, that the MU found themselves at odds with the primarily secular women's movement during the 1920s and 1930s. The need for divorce law reform was part of a set of changes to family law that also included arrangements for guardianship and pensions, which many women supported. The Matrimonial Causes Act of 1857 had set a double standard: men were able to petition for divorce on the grounds of adultery alone while women had to prove an aggravating factor, such as cruelty, rape or incest. A 1912 Royal Commission had agreed that the grounds for divorce should be put on an equal footing between the sexes, and a majority had recommended additional grounds for divorce including incurable insanity, habitual drunkenness and imprisonment. Nothing had been enacted before war broke out. The attitude of the Devon MU was demonstrated by the case brought forward in 1918 to the Council by the Hon. Lady Acland. Acland reported the case of a Presiding Member 'who had expressed herself in favour of divorce and remarriage'. The Council agreed that 'such members should

---

57. An undated note in Mary Thompson's Diary (DHC 7137G) shows her on the Speakers' List for that topic in 1930, agreed by the Speakers' Conference.
58. Emily Acland, wife of Admiral Sir William Acland, not to be confused with her distant cousin by marriage, Eleanor Acland, subject of another chapter.
59. DHC 7137G, *EDMU Council*, 29 September 1917.
60. *WT*, 16 April 1926, p. 8. She repeated the statement when opening a church school extension, reported in *WT*, 7 September 1928, p. 9.
61. *WMN*, 28 November 1928, p. 7.

resign'.[62] Cecil herself described divorce law reforms as 'dreadful'. She told
the Okehampton Women's Bible Class that '[s]he was strongly of opinion that
there was not a large number of cases of married unhappiness. She could
speak from many years of experience.'[63]

The MU Central Council took the view that women should be asked as
part of their membership to subscribe to Object One. This was to be footnoted
on the membership card with the explanation that it 'affirms the permanence
of the relationship between husband and wife'. Many branches had felt this
was not enough, wishing the wording to include more absolute terms such
as 'indissoluble'.[64] In Devon the Council had supported a rewording which
used the terms 'a lifelong and indissoluble union', although when a vote was
taken in 1923 almost one third of the branches present (eleven out of thirty-
seven) voted against such a hard-line position.[65]

The Matrimonial Causes Act 1923 removed the need to prove an aggravating
factor. Although this bill had the support of the Archbishop of Canterbury,
who argued that he would always support proposals to remove inequalities,
the MU felt unable to support it, although they eventually agreed not to
oppose it.[66] Pressure continued to grow for further reform, and the MU
remained vigilant. An action plan to oppose any bill was devised and agreed
at the end of 1930. Each Diocesan Secretary was to keep a set of envelopes
addressed to members ready to communicate with them and a draft letter
ready to send to MPs. Code messages were agreed on what approach should
be taken on a particular issue.[67] Gradually the MU softened its position into
an acceptance of separation (with appropriate provision) in cases such as those
where one party suffered from prolonged psychiatric problems. Cecil, by this
time a member of the National Council of the MU, was clear that all members
should accept this, and argued in 1931 that existing members should be
required to sign cards pledging that they accepted the guidance of the MU.
'She would rather have a more united band of five thousand less than five
thousand of the fifteen thousand wavering members,' she said.[68]

The growing secular movement for the increasing availability of information about and access to contraceptives also found the MU at odds with

62. DHC 7137G, *EDMU Council*, 18 October 1918.
63. *WT*, 28 March 1918, p. 9
64. Moyse, *History of the MU*, pp. 121–22.
65. DHC 7137G, *EDMU Council*, 19 October 1923.
66. Moyse, *History of the MU*, p. 122.
67. DHC 7137G, *EDMU Council*, 5 November 1930.
68. *DEG*, 20 October 1931, p. 8.

other women's organizations. Their view was that Object One required acceptance that the first purpose of marriage, as defined by the Book of Common Prayer, was 'the procreation of children', and that it was wrong to limit it. They also felt that the availability of 'artificial birth control' tempted women into immorality. Exeter Diocesan Council noted in 1929 the request from the Central Watch Committee to take steps to oppose the spread of 'propaganda in favour of Birth Prevention and display and sale of contraceptives in shops'.[69]

This was an issue in which Cecil and her husband were both very personally involved. The bishop wrote in the *Exeter Diocesan Gazette* that autumn expressing concern, in eugenic terms, about the falling birth-rate, especially amongst those who had 'shown their mental efficiency by becoming members of learned professions' and urging 'the joy of large families'.[70] Meanwhile the Exeter and District Society for Equal Citizenship, at the prompting of city councillor and midwife Mrs Rachel Allen, had begun in 1928 to press the City Council to 'allow scientific information on birth control to be given to married women at maternity clinics and welfare centres'.[71] When their pressure was ignored, they decided to hold a public meeting to discuss the establishment of a Women's Welfare Clinic in the city where services would be provided on a voluntary basis. The meeting, held on 21 October 1929, was chaired by Lady Acland (Eleanor Acland, subject of another chapter in this collection) and Cecil not only attended but spoke in opposition to the proposal. Cecil asked 'if it would not be much better to improve housing conditions whereby people would be made much happier than to diminish the number in families'. Acland agreed, but felt that 'such a happy state' was 'a long way off'. Cecil then asked 'if it was not a fact that people who had long families were healthier and happier when they reached old age'. Allen replied that 'she was one of a family of eleven, and did not wish any women to have to work as her mother had had to do'.[72] The meeting voted in favour of the establishment of the clinic.

By 1931, however, the MU central committee considered that the subject had become 'acutely controversial' and advised that no public or branch meetings on the topic should be held by the MU, nor should official speakers accept invitations to advise.[73] The bishop, however, was not bound by such guidance, and he returned to the topic in 1933. The volume of

---

69. DHC 7137G, *EDMU Council*, 27 May 1929.
70. Quoted in *DEG*, 21 October 1929, p. 7.
71. *DEG*, 7 March 1928, p. 8.
72. *DEG*, 22 October 1929, p. 6.
73. DHC 7137G, *EDMU Council*, 30 January 1931.

correspondence he received in reply to a public letter he wrote led Cecil to write a response in the *Exeter Diocesan Gazette*. She wrote about her own experience of the 'intense agony' of giving birth nine times, but argued, as described above on page 139, in favour of large families. She also claimed that in her parish work she had found that women with big families were not the ones who 'lost their health earliest', and indeed that poor health often resulted from 'thwarted motherhood'.[74]

The issue returned again for discussion at the Devon Council of Women in 1933 where Councillor Mrs Clara Daymond from Plymouth (subject of another chapter in this collection) put forward and won a resolution recommending all local authorities to open or arrange to fund referrals at birth control clinics. Cecil, present at the meeting, maintained her opposition, suggesting that later children were healthier than the eldest, and that what was really wanted was improved housing rather than the limitation of 'citizens for the nation'. She cautiously said, in response to the lecturer from the Eugenics Society, who advocated selective sterilization, that she had not made up her mind on the subject, as she was 'not convinced it would not increase immorality'. The Council as a whole passed a resolution that 'voluntary sterilisation if legalised and carefully safeguarded ... could be usefully employed to reduce the incidence of grave hereditary defects'.[75]

Some causes in Devon did, however, attract support from the MU as well as other women's organizations. One of these was the need for the appointment of women police officers, a proposal against which the three police forces in the county, Devon, Exeter and Plymouth, were united. Cecil brought to the MU Council in October 1926 a resolution expressing emphatic support for women police, 'believing it to be a step forward in the interests of morality and good behaviour'.[76] This was supported, with only one contrary vote, and in December 1929 Cecil joined a deputation from the Devon Council of Women to lobby the Devon County Council Joint Standing Committee (responsible for the county police force) to provide women police. Cecil stated that '[s]he supported the proposal with all her heart, especially in regard to the interrogation of small children by police officers. Sometimes a child's nerves were affected all its life by a feeling of terror experienced when young.'[77] She also claimed, from her own

---

74. *Exeter Diocesan Gazette*, June 1933.
75. *DEG*, 10 November 1933, p. 3.
76. DHC 7137G, *EDMU Council*, 8 October 1926.
77. *DEG*, 1 December 1926, p. 2.

experience, that it was important that women should deal with cases relating to fallen girls and prostitutes. The County Council were not, however, persuaded.

Cecil had also intended to join a similar deputation to Exeter City Council, but was ill and could only write a note expressing her support, again emphasizing that 'women were more suitable to take evidence from women' and that their manner was 'calculated to soothe the terrors of a child ... so that the truth of the story is forthcoming'.[78] Exeter City Council, like the County Council, decided not to introduce such a change.

The MU was concerned about poor housing, and took measures to exercise pressure on providers.[79] Ottery St Mary MU, for example, resolved to seek the election of two representatives to the local Council.[80] Cecil herself supported the local Church Army housing initiative and became a director of the Exeter Workmen's Dwellings Company.[81]

The MU Diocesan Council saw the need for broadening the appeal of membership to different groups of women. Members were urged to help support Women's Institutes and Village Clubs, even though these were founded on non-sectarian principles.[82] Recognizing their own primarily middle-aged, primarily middle- and upper-class membership they took steps to broaden their appeal. The Council decided in 1918 to make sure that each Archdeaconry nominated two 'working women' as delegates.[83] This was implemented by a requirement that every branch committee should be asked to send a representative from the 'farmers, tradesmen and labouring class' to the Deanery Committee, from whom the Council representatives should be chosen.[84]

Attitudes from the past lingered on, however. The veteran Mrs Knight-Bruce proposed to the Exeter Diocesan Conference in 1919 that each member of the MU should do 'spiritual work among those of her own class and practical work among those who were not so well-off', indicating her own assumption that spiritual work was not relevant amongst the poorer sections of society.[85] Recommendations for campaigning, however, now

78. WT, 31 December 1926, p. 8.
79. Discussed at the MU Speakers' Conference, reported in WT, 17 March 1921, p. 2.
80. DHC 7137G, EDMU Council, 6 February 1925.
81. DEG, 27 June 1925, p. 4; 13 October 1926, p. 5.
82. WT, 11 March 1919, p. 6, reporting on the Annual Conference of the Exeter MU; DHC 7137G, EDMU Council, 31 May 1919.
83. DHC 7137G, EDMU Council, 15 February 1918.
84. DHC 7137G, EDMU Council, 18 October 1918.
85. WT, 11 March 1919, p. 6.

included not only 'drawing-room' meetings, but 'cottage' meetings, although evidence has yet to be found showing that cottage meetings did occur.[86]

The question of subscriptions also showed the move towards equality of status. Before the war poorer women had been able to join without paying a subscription, and this deficit in funding was made good by other, better-off members paying more. Now a new measure was introduced that the subscription, sixpence per annum, should be paid by all. Wealthier members were urged to donate additionally to the central funds of the MU. Cecil explained this to the Exeter Archdeaconry Conference in 1920:

> The MU must be self-supporting and this could only be brought about by all the members putting their shoulders to the wheel and helping in meeting the expense. Wherever she had been in the diocese she found the proposal was greeted with absolute pleasure and the members were delighted to help in some small way. 'At the same time', said her ladyship, 'we cannot entirely do without the larger gifts which the richer members of the Society have always been accustomed to give and I hope they will be offered freely'.[87]

In order to draw in younger members, the Central Council resolved that each diocese should form a committee, to work with 'younger women of all classes'.[88] This was to become the 'Fellowship of Marriage', and its local foundation was announced by Cecil in the MU magazine for 1921, referring to the requirement that 'we must see to it with unceasing diligence that our young people shall fully understand the sacredness of the married state and the solemnness of the vows they take'.[89] The group was convened in 1922. A major conference to promote the Fellowship was held in 1925, at which Cecil presided, where the speaker from the Central Council explained the aim was to 'make religion a real thing so that the members should have something to pass on to their children [and to help] towards clear thinking and principles among the members and to enable them to understand pending legislation, especially in regard to women and children'.[90]

Lack of further reference to this group (although it continued to maintain a presence on the Diocesan Council) demonstrates the comparative failure of

---

86. *DEG*, 11 October 1919, p. 3.
87. *DEG*, 4 June 1920, p. 6.
88. DHC 7137G, *EDMU Council*, 14 October 1921.
89. DHC 7137G, *MU Magazine*, 1921–1922.
90. *DEG*, 20 May 1925, p. 4; 21 May 1925, p. 8.

the MU to engage with the younger generation. It appears to have been in abeyance by 1930 when a proposal was made to restart it, though this does not appear to have happened.[91] The MU was also criticized from within for failing to reach 'that large body of population in the suburbs of the great cities and in bungalow towns'.[92] It is true that many of the new branches in Devon were from traditional small parishes and towns, but there were also new urban branches, for example, those for Plymouth St Matthias and Plymouth St Augustine reported in 1934, showing that efforts were being made to correct the balance.[93]

The Bishop's Death

Nineteen thirty-six was the Diamond Jubilee of the foundation of the MU. Arrangements to celebrate it in Exeter included a service in the cathedral, to be repeated on consecutive days so that all branches could attend, followed by festivities in the Bishop's Palace gardens. It was, as the *Western Morning News* put it, a 'tragic stroke of fate' that the bishop, who had been ill for some weeks, died on the very morning of the first service. Arrangements for the Jubilee were hastily changed, with all entertainments cancelled, and the blue-veiled members processed into the cathedral without their banners. During the service Prebendary Warren expressed on behalf of them all their prayers for 'your president, who has always been a good friend to you and to us all, and such a splendid helpmeet to the Bishop'.[94] The bishop's funeral went ahead the next day at a private service in the Lady Chapel, followed by a night vigil, with the coffin, surmounted by a full-length cross of roses from Cecil, taken the next day back to Hatfield for interment.

Afterwards, within weeks, Cecil decided that she would not remain in Devon but would move to London, to be closer to her children. Upon her retirement an appreciation of her work appeared in the MU Magazine. The author wrote:

> Through long years she has served our Union, never sparing herself for one moment to make 'all things well' … She is known to every

---

91. DHC 7137G, Minutes of the MU Executive Committee, 5 November 1930.
92. Mrs Corfield, Chairman of the Religious Education Committee, speaking to a Diocesan conference reported in *DEG*, 1 November 1928.
93. DHC 7137G, *EDMU Council*, 8 July 1934.
94. *WMN*, 25 June 1936, p. 4.

branch, being always ready to go to any which asked her. Her wise
and thoughtful addresses have been loved for their homely applications to the needs of everyday life. To workers she has always been
so accessible and so ready to enter into difficulties or problems,
and she has never failed to give a sense of personal interest and
sympathy with the smallest matter.[95]

Such a tribute, recognizing the depth of her personal commitment, must
surely have pleased Cecil for, as she had once said of the MU, that was 'the
piece of work in her life which she could not help loving best, for she
loved all mothers'.[96]

Her London home was a quiet flat in Cadogan Square and as a Life Vice-
President of the MU she continued her work in giving addresses to local
branches. She also worked in a voluntary capacity for clergy widows and
orphans. She survived her husband by eight years, dying in 1944 in a cottage
at Hatfield next door to the parsonage where she and William had lived long
before.

Cecil was probably one of the best known women in Devon during the
1920s and 1930s since she travelled widely around the diocese, not only to
the towns but to the smallest of Devon parishes, over 350 of which had an
MU branch by the end of the 1930s. Her position did derive from her husband's
office, but she had the freedom to develop her role in ways that accorded
with her own interests.

Drawing on her deep-seated Christian faith, when she came to Devon she
'consecrated all her gifts and power to work for the people of this Diocese'.[97]
She came from an aristocratic family and had married into one of even higher
rank. This gave her a social standing which translated into a belief that her
views and ideas were of importance, and she used this in combination with
the new opportunities in church governance to work not only at diocesan
level but nationally. Her principal interests were in issues relating to women
and children and she worked within the framework set by the church, through
the MU, to further those concerns. With her peers in secular organizations,
she made her voice heard on the issues of the day, where she was often in
agreement with their priorities (such as women police or better housing)
though sometimes at odds (as over contraceptive services). Although she would

95. DHC 7137G, *MU Newsletter*, September 1936.
96. *WMN*, 3 June 1932, p. 5.
97. *WT*, 26 May 1944, p. 4.

not have described herself as a feminist, and once said that she was an 'early Victorian' and believed 'in the headship of the husband in the home', her advocacy of new opportunities for girls and better living conditions for all women should enable her to be recognized for the contribution she made to the acceptance of women in leading roles.[98] 'She will be remembered', her obituarist wrote, 'as an example of fine public service.'[99]

98. *DEG*, 23 February 1934, p. 19.
99. *WT*, 26 May 1944, p. 4.

CHAPTER SIX

Georgiana Buller (1884–1953)

JULIA NEVILLE

Georgiana Buller, photographed by Walter Stoneman in 1930

When Sir Redvers Buller, Devon's greatest nineteenth-century general, died in 1908 his funeral was attended by mourners from the three worlds he had served: the estate, the army and the county.[1] The two miles between his home at Downes and the church in Crediton were lined on either side by people paying their respects to 'the great soldier, the kindly squire, the good neighbour, the friend of all that were needy'.[2] His coffin was borne on a Field Artillery gun carriage covered with a Union Jack on which rested his sword,

---

1. An earlier version of this text was published as J. Neville, 'Noblesse Oblige: Dame Georgiana Buller and Services for Disabled People in Twentieth-Century Devon', in *Aspects of Devon History: People, Places, Landscapes*, ed. by J. Bliss, C. Jago and E. Maycock (Exeter: Devon History Society, 2012), pp. 387–99. The author extends her thanks to Devon History Society for their agreement to her use of that material as the basis for this chapter.
2. C.H. Melville, *Life of General the Right Hon. Sir Redvers Buller*, Vol. II (London: Arnold, 1923), p. 288; *The Times*, 6 June 1908, p. 14.

Julia Neville, 'Chapter Six: Georgiana Buller (1884–1953)' in: *Devon Women in Public and Professional Life 1900–1950: Votes, Voices and Vocations*. University of Exeter Press (2021). © Julia Neville
DOI: 10.47788/KDUK1795

his plumed busby and a wreath of yellow roses from his only child, Georgiana. Behind the coffin came Biffen, the general's horse at the relief of Ladysmith, his master's empty boots reversed in the stirrups. Then came Georgiana, accompanied by her stepbrother and stepsisters. Buller's widow, Lady Audrey, as was the custom, did not attend. The church was full; simultaneous memorial services were held in Aldershot and in Exeter Cathedral; and a general's seventeen-gun salute marked his interment in the family vault.

The Devonshire Red Cross Organization

After the funeral, Georgiana Buller needed to make a new life. When her father had retired in 1902 she was almost 20 and though, following convention, she had 'come out' and been presented at court, she had in practice become her father's assistant at Downes, helping him in the administration of the estate where 'he knew every blade of grass ... had planned every cottage and had known every labourer from his youth' and in his work for Devon County Council.[3] She had even taken a shorthand certificate in order to act more efficiently as his secretary.[4] When he fell ill with the cancer that killed him, she had helped to nurse him.[5] Nonetheless, although she was her father's only child, the Downes estate passed to the nearest male heir, her uncle Tremayne. She and her mother moved out of Downes into a house in nearby Newton St Cyres let to them by local landowners, the Quickes. They found some occupation in planning memorials to Sir Redvers and in discussions with his biographer, but neither these tasks nor her enthusiasm for hunting could provide sufficient occupation for an active and intelligent young woman. Nor were Georgiana and her mother entirely compatible as companions. Lady Audrey took on the presidency of the Exeter branch of the League for Opposing Women's Suffrage, while Georgiana, at least on one occasion, was part of a platform party for the Exeter branch of the National Women's Suffrage Society.[6] Georgiana needed an occupation.

By a fortunate coincidence, the Territorial and Reserve Forces Act, incorporating the Volunteers and the Militia into a new Territorial Force based on county boundaries, had been passed only a year before Redvers Buller's death. Its implementation included the establishment of civilian organizations, also

3. Ibid.
4. Devon Heritage Centre Exeter (DHC), Buller Family Papers 2065M add F357.
5. Melville, p. 282.
6. *Western Morning News (WMN)*, 7 April 1914, p. 7; *Western Times (WT)*, 17 March 1910, p. 2.

county based, formed under the aegis of the Red Cross and known as Voluntary Aid Detachments. The idea of volunteers 'behind the lines' who could carry out transport duties, provide rest stations and staff auxiliary hospitals in support of the professional medical corps had been General Buller's own, first put in place during the South African War. Lady Audrey and her daughter had both attended the initial meeting for a Devonshire branch of the organization in July 1907: Lady Audrey became a Vice-President and Georgiana Buller the Assistant County Director for Exeter. The Exeter detachments became a major source of occupation for Buller, involving her in recruitment, training and fundraising. As she later recalled, she began her recruitment programme west of the Exe, in the St Thomas area of the city where the Bullers were significant landowners and her name would attract support.[7] By 1913 her organizational skills had secured her the post of Deputy County Director.[8]

On 4 August 1914 Britain went to war. The declaration of war was followed almost at once by a call for additional hospital beds to supplement those already run by or planned for the Royal Army Medical Corps (RAMC). The Devon Red Cross Director, Mr J.C. Davis, received a telephone call instructing him to set up three hospitals immediately. One of these was in Torquay, but the other two were in Exeter and fell to Buller to commission.

The work involved in commissioning was intense. Negotiations had to be undertaken to release the buildings from their original purposes to the Red Cross. What was to become Exeter's Hospital No. 1 was the West of England Eye Infirmary, and required the Governors to decant their inpatient services to the Royal Devon and Exeter Hospital (RD&EH). Hospital No. 2, the Episcopal Modern School for Girls, was fortunately empty for school holidays and could be quickly emptied for commissioning. Alert to future needs, Buller also opened negotiations with the Exeter Poor Law Guardians about a Hospital No. 3, their newly built Children's Home.[9] Her foresight was admirable: Hospital No. 3 was indeed brought into use only a few months after the first two.

The hospital staff, a complicated mix of local Red Cross volunteers supplemented by additional trained nurses and paid ancillary staff, needed to be called up or employed, and an arrangement negotiated for at least some of the volunteers to gain experience of hospital nursing by secondment

7. *Devon and Exeter Gazette (DEG)*, 12 November 1937, p. 8.
8. British Red Cross Archive (BRCA), 1293/1, Minute Book, Devonshire Branch; DHC 2065M add F357.
9. *DEG*, 12 August 1914, p. 4.

to the RD&EH.[10] Equipment and supplies needed to be requisitioned, purchased or called in on loan. Householders in Exeter had promised to lend equipment in case of necessity, but many people defaulted on their promises. 'Some of them', Buller said caustically, '—living in quite big houses too—could not spare us as much as a kitchen chair when asked to do so.'[11] She continued to appeal in the newspapers for items as varied as slippers, hearth-brushes, fish kettles, tables, a screwdriver and cupboards.[12] Arrangements were also needed for the continuing supply of items such as nightwear and underwear for the men, bedlinen, household linen, cloths and dusters. Buller worked with the Mayoress of Exeter to set up a Red Cross Linen League with a central workroom staffed by volunteers and a network of working parties around the county to sew the items required.[13] Transport, a mix of covered waggons and motors, needed to be in place and ready to meet ambulance trains at the station. Somehow, and no doubt as a result of Buller's earlier focus on training for her Voluntary Aid Detachments, all was ready within three weeks, before the end of August.[14] On 11 September 1914, they were formally inspected by the Deputy Director of the RAMC (Southern Command) and designated as civilian hospitals attached to the military base in Plymouth.[15]

The first patients arrived in a convoy on 4 October and were transferred to Hospital No. 1. Most of them had been moved on from the military hospital in Devonport and so were 'walking wounded', convalescents.[16] As casualties mounted, however, it was recognized that the Exeter hospitals were able to provide skilled consultant surgeons. Many of the voluntary consultants at the RD&EH had also volunteered to work for the Red Cross. It was also recognized that the rail journey from Southampton (the western disembarkation point for casualties) to Exeter took an hour less than the journey to Plymouth. The RAMC accepted that it would be prudent to make use of the Exeter hospitals as first-line hospitals, receiving patients direct by ambulance train from Southampton.[17] In November 1914, Buller opened a third hospital, at less than forty-eight hours' notice, then in February 1915 a fourth, and in

10. *DEG*, 29 August 1914, p. 4.
11. *WT*, 25 August 1914, p. 3.
12. *DEG*, 12 September 1914, p. 3.
13. *WT*, 10 August 1914, p. 4.
14. *WT*, 25 August 1914, p. 4.
15. *DEG*, 12 September 1914, p. 3.
16. *WT*, 8 October 1914, p. 2.
17. *DEG*, 31 March 1915, p. 3.

May 1915 a fifth, taking the total number of beds in the Exeter hospitals to almost 600.[18] On average at that point the hospitals were admitting about one hundred patients a week, with several ambulance trains disgorging a mix of 'cot cases' and ambulant cases, a pace that was to continue until the end of the war.[19]

In addition to her role as Director of the Exeter War Hospitals, Buller retained countywide responsibilities as the Deputy Director for the central organization of support services. This required keeping track of all patient movements, organizing the medical boards that assessed the soldiers' futures, discharging them as soon as possible (provided with twelve items of clothing) to other places in order to free beds for the next convoy, and supporting relatives. The organization also had to be scrupulous in record and account-keeping in order to claim the War Office subsidy made to the Red Cross on the basis of the actual number of patients treated per day. As well as patient records, the central office was responsible for catering supplies, medical and surgical stores, information, and the co-ordination of transport on behalf of all the hospitals.[20]

The War Office payments by no means covered the cost of the services the Red Cross provided, and there was a constant need to raise funds in which Buller necessarily became involved and which continued throughout the war. She wrote letters of appeal for funding or used her contacts at the local papers to publicize the latest cause.[21] She worked with interested committees such as the Red Cross Children's Guild, the Devonshire Patriotic Fund, and the Christmas Appeal Committee.[22] She persuaded local organizations such as the Exeter Literary Society to fundraise for particular items, in this case a machine for 'exercising stiff joints and muscles', and appealed to farmers to supply '200 to 300 rabbits weekly' for food for the hospitals.[23] 'Not a penny was unnecessarily spent', she told fundraisers at a 'Monster Rummage Sale' in 1917, 'but ... they did not grudge anything, because their standard from the

18. T. Bowser, *The Story of British VAD Work in the Great War* (London: Imperial War Museum, 1917), p. 95; 'War Hospitals in Devon', *British Medical Journal* 2852 (28 August 1915), pp. 336–38.

19. DHC 2065M add 7 Box 2767. Details of convoys from 7 October 1914 to 6 July 1917.

20. *DEG*, 30 July 1919, p. 1; also described in detail by W. Fothergill Robinson in articles published in *WT*, 31 March 1915, p. 3; 7 April 1915, p. 3. Robinson, who worked for the Devon Red Cross, notes that this was unusual amongst County Red Cross organizations and had been well thought out before the war.

21. E.g. *WT*, 8 October 1914, p. 2; 14 October 1916, p. 4; *DEG*, 25 August 1916, p. 9 (hostel for relatives).

22. *DEG*, 18 August 1916; p. 8; *WT*, 24 November 1916, p. 11.

23. *WT*, 3 April 1916, p. 6; 17 February 1917, p. 2.

first had been to give to the men ... everything the public would want their nearest and dearest to have when wounded'.[24]

The Lord Lieutenant, Earl Fortescue, thought that Buller had aspirations to be a Florence Nightingale, but it was not the clinical side of Red Cross work that interested her. Her focus was always, as her father's had been, on doing the best overall for the men who came under her care. In 1917 she spoke about her motivation:

> she particularly regretted that the demands of the VAO administra-
> tion work made it impossible for her now to be in and out of the
> hospital wards as she used to be. That still remained the work that
> she liked best ... More than that, she knew that in discharging
> anything it was in her power to do for the British soldier she would
> be carrying out the wishes of her father. She knew that if General
> Buller were with them now his first thought would be, as it always
> had been, for the welfare of his men.[25]

The letters that she preserved in her archive from patients and their relatives speak of their gratitude for 'all the trouble you took', 'your great kindness in our bereavement'.[26] Although sometimes the soldiers chafed under the strict regime, they did appreciate her. 'So extremely kind and nice is Miss Buller that anyone who comes to the hospital in Exeter gets quite endeared to her great, kind heart', wrote one of the soldiers in a piece for the *Western Times* at the end of 1915.[27] Mrs Mildmay, who had taken convalescent soldiers from Exeter into her home at Flete, said that they were 'full of praise and appreciation for their treatment ... Men talked of the Exeter Hospitals as "Paradise"'.[28] A Yorkshireman wrote to the *Gazette* with an unsolicited tribute: 'Were all places like the hospitals in Exeter the lot of the wounded soldier would indeed be an enviable one, but alas! this is far from the case ... [in many hospitals] the atmosphere is too frequently between that of a prison and a workhouse.'[29] The men knew who drove the organization: 'B for Miss Buller, who makes the thing go', ran the 'ABC of Hospital No. 1' printed in the hospital magazine.[30]

---

24. *DEG*, 2 August 1917, p. 3.
25. *WT*, 19 March 1917, p. 2.
26. DHC 2065M add 7 Box 2767; DHC 2065M add F357.
27. *WT*, 31 December 1915, p. 5.
28. *DEG*, 31 January 1920, p. 4.
29. *DEG*, 10 June 1918, p. 2.
30. DHC 2065M add F357, *Tittle-Tattle, Hospital No. 1 Magazine*, June 1916, p. 15.

To her staff, however, she was not so sympathetic a figure. She attracted both admiration and loathing. Many of the doctors she worked with respected her, as the confidence they placed in her after the war was to demonstrate, but on one occasion she provoked a row at Hospital No. 1 which drew resignations from three of the volunteer doctors, unaccustomed to their professional status being challenged by a lay person in the interests of efficiency.[31] She took the blame for perceived hardships. 'Everyone loathes Miss Buller', Margaret Kelly, a Red Cross volunteer nurse, confided to her diary when, in November 1914, Buller issued an edict that the volunteer cooks would have in future to do their own washing-up rather than leave it for the (paid) charwomen to do.[32] Buller herself was rather disparaging about the quality of the women who volunteered during the early phase of the war. She described her concerns at a prize-giving at Crediton High School in 1915, reflecting on the interviews she had had with potential recruits:

> She had been much struck by the few girls who were able to perform the duties they wished to discharge … it struck her as rather sad that there should be so many people who, now they wanted to help, were so incapable of helping … Only lately had we realised that women had got to know how to do things thoroughly just as much as men.[33]

She appointed women to positions such as that of Registrar that were generally held by commissioned officers, and was proud of her team of women staff for freeing up men for active service. She was also proud that their costs were below the national average.[34]

The Devon author E.M. Delafield, popular in later life for her columns as 'The Provincial Lady' in *Time and Tide*, always denied that 'Miss Vivien' in her novel, *The War Workers*, was based on Georgiana Buller, but many people thought they recognized the portrait. Delafield had worked on the team at Buller's headquarters in the Exeter War Hospitals and although her fictional setting was called a 'Midlands Supply Depot' the account of Miss Vivien tackling her morning post sounds very much like Buller's daily tasks:

---

31. *WMN*, 4 March 1918, p. 5.

32. M. Kelly, *Margaret's WWI Diary*, 29 November 1914 <https://kelly-house.co.uk/margarets-ww1-diary-100-years> [accessed 20 January 2015].

33. *WT*, 15 December 1915, p. 2.

34. *WT*, 2 August 1917, p. 2.

> Transport wanted for fifty men going from the King Street Hospital
> today—and they want more sphagnum moss ... Hospital
> accounts—that can go to the Finance Department ... The Stores
> bill—to the Commissariat ... Look me up the War Office letters
> as to Petrol regulations ... Here are some more of those tiresome
> muddles of Mrs Potter's. I told her about all those people on
> Monday ... Why on earth hasn't it been arranged? Nothing is ever
> done unless one sees to it oneself![35]

In 1916 the War Office decided to take more of the Red Cross Hospitals into
direct administration in order to increase their efficiency. The Exeter War
Hospitals were amongst this group and were officially detached from the
Devon Red Cross organization, although in practice, since hospitals had to
work together over transfers for convalescence and medical boards, they
remained interdependent.[36] Buller was the only woman hospital administrator
to be kept in place by the War Office to run a group of military hospitals, a
fact of which she was immensely proud all her life.[37]

The Lord Lieutenant might have hoped that this separation of responsibilities would have eased the difficult relationship between Buller and the
Devon Red Cross Director, Mr Davis, into which his wife (who chaired the
county committee) and he himself were reluctantly drawn. Davis was a North
Devon neighbour of the Fortescues, retired from the Indian Civil Service,
and had built up the Red Cross in Devon from its inauguration. He was
'methodical and business-like', though 'a little slow and precise'. Buller was
the daughter of Sir Redvers, a fellow landowner, and had inherited, Fortescue
felt, his 'capability and some obstinacy'.[38] She was impatient with Davis's
approach and wanted to run her own show. Each of them complained to the
Fortescues about the other.[39] The War Office took Buller's part, rather to

35. E.M. Delafield, The War Workers (London: Heinemann, 1918), pp. 29–30.
36. WT, 21 July 1916, p. 7 records the transfer of Davis and the county organization from 10 East
    Southernhay to 17 Bedford Circus.
37. She included it in biographical entries, e.g. for the magistrates' directory, The Magistrates of
    England and Wales: Western Circuit: Cornwall, Devonshire, Dorsetshire, Hampshire, Somersetshire, Wiltshire
    (Hereford: Jakemans, 1940), p. 48.
38. R. Batten (ed.) A Lord Lieutenant in Wartime: The Experiences of the Fourth Earl Fortescue during the
    First World War, Devon and Cornwall Record Society, new series 61 (Woodbridge: Boydell, 2018),
    pp. 51–53.
39. See correspondence in the Lord Lieutenant's files, DHC 1262M/0/0/LD/145. It appears that
    Davis managed to annoy other subordinates too.

Davis's annoyance. He suspected, perhaps correctly, that her father's former colleagues influenced their actions.[40]

Running hospitals for the War Office rather than the Red Cross proved a mixed blessing. Worries about how to find sufficient medical staff were eased: although some of the original consultant surgeons had volunteered for front-line duties, the RAMC were now responsible for substitutes. Military discipline and organization meant that logistics became more straightforward, but also sometimes led to local friction.

The number of beds increased gradually from May 1915 onwards, rising by the addition of temporary accommodation in huts or marquees, and then by the addition of a sixth and a seventh hospital in 1917, to a total of 1,400 beds. Nineteen seventeen also saw the closure of some of the smaller peripheral convalescent hospitals to release staff for the first-line hospitals. To accommodate the extra numbers, some convalescent soldiers in Exeter found themselves billeted with local residents.[41]

By 1919, when the hospitals were decommissioned, over 35,300 patients had been treated in the Exeter War Hospitals, staying on average twenty-five days each. Only 256 hospital deaths were recorded. If Davis could not bring himself to cite their achievement in his speech at the 1919 commemoration of the work of the Devon Voluntary Aid Organization, the local press had no such inhibition. A fortnight later Exeter's news-papers celebrated 'Exeter War Hospital, Birth, Growth and End' with a front-page story:

> Well may Devon and Exeter be proud of the work which has been
> quietly accomplished during the past five years by the officials,
> matrons, nurses, general duties, and numerous others ever willing,
> however tired they might be, to do their utmost to heal and ease
> the pain of our wounded and sick who had faced the foe abroad
> for the honour of the Empire.[42]

Sir Henry Davy, who had been consulting physician to the RAMC's Southern Command throughout the war, and in that capacity had visited numerous hospitals, wrote that '[t]he Exeter War Hospitals, under the direction of Miss

---

40. Batten, *Lord Lieutenant in Wartime*, pp. 52–53.
41. DHC 2065M add F357, typescript headed *Exeter War Hospitals*, p. 2; *WT*, 26 April 1918, p. 8.
42. *WT*, 12 July 1919, p. 1; *DEG*, 30 July 1919, p. 1.

Buller, equalled, if they did not surpass, all the other hospitals I visited, both in the work done and in general organization'.[43]

It was not until 1920 that Georgiana Buller herself stood down. She had already received the distinction of the Royal Red Cross for her work, and now she was awarded the new honour established by the King, that of a Dame of the British Empire.[44] Local admirers raised funds to present her with a testimonial and a pearl necklace.[45] She had been described as 'indefatigable and inexhaustible' by Colonel Mackay of the RAMC in 1915, but now, exhausted by her efforts and still in pain from a hunting accident before the war, she retired to convalesce at Sidmouth.[46]

'Broken Blossoms': Georgiana Buller and the Princess Elizabeth Orthopaedic Hospital

During the summer of 1927,[47] a small boy in a wheelchair pushed by his mother could regularly have been seen making his way towards the building site at Gras Lawn on the corner of Exeter's Wonford and Barrack Roads. He had been told that the new building was to be a hospital for people like him and he wanted 'just to be sure it's really there'.[48] Down to the site too, no doubt, came Georgiana Buller, now living at Bellair on Topsham Road, only a few hundred yards away. She had become the President of the Devonian Association for Cripples' Aid, the body that was developing the future Princess Elizabeth Orthopaedic Hospital.

Buller had become involved in this initiative after an approach by her own doctor, Henry Andrew, and a medical colleague from War Hospital days, Brennan Dyball, a surgeon at the RD&EH who had developed an interest in the new specialism of orthopaedics and who had worked with Buller as the medical 'Officer Commanding' for several of Exeter's War Hospitals. Buller had become interested during the war in the rehabilitation available for soldiers

43. *DEG*, 31 January 1920, p. 4.
44. *DEG*, 24 February 1917, p. 5; *WMN*, 24 November 1920, p. 4.
45. *WT*, 21 February 1921, p. 2.
46. *WT*, 6 March 1915, p. 3; residence at Sidmouth first referred to in March 1920 (*Derby Daily Telegraph*, 16 March 1920, p. 1). Buller's mother moved away from Devon in June 1920 to live in Salisbury. Buller herself moved into Marsley House in Sylvan Road, Exeter, together with Annie Whatley, who had been first her childhood nurse and then her lady's maid.
47. 'Broken Blossoms' was the headline of the appeal made in the *Devon and Exeter Gazette*, prefacing a column on 'Devon's Duty to her Crippled Children. How You Can Help', *DEG*, 5 November 1926, p. 5.
48. DHC 6181G, Devonian Orthopaedic Association (DOA), *First Annual Report* (1927), p. 9.

who had lost their limbs. She supported the development of occupational therapy activities in the hospitals and encouraged soldiers to exhibit and sell their work. At the end of the war she had attended a talk on the Italian Army initiative for total rehabilitation of disabled servicemen, but after her own health broke down she had been unable to pursue this further.[49]

Dyball's inspiration was the 'National Scheme for Crippled Children'. Its sponsors were practising orthopaedic surgeons who had published their proposal in the British Medical Journal in 1919. They described how 'the majority of children suffering from crippling diseases and deformities of all kinds' lay 'out of sight in their homes … in workhouses, or collected in homes for crippled children'. Three-quarters of these children, they claimed, could be cured by surgical treatment, and an even greater proportion enabled to be more active.[50] The Chief Medical Officer rejected their proposal to make provision of orthopaedic hospitals a statutory requirement, and it was left to the voluntary sector to make the scheme work. A Central Committee for the Care of Cripples was established in 1919, and a national scheme was published in 1924.[51]

In 1925, at the prompting of Andrew, Dyball and Mrs Jessie Loch, who had also worked with Buller at the War Hospitals, a Devon and Cornwall Association for the Care of Cripples was established. It was then agreed that the two counties formed too large an area for a single service. A line was drawn from Bude to Torquay and then at a meeting addressed by Buller on 31 August 1925, attended also by Lady Clinton and Mrs E.M. Acland (subjects respectively of other chapters in this collection), the Devonian Association for Cripples' Aid (DACA) was launched to serve the eastern sector.[52] Lady Clinton subsequently chaired a public meeting in Exeter in support of the initiative.[53] Acland was again present, and Lady Florence Cecil (another chapter subject) sent her apologies.

Many of the fundraising events were organized locally by supporters engaged at the inaugural drawing-room meeting and otherwise, but Buller seems to have been ubiquitous. She spoke at fundraising events such as the 'Fancy Fair

49. WT, 26 November 1918, p. 6.
50. R. Jones and G.R. Girdlestone, 'The cure of crippled children: proposed national scheme', British Medical Journal (11 October 1919), pp. 457–60.
51. G.R. Girdlestone, The Care and Cure of Crippled Children (Bristol: John Wright & Sons, 1924).
52. R. Cooter, Surgery and Society in Peace and War (Basingstoke: Macmillan, 1993), pp. 155–58; DHC 2065M add F357. The Association later extended its work to South West Devon and North Cornwall.
53. DEG, 5 December 1925, p. 6.

for Crippled Children', organized by the South Molton Voluntary Organization, and the 'Little Cripples' Bazaar', organized by Exeter Rotary Club.[54] She addressed societies and events such as the Ladies Luncheon of Newton Abbot Rotary Club and wrote a letter published in the national press to attract support from Devonians across the country.[55] Schools were mobilized to raise £500 to name a cot.[56] Organizations which had previously supported the Exeter War Hospitals, such as the Devon Farmers' Union, were appealed to for their support with this new venture.[57] She used her networks to identify individuals who could help with particular aspects of the programme. Calmady-Hamlyn (subject of another chapter in this collection), for example, was asked to supervise a weight-judging competition for a Shetland pony donated by Miss Chichester of Arlington Court.[58] For the next two years, fundraising was Buller's principal activity. The target set for the hospital building fund was initially £15,000 (over £950,000 at today's prices), all to be raised from charitable sources, though local authorities were expected as part of their responsibilities for education for children with special needs to contribute substantially to the running costs.

Buller was involved in selecting the site and in developing the plans. In an astonishingly short time, just over two years, the Princess Elizabeth Orthopaedic Hospital, with forty beds, was opened by the Duchess of York, who graciously permitted it to be named after her infant daughter, the future Queen Elizabeth II. In fact, on opening day the hospital was not quite finished and local children were recruited to play the parts of patients. Buller had refused to let the date slip, reputedly saying that the opening would go ahead, even if all they could open was a bathroom.[59] The first patients were admitted on 16 December 1927.[60]

Rosemary Sutcliff, the children's author, was treated at the Princess Elizabeth Orthopaedic Hospital in the early 1930s. She remembered it as 'Mr Capener's kingdom'. (Norman Capener had been appointed surgeon-in-charge in 1931.) She described its 'fresh-air' approach to treatment:

---

54. *WMN*, 9 April 1926, p. 6; *DEG*, 12 November 1926, p. 15.

55. *DEG*, 26 April 1926, p. 4.

56. *DEG*, 29 March 1926, p. 3.

57. *DEG*, 17 September 1926, p. 6.

58. *DEG*, 14 September 1926, p. 4. Proof of the reach of the appeal is shown by the fact that entries for this event came from as far afield as Ireland, Scotland and Canada (*WT*, 12 November 1926, p. 12).

59. DHC, Westcountry Studies Library, Exeter Heritage Project, *Working Lives: The Careers of Seven Exeter Women* (Exeter: Exeter City Council, 1987), p. 24.

60. DHC 6181G, *DOA First Annual Report* (1938), p. 9.

All down one side the wards were completely open ... lovely in the fine summer weather, but murder in the winter ... worst of all in wild weather, when canvas screens had to be shipped all down the open side ... [T]he rain spattered in over the top of the screens and the canvas bellied like the sails of a ship at sea, and the wind set the unshaded lights that hung on long flexes from the khaki-painted iron roof girders swinging wildly.[61]

The hospital provided children with access to inpatient treatment, reha-bilitation and education, admitting in its first year seventy-four boys and fifty-one girls, and numbers then rose rapidly, promoting the need for further extension, on-site and off-site, in 1932 and 1934.[62] It was supported by a network of local centres based in Barnstaple, Exeter, Honiton, Okehampton, Tiverton and Torquay, and later in Launceston and Kingsbridge. Each centre had a committee to run it and a local voluntary secretary (always a woman) and was visited by a nurse fortnightly and a surgeon once a month to under-take assessments and reviews.[63]

Buller in a Wider Context

Once she had returned to Exeter, Buller resumed her place as a member of the county gentry, a 'Buller of Downes', with the status and obligations associated with that position. She became a member of the cathedral congre-gation and a committee member of the Friends of Exeter Cathedral, took parties to the Devon County Ball and to county fundraising events, and supported a number of charities and good causes such as the Church Army Housing scheme, the Devon Voluntary Hospitals Committee, and the Industrial Christian Fellowship.[64] She was also invited to various civic functions, such as the reception for the Devonshire Association visit.[65] Her background in hospital management made her a valued member of the RD&EH's court of Governors.[66]

61. R. Sutcliff, *Blue Remembered Hills* (Oxford: Oxford University Press, 1988), pp. 86–87. Originally published in 1983.
62. *DEG*, 18 March 1932, p. 7; 30 September, p. 20; *WT*, 29 March 1934, p. 10.
63. *WT*, 14 October 1927, p. 9.
64. *DEG*, 2 December 1929, p. 7; 9 January 1929, p. 7; *WMN*, 17 May 1927, p. 5 (with Lady Florence Cecil); *DEG*, 17 September 1927, p. 4; 25 April 1928, p. 4.
65. *DEG*, 25 June 1931, p. 5.
66. *DEG*, 27 February 1931, p. 9.

In October 1928, once the Princess Elizabeth Orthopaedic Hospital was fully operational, Buller was appointed as a magistrate on the Exeter bench. She often sat with a fellow woman magistrate, Lady Radford. As the practice of youth justice evolved, they and Exeter's few other women magistrates became increasingly involved in juvenile court work, particularly after the implementation of the provisions of the Children and Young Persons Act 1933, with its emphasis on 'reclaiming young offenders to good citizenship'.[67] This approach paralleled the 'Crippled Children' initiative of hospital treatment and training for employment by seeking to ensure that as many people as possible, no matter what their disadvantage or disability, could play their role as self-supporting members of society. She also became a member of the national Council of the Magistrates' Association.[68]

When, in 1936, a Home Office Departmental Committee reported on the development of social services within the courts, Buller initiated the holding of a South West regional conference among magistrates the following year to discuss the changes.[69] The discussions there revealed that the Exeter service was pioneering the integration into the courts system of a psychiatrist. Buller also helped publicize the changes more widely, for example by speaking to local teachers in the Exeter and District Teachers' Association.[70]

Her concern for assisting disadvantaged members of society back to citizen-ship also came out in her support for the Devon League of Workfinders. This 1930s Devon initiative, started by the Bishop of Exeter, aimed, in the absence of any formal government initiative, to rehabilitate workless men on the tramp from place to place. It offered support ranging from the most basic of provi-sion, a pair of boots or a day's work, to an extended stay in the Blackborough Home for Young Wayfarers in East Devon which aimed to prepare the men for full employment. Buller joined the League when it was founded at the peak of unemployment in 1932 and served on the committee.[71] Some of these men were former soldiers whose plight was naturally close to Buller's heart, and this may have been what attracted her support.

As a magistrate and thus the holder of a public appointment, Buller became eligible for membership of the rather unusual Devon branch of the

---

67. K. Bradley, *Juvenile Delinquency and the Evolution of the British Juvenile Courts, c.1900–1950* <https://archives.history.ac.uk/history-in-focus/welfare/articles/bradleyk.html> [accessed 16 May 2020].
68. DHC Westcountry Studies Library, folder of Buller press cuttings and other items.
69. *DEG,* 19 March 1937.
70. *DEG,* 12 November 1937.
71. *WT,* 27 January 1933.

National Council of Women, the Devon Council of Women on Public Authorities (DCW). Its membership was confined more narrowly than that of the usual geographically based branch. As described in the chapter on Sylvia Calmady-Hamlyn (p. 216), it had been founded in 1923 following a conference held in Exeter to promote the appointment of more women in public services. Its aim was principally to help women in new positions, or positions where there were few other women, by programmes of education and discussion. The men who undertook roles as councillors or magistrates had well-established networks of clubs and discussion fora where they could debate current affairs; women were not eligible to join many of these.

Buller had earlier been involved in the initiative begun by the DCW to lobby local authorities for the appointment of women police. She is listed as present at the meeting that the DCW organized in Exeter in February 1928 to increase pressure on local authorities to appoint women police.[72] Her name appears in a personal capacity rather than, like most of the others, as a representative of an organization. In moving the vote of thanks, she said:

> It was her belief ... that there were not any people who really opposed the introduction of women police. It was said that a special kind of woman must be obtained. This was true in nursing and supremely so in teaching, but no one suggested this work should not be done by women because of that.

The initiative, as described elsewhere (pp. 151–52) was unsuccessful, and once she became a magistrate Buller took no further part in the lobbying on this topic. She did, however, join the DCW when she became a magistrate. This was only shortly before, with the reduction in numbers of Poor Law Guardians, the numbers eligible for the organization were drastically reduced. The smaller number of opportunities for elected public service that resulted from the abolition of Boards of Guardians meant a real loss of opportunities to women and the DCW became less viable, with difficulties in finding women willing to take office. Buller would nonetheless have found the topics on the half-yearly agenda often relevant to her role as magistrate.

---

72. *WMN*, 2 February 1928, p. 3. She was asked to move the vote of thanks to the chairman, suggesting that she had been involved earlier in the arrangements. Once she was appointed as a magistrate, however, she does not seem to have played any further part in the lobbying.

The group discussed, for example, the Public Places Order to control soliciting; legal advice for those on Public Assistance; and the cinema and its impact on children.[73]

Buller does not seem to have become involved in party politics in the interwar period. Her father had been a Liberal Unionist, and she lent her support to Eleanor Acland when Acland stood in Exeter as a Liberal candidate in 1931. But she seems to have been closer in spirit to those members of the women's movement who were interested in new, less 'party-led', ways of politics. From 1919 Exeter had been represented in Parliament by Sir Robert Newman, a Conservative politician and strong supporter of the women's suffrage movement and, in the 1920s, a reliable advocate for programmes of social reform. His reformist tendencies led him into conflict with the Conservative government, and after the General Strike the Conservative Party in Exeter determined to look elsewhere for a candidate for the next General Election. A group of Newman's supporters, including a number of women who had worked with him on the reform agenda, determined to support him as an independent candidate for the seat. Buller does not seem to have played a part in the initial organization of this move, but she had known Newman for many years, and he had been vocal in his support for the Orthopaedic Hospital. She responded to the advertisement for supporters by writing a letter that was read out at the public meeting which formed the Independent Parliamentary Association in support of Newman. In this she stated:

> I have voted for Sir Robert Newman in the past, and intend doing so in the future if opportunity occurs, because I believe he can be relied upon to put honesty before political expediency when these two things clash, as on various occasions they must do. In my opinion it is not in the interests of the country that Parliamentary representatives should place party loyalty above all other considerations. I believe that the number of those, who like Sir Robert Newman, claim some liberty of judgement, will increase.[74]

---

73. DHC Westcountry Studies Collection, Special Collections F6, *Scrapbooks of Juanita Maxwell Phillips*, 11 November 1931 (Vol 1, p. 25); 18 May 1933 (Vol. 2.28–2.31), 10 December 1936 (Vol. 7.51) & 17 December 1937 (Vol. 9, p. 38).
74. *DEG*, 11 November 1927, p. 16.

Over the next two years she supported his candidature, appearing on the platform and chairing public meetings, particularly those of the women's branch of the Association, to endorse his candidature.[75] Newman was successfully elected in 1929 and served for two years, determining to retire in advance of the 1931 election. Buller expressed the thanks of the Independent Parliamentary Association to him for his services but, though her name was briefly touted in the press as a successor, she chose not to take up a political career.[76]

'No Man is a Cripple Until He is Crippled in Spirit': Buller and St Loye's College

In addition to these other duties Buller continued to play a full part in the management of the Orthopaedic Hospital and the supporting outpatient clinics. It was she with whom the county Medical Officer of Health crossed swords when he sought to exercise the right to agree which patients should be admitted at the county's expense, and she of whom the chair of the County Finance Committee once exclaimed in exasperation: 'A certain lady is trying to rule the County Council'.[77] Buller and her committee, who knew that adults also could benefit from orthopaedic surgery, wished to extend the remit of the Orthopaedic Hospital to adults. This was not a development for which the county had budgeted. In March 1934, Robert Newman, now Lord Mamhead, and a County Alderman, forced a debate on the issue within the County Council, prompting the Finance Committee chair into his exasperated exclamation. Three months later, however, enough money was indeed found to increase admissions.[78] After this episode Buller and her vice-chair, John Radcliffe, changed places. At the end of 1935 Radcliffe took on DACA and the hospital, and Buller turned her attention to a new project, one that the Association had been promising to tackle ever since its first beginnings: the broader welfare of disabled people, and in particular their training for employment.[79]

A Vocational Training Department (staffed by volunteers) had been established at the hospital from the start. It made slow progress, however. Employers

75. *DEG*, 10 December 1927, p. 8; 3 November 1928, p. 8; 25 May 1929, p. 7.
76. *DEG*, 31 January 1931, p. 8.
77. DHC 2609F HM1, *Minutes of the Devonian Orthopaedic Hospital*, 17 April and 30 October 1930; *Express and Echo (E&E)*, 9 March 1934, p. 6.
78. Ibid.; *E&E*, 16 June 1934, p. 3.
79. DHC 6181G, *DOA Annual Report for 1935* (1936), p. 2; *DEG*, 5 April 1935 p. 10.

were reluctant to offer placements and there were limited opportunities for home working, although crafts such as 'Italian embroidery' were tried. A first meeting about a possible project to create a training college that could run accredited courses to prepare people with disabilities for work was chaired by the Mayor of Exeter on 1 July 1930, but little had been achieved by 1935. Georgiana Buller had chaired the national Central Council for the Care of Cripples in 1932 and helped to establish the first training institute at Leatherhead, the 'Cripples' Training College', now Queen Elizabeth's Foundation for Disabled People. Once she took charge of the Devon project its impetus changed. A regional group representing the six counties in the far South West began to plan in earnest for St Loye's Training Centre for Cripples, later St Loye's College.[80]

As had been the case for the hospital earlier, an intensive period of fund-raising then took place. Millbrook House on Exeter's Topsham Road was acquired, and a hostel and workshops converted or built. In a phrase to which Buller was to return to sum up her life's work she described the college as 'transformed from a castle-in-the-air into a building of bricks and mortar'.[81] The first trainee moved in on 8 July 1937 and the twenty-five places for male trainees were rapidly filled. The college offered training in watch and instrument making and repairs, and in catering and gardening. Demand was so high that by June 1938 there was a waiting list of twenty-four men from the South West and beyond.[82]

Trainees came with different backgrounds and disabilities. The first four who found permanent employment were a 33-year-old man who had had infantile paralysis, trained as a gardener; a 32-year-old man with a tubercular hip and a 16-year-old with osteomyelitis, who went into watch-making; and a 20-year-old who had lost a leg and became an instrument maker. One of the first graduates later reflected on his experience at St Loye's: 'I can only say that the training I received has been the greatest thing in my life. It has got rid of my inferiority complex, established me on an equal footing with other people, and given me a certain amount of independence, which is best of all.'[83]

Plans to develop the college accelerated. The neighbouring property, Fairfield House, came onto the market and, as Buller put it, it was 'now or

---

80. *DEG*, 20 November 1936, p. 20.
81. DHC ZAKZ, St Loye's College *First Annual Report* (1937); *Second Annual Report* (1938).
82. Ibid.
83. DHC ZAKZ, St Loye's College *Third Annual Report* (1939).

never' to create space for women trainees, another 'castle-in-the-air' made real. War came: the college's potential to help meet the need for additional labour was recognized and it was approved for work of national importance by the Ministry of Supply and the Air Ministry.[84] Ernest Bevin, the Minister of Labour, reputedly after a personal appeal from Buller who remembered him as Ernie, a small boy scrumping apples on the Downes estate, agreed to pay tuition fees for the students. St Loye's College was confirmed on its seventy-year life as a specialist college.[85]

Buller continued to guide St Loye's in the new post-war world of the Welfare State. She also became involved in the creation of the new National Health Service, which took over the administration of the Princess Elizabeth Orthopaedic Hospital. She was appointed as a member of the new Hospital Management Committee responsible for running both the RD&EH and the Princess Elizabeth Orthopaedic Hospital. In this role she helped to create the pressure on the Regional Hospital Board for the planning of new hospital buildings for Exeter.[86]

A Woman of Great Gifts

Dame Georgiana Buller was a woman of great gifts. When she died in 1953 the St Loye's Annual Report described her as 'a master of strategy and tactics with powers of persuasion which few could resist'.[87] Norman Capener, her long-term associate, remarked:

> Whatever Dame Georgiana put her hand to she did superlatively well. She was a Justice of the Peace and she had a keen interest in music, drama and the arts … Dame Georgiana was a most able chairman of committees: orderly, coldly logical and quick in repartee. She was patient and kindly when working with those she liked or respected but ruthlessly direct and impatient with those who by foolishness, thoughtlessness, incompetence or obstinacy stood in her way.[88]

---

84. *E&E*, 3 November 1939.
85. DHC ZAKZ, St Loye's College, *Second Annual Report* (1938), *Fourth Annual Report* (1940).
86. *DEG*, 20 October 1950, p. 8.
87. DHC ZAKZ, St Loye's College, *Annual Report for 1953*.
88. N. Capener, 'In Memoriam Dame Georgiana Buller', *Journal of Bone and Joint Surgery*, 35 (1953), pp. 573–74.

Buller used her gifts to create three great twentieth-century services for people with disabilities in Devon: the Devonshire Association for Cripples' Aid, the Princess Elizabeth Orthopaedic Hospital, and St Loye's Training College. All three were pioneering ventures which paved the way for their still-existing successors: the Devonian Orthopaedic Association (incorporated into Devon Community Foundation), the Princess Elizabeth Orthopaedic Centre at the Royal Devon and Exeter NHS Foundation Trust, and the St Loye's Foundation, now known as Step One. Nonetheless Buller was a woman of her time, and the conventions of her generation shaped the way in which she used her gifts. As she was not by nature a radical her work in Devon was bounded by the ideas, practice and attitudes of the times through which she lived. This shaped the expectations of what women could do; the way in which her voluntary organizations had to work; and the nature of the opportunities she was able to create for disabled people.

Buller was born into a late Victorian world. She grew up in a well-to-do, well-connected county family. In her father she observed a devotion to service, a strategic grasp of direction and ruthless attention to detail combined with a personal interest in and concern for those dependent on him. Her mother was a great charitable patron in the way then expected of a lady, serving on committees and lending her name to appeals or fundraising events to encourage others to give. Although Georgiana herself was unconventional enough as a teenager to write a play called *The Prude's Prejudice or The Triumphant Bicyclist*, in which she played a man, she never sought to do anything other than to work within the framework of the county society into which she had been born.[89] The Great War gave her an opportunity to learn what she was capable of and, like many other young women, she took it. Her war service became a foundation for unpaid but full-time public service thereafter.

The world of welfare in which she worked was itself evolving. The roles of voluntary organizations and of local authorities and central government were shifting. Responsibilities for the welfare of those who could not afford to pay for their care had once been sharply divided between the patronage of the charitable and the hated Poor Law. By the mid-twentieth century a 'New Philanthropy' was emerging, a partnership between the state and the voluntary sector under which the state took greater responsibility for resourcing welfare services and voluntary organizations accepted state funding for some of the service they delivered. Voluntary organizations came to derive as much as a third of their income from statutory agencies. This developing relationship

89. DHC 2065M.

frequently generated friction, with the statutory sector seeking to set policy for provision and voluntary organizations seeking to continue the freedom of action to which they were accustomed. Such tensions are evident in the difficulties that Devon County Council and the DACA experienced over the development of orthopaedic treatment for adults.[90]

The services that Buller helped create at St Loye's College have been superseded by newer ideas about supporting people with disabilities to lead a normal life. Borsay has described the mid-twentieth century as the period of 'Growth of Collectivism' in services for disabled people.[91] A philosophy of 'economic rationality' prevailed that valued equipping disabled people for economic independence as the highest goal and considered that this could be most effectively delivered in special institutions offering a narrow range of possibilities. St Loye's College fitted this now discarded model: but the limitations on what it offered were a practical response to the possibilities in a particular time and place. They illustrate Buller's pragmatism, rather than the limits of her imagination.

Buller herself described her talent as making a reality of 'castles-in-the-air'.[92] It was the very talent that her father had exercised to the full, comprehending the strategic objective and marshalling the resources to achieve it. 'She made positively toy soldiers of the War Office; they did whatever she wanted them to do', said one of her former colleagues.[93] Her obituary in the St Loye's Annual Report stated that 'she worked unceasingly to persuade Government Departments, Local Authorities and private citizens that her ideas were practical politics'.[94] She herself modestly underplayed those roles. 'Nothing ever gets done unless you shout long and hard for it', she said, picturing herself as an 'agitator', and shout long and hard for the causes she supported she did indeed.[95] The lives of many disabled people in Devon were the richer for it.

90. G. Finlayson, 'A Moving Frontier: Voluntarism and the State in British Social Welfare, 1911–1949', *Twentieth-Century British History*, 2 (1990), pp. 183–206, DOI <https://doi-org.uoelibrary.idm.oclc. org/10.1093/tcbh/1.2.183>; E. Macadam, *The New Philanthropy* (London: G. Allen and Unwin, 1934).
91. A. Borsay, *Disability and Social Policy in Britain Since 1750: A History of Exclusion* (Basingstoke: Palgrave Macmillan, 2008).
92. *WMN*, 14 July 1950, p. 4.
93. Robert Jones, speaking at the opening of the Princess Elizabeth Orthopaedic Hospital, *WMN*, 17 November 1927.
94. DHC St Loye's Annual Report for 1953.
95. *E&E*, 16 November 1927; H. Harvey, *Towards a Better Provision Fifty Years On: The Royal Devon and Exeter Hospital, 1948–1998* (Exeter: RD&E NHS Foundation Trust 1998), p. 51

An earlier version of this chapter was published in Aspects of Devon History: People, Places and Landscapes *in 2012. The author extends her thanks to Devon History Society for their agreement to her use of that material as the basis for this chapter.*

CHAPTER SEVEN

Jane Grey Clinton (1863–1953)

JULIA NEVILLE AND HELEN TURNBULL

Jane Grey Clinton, photograph published in *The Sphere*,
19 June 1920

Jane Grey McDonnell, known to her friends and family as Jenny, was one of
the daughters of Mark McDonnell, fifth Earl of Antrim, and his wife Jane,
formerly Macan. She was born in Glenarm Castle, County Antrim in 1863,
the ninth of ten children. When she was 6 her father died and was succeeded
by Jenny's eldest brother William, aged only 18. The family continued to live
at Glenarm, and when Jenny came to write an account of her childhood, she
called it *Happy Hours in an Irish Home*, a tribute to their family life.[1] In 1875,
however, William married, and Jenny, her mother and sisters moved to live
in Lowndes Square in London's Belgravia.[2]

---

1. J. Grey Hepburn-Stuart-Forbes Trefusis, Baroness Clinton, *Happy Hours in an Irish Home*
   (Edinburgh: William Brown, 1938).
2. A. Austin, *The History of the Clinton Barony, 1299–1999* (Exeter: Lord Clinton, 1999), p. 206.

Julia Neville and Helen Turnbull, 'Chapter Seven: Jane Grey Clinton (1863–1953)' in: *Devon Women
in Public and Professional Life 1900–1950: Votes, Voices and Vocations*. University of Exeter Press
(2021). © Julia Neville and Helen Turnbull DOI: 10.47788/KNNY1057

Clinton once became nationally famous for reminiscing that in her childhood she had 'thirty-six governesses' which she felt had meant that her only 'worthwhile education' had been in modern languages. She made this statement when addressing a school Speech Day in 1922, using it to highlight the importance of education. It was reported by the *Devon and Exeter Gazette*, and immediately picked up by local papers around the country for further publication, rather like a modern retweet.[3] She also owed her musicality to her upbringing, and was ready in later life to entertain groups with a song such as 'Molly Malone' at the piano, to conduct community singing with her baton, or teach the members new and amusing songs.[4] Her mother also encouraged a spirit of enterprise. She and her sister were allowed on their Saturday half-holiday to use a model printing press they had been given and produced (with the aid of some 'quite distinguished contributors') a little newspaper called the *Lowndes Square Chronicle*. They sold the paper and earned enough money with it to maintain 'a cripple' for four years.[5]

In 1886 Jenny married a distant cousin, the Hon. Charles Forbes-Trefusis, eldest son of the Devon premier peer Lord Clinton.[6] He had already inherited his mother's property at Fettercairn House in Kincardineshire and was heir to the properties of his uncle, the Hon. Mark Rolle, at Stevenstone and Bicton, in addition to the Clinton estate at Heanton Satchville in North Devon. The couple made their home at Fettercairn House and took up the traditional roles of the gentry in a farming community: Charles took an interest in local agriculture, served as a Poor Law guardian, and made a start on his political career by securing election (unopposed) to the new County Council, whose Convenor he became in 1898. Jenny visited the sick; supported good causes such as the local nursing association which employed a district nurse; helped raise funds for the parish hall; took part in raising poultry, for which she won prizes; and brought up their two daughters, Harriet (b. 1887) and Fenella (b. 1889).

At their golden wedding in 1936 Charles was asked the traditional question about what makes a successful marriage. He replied that 'to be happily married people should have the same interests and, so far as possible, work in the same

---

3. *Devon and Exeter Gazette (DEG)*, 19 December 1922, p. 5.

4. *Western Times (WT)*, 29 January 1915, p. 9; 13 May 1927, p. 9; *DEG*, 20 May 1927, p. 3.

5. *Western Morning News (WMN)*, 23 November 1932, p. 3. Clinton related the anecdote to the reporter interviewing her about producing a 'Chronicle' to sell to raise funds for the Devonshire Nursing Association.

6. *Pall Mall Gazette*, 1 June 1886, p. 8.

forms of personal service … There must be no question of obedience or mastery. No two people can always concur, so they must agree to differ and practise mutual forbearance.[7] It was a relationship grounded in respect for the other party, and thus one which enabled Jenny to develop her own role in Devon's voluntary organizations.

Charles's father died in 1904, and Charles became the twenty-first Baron Clinton, inheriting over 14,000 acres in north-western Devon. This drew the family down to Heanton Satchville in Huish, the centre of the estate. He resigned his Scottish offices and almost at once became a Devon JP and County Council alderman. He also took his seat in the House of Lords. Lady Clinton assumed in North Devon the roles she had performed at Fettercairn: visiting the sick poor in the villages on the estate and in Torrington Workhouse, entertaining the tenantry to a Christmas tea and providing them with gifts.[8] The family commitment to Devon was strength-ened when in 1907 Mark Rolle died and Charles inherited the Rolle estate in East Devon, amounting to a further 70,000 acres.[9] Although the Clintons knew Bicton well, as they had often been the guests of Lady Rolle there, they did not immediately take up regular residence. In fact Lord Clinton, concerned about death duties, laid off staff there, although he also embarked on a renovation programme.[10] He, Jenny and their daughters divided their time over the next few years between Heanton Satchville, Fettercairn, and London (during the season). They paid a few visits to Exmouth, where it appears they stayed at the Imperial Hotel.[11]

Lord Clinton became a leading figure in the Country Landowners' Association, formed to combat the proposals of the Liberal Government for land reform, and was also appointed to the Council of the Duchy of Cornwall. Lady Clinton took on the role of Ruling Councillor of the Bicton Habitation of the Primrose League in succession to her aunt.[12] She had earlier become a member of the Devonshire Nursing Association Committee, representing

7. *WMN*, 2 June 1936, p. 4.
8. *North Devon Journal (NDJ)*, 9 August 1906, pp. 7–8; *WT*, 28 May 1907, p. 3.
9. Austin, *Clinton Barony*, pp. 208–09.
10. *North Devon Gazette (NDG)*, 12 November 1907, p. 2; *DEG*, 8 September 1909, p. 2.
11. *DEG*, 9 July 1912, p. 10.
12. The Primrose League was a campaigning organization within the Conservative and Unionist Party that brought many women into political activism before they were granted the Parliamentary vote, and set out to appeal broadly across the class spectrum, see Stephen Luscombe, *The British Empire: The Primrose League* <https://www.britishempire.co.uk/article/primroseleague.htm> [accessed 30 December 2019]; *DEG*, 9 July 1909, p. 3.

the branch at Huish.[13] From Bicton she instituted a district nursing scheme for the parishes around Bicton: Colaton Raleigh, Newton Poppleford, Harpford and Venn Ottery.[14] She also became President of the Budleigh Salterton Nursing Association.[15] Much of her time was probably occupied, however, with launching her daughters into society and securing their marriages. Harriet married Henry Nevile Fane in 1910 and Fenella married the Honourable John Bowes-Lyon (brother of the future Queen Elizabeth, consort of George VI) in 1914.

Early Activism and the First World War

The Rolle estate included the town of Exmouth, where the family were lords of the manor. Edwardian Exmouth had expanded beyond the original fishing port to take in the village of Littleham, and reached out along the coast road east lined with smart houses for those with private means, including many retired from the colonial service and the armed forces. Exmouth seems to have expected a continuing involvement from the Clintons, but they were initially cautious. Lord Clinton, for instance, declined an invitation to become patron of the Exmouth Regatta.[16] The cachet of the Clinton connection was not to be lightly foregone, however. Knowing that the Clintons were due to come to Exmouth for the dedication of the extension to Holy Trinity Church, which Mark Rolle had commissioned, Exmouth Urban District Council determined to make a civic occasion of their visit in 1908 and to present them with a congratulatory address.[17] It was a festive occasion. The bishop consecrated the chancel; Lady Clinton planted a tree; the Council held an 'At Home' at which they presented the Clintons with the illuminated address; and Lord Clinton in return presented the town with the Manor Grounds for 'free use and free enjoyment for ever' as a memorial to Mark Rolle.[18]

Gradually the Clintons were drawn into patronage, and then to a more active role in the town's activities. In 1908 Lord Clinton became President of the Constitutional Club and a patron of the Dispensary.[19] Then Lady Clinton

---

13. *DEG*, 16 February 1906, p. 2.
14. *DEG*, 25 February 1910, p. 9.
15. *DEG*, 30 July 1913, p. 4.
16. *NDG*, 16 July 1907, p. 5.
17. *DEG*, 11 October 1907, p. 16.
18. *WT*, 31 October 1907, p. 2.
19. *DEG*, 28 January 1908, p. 8; 30 January 1908, p. 4.

became associated with one of the two major movements that were to dominate her life: the Girl Guides. In 1908 General Sir Robert Baden-Powell had published *Scouting for Boys*, and so instigated one of the most successful youth movements of all time.[20] The handbook was based, as the first historian of the Girl Guide movement describes, on his ideas for a youth scheme intended to 'encourage discipline, unselfishness and good citizenship' by developing 'woodcraft, observation, loyalty, chivalry, courage and endurance'.[21] He set up a central office to provide advice to boys and their leaders, and the movement grew apace.

Many girls, excluded from the formal scheme, nonetheless set up their own groups of 'Girl Scouts'. Although Baden-Powell initially resisted the idea that girls should form part of the scouting movement, he was impressed by their enthusiasm, and in 1909 these informal initiatives led to the founding of a new organization, the Girl Guides. Baden-Powell asked his sister Agnes to take on the task of transforming the informal arrangements for Girl Scouts into a separate organization.[22] In 1910 a central committee was established. By that time, a 'troop' of Girl Guides was already in existence in Exmouth. Its first Captain was Miss Faulkner.[23] It was probably she who approached Lady Clinton for permission to name the troop the 'Clinton Troop', and thus engaged Lady Clinton in agreeing to become a Vice-President.[24]

The *Exmouth Journal* wrote approvingly about the new organization, considering it should be 'of immense value in the improvement of the physical and moral character of the girls of the nation' as 'the lack of character training among all classes of girls is painfully apparent'.[25] It also noted that part of the training was that 'the girls are taught cooking, nursing, dairy work and the making of clothes, as well as dozens of other arts which go to make up the attributes of a complete housekeeper'.[26] This was rather far from the appeal of the 'woodcraft' that had attracted the early Girl Scouts, but an emphasis on fitness was maintained by drill, and the girls also learned semaphore, Morse

---

20. R.S. Smyth Baden-Powell, *Scouting for Boys: A Handbook for Instruction in Good Citizenship* (London: C. Arthur Pearson, 1908).

21. R. Kerr, *Story of the Girl Guides, 1908–1938* (Edinburgh: Clark Constable, 1976), p. 23. Originally published in 1938.

22. H.D. Gardner, *The First Girl Guide: The Story of Agnes Baden-Powell* (Stroud: Amberley Publishing, 2011), pp. 62–67.

23. *Exmouth Journal (ExJ)*, 18 June 1910, p. 8.

24. *ExJ*, 23 July 1910, p. 5.

25. Ibid.

26. Ibid.

code and ambulance work.[27] The organization, like the Boy Scouts, drew widespread support from those interested in 'citizen training', with elements grounded variously in militarism, education and Christian ethics, but differing in its combination of activities from the traditional Sunday School movement and its 'brigades', the army-related 'cadet companies' and the organization of social clubs such as the Girls' Friendly Societies.[28]

The first record of Lady Clinton with the Exmouth troop is in February 1912, when she is referred to as 'President'. This was a 'visit of inspection' during which the girls demonstrated cookery, laundry work and dressmaking, and ambulance work.[29] Clinton seems to have been impressed. She commented that she had heard criticisms about the Guides, 'which could only have come from those who knew nothing about the movement'. Her speech demonstrates what she thought was important:

> now that women were coming so much to the fore, they needed to be well equipped to be genuine workers, and especially so when so many were going abroad or to the Colonies. Membership of the Girl Guides so well fitted them to do all the work that women should do in the world, particularly in the way of nursing, cooking and laundry work.[30]

Her emphasis is definitely on domestic skills. However, she also refers to the needs of the Empire. This was very much in line with the thinking of the Baden-Powells. Agnes and Robert published *The Handbook for Girl Guides, or How Girls Can Help Build the Empire* in 1912, and this includes a section on 'Women, Travel and Empire' with chapters such as 'Frontier Life'.[31]

Clinton's commitment to the needs of the Empire was a strong part of her set of beliefs as a long-serving Ruling Councillor in the Primrose League. She refers also to 1912 as a time when women were 'coming to the fore'. This may be a reference to the greater prominence given to the talents of women during the debate about women's suffrage. Lord Clinton was himself a supporter of the League for Opposing Women's Suffrage, but Lady Clinton's

27. *DEG*, 31 March 1911, p. 6.
28. A. Warren, 'Sir Robert Baden-Powell, the Scout Movement and Citizen Training in Great Britain, 1900–1920', *English Historical Review*, 101 (1986), p. 390.
29. *DEG*, 26 February 1912, p. 3.
30. Ibid.
31. A. Baden-Powell, with R. Baden-Powell, *The Handbook for Girl Guides, or How Girls Can Help Build the Empire* (London: Nelson, 1912).

personal position is less clear.[32] She later referred to herself as a 'convert' to the enfranchisement of women.[33]

By the spring of 1914, the Clintons had decided to live at least part-time at Bicton. Guiding was spreading in Devon as it had done nationally. When Miss Prichard of Exmouth gave a cup to be competed for by Devon Guides in May 1914 troops from Exmouth, Exeter, Torquay and Topsham all entered the competition. Lady Clinton presented the trophy, saying that 'she thought the physical side was very important' but 'the more homely part of the training was of greater importance still. What could be more splendid work than that of sewing, cooking, laundry and nursing? Could anyone be more unhappy than an incapable and helpless woman?'[34] That summer Clinton was appointed County Commissioner for Devon, a role in which, as the first historian of the Girl Guide movement suggested, she became 'loved and honoured far beyond the bounds of her own county'.[35]

Although the First World War began soon after her appointment, and Guides were asked to give time to supporting other voluntary organizations in their wartime efforts, for example by fundraising for Belgian Refugees or the Red Cross, the movement continued to flourish in its own right.[36] In June 1915 Miss Baden-Powell herself, as Chief Guide, came to Exeter to inspect local Guides at a rally, with Lady Clinton in attendance. The rally was attended by Guides from seventeen Devon companies and one from Taunton.[37]

Lady Clinton's involvement in Guiding became a substantial commitment of her time during the war as she used her networks to develop the movement. This was in addition to other wartime commitments. She had family responsibilities towards members on active service. When war was declared in early August 1914 Lord Clinton was immediately absorbed into military duties with the Royal North Devon Yeomanry. As he was already 50 he was not posted to the front but remained in the UK. His initial remit was for recruitment, particularly in North Devon, and he was then made responsible for training and for preparations in case of invasion. In May 1915 one of the

---

32. He announced his intention of attending the Anti Suffrage Rally at the Albert Hall in 1912 (*WT*, 30 January 1912, p. 5) and sent apologies 'as a sympathiser' to an Exeter meeting in 1913 (*DEG*, 4 February 1913, p. 10). Lady Clinton did not join her husband either in attendance or in sending apologies.
33. *WMN*, 12 April 1930, p. 9.
34. *DEG*, 5 May 1914, p. 10.
35. Kerr, *Story of the Girl Guides*, p. 79.
36. *DEG*, 3 August 1915, p. 7; 13 December 1915, p. 3.
37. *DEG*, 4 June 1915, p. 4.

Clintons' sons-in-law was wounded, and a few months later Lord Clinton's step-brother was killed in action.[38]

Clinton played her part alongside other aristocratic and gentry women from the county, work led by Countess Fortescue, wife of the Lord Lieutenant. She promoted local registration of women for employment, encouraged women to join the Women's Emergency Corps, and from November 1915 lent her home at Bicton as an auxiliary Red Cross hospital.[39] As she told Exmouth women, 'No true woman would hold back … they would not be one whit behind the Germans in their patriotism.'[40] She also became involved in the Women Signallers' Territorial Corps, an organization that trained women to take the place of soldiers and release more men for active service.[41] Not much is known about this organization, and it was probably superseded by initiatives such as the Women's Auxiliary Army Corps later in the war.

Clinton's appointment as a Guide Commissioner carried with it a national role as a member of the governing Council, and she is named as such on the Royal Charter issued in 1922.[42] Her first task, however, was to recruit a set of District and Divisional Commissioners for Devon and to support the establishment of additional 'troops'.[43] Clinton appointed commissioners in her own mould. By 1916 she had appointed Lady Acland, wife of Admiral Sir William Acland, as the District Commissioner for Torquay.[44] In 1917 she persuaded Nancy Astor, then the wife of a Plymouth MP, to call a meeting in Plymouth about establishing the movement there, for which they received the support of two local aristocratic ladies, Lady Mary St Edgcumbe and Lady St Aubyn.[45] Astor became Clinton's latest Divisional Commissioner. Then Mrs Mildmay of Flete was recruited as the Totnes Divisional Commander; Miss Davie as District Commander for Barnstaple; Mrs Kendall King, wife of a former mayor, Divisional Commander for Exeter; and Lady Albertha Lopes the Divisional Commander for Tavistock.[46] These were the wives, sisters and

38. *DEG*, 15 May 1915, p. 3; *WT*, 28 October 1915, p. 3.

39. *DEG*, 4 Mar 1915, p. 5; 1 June 1915, p. 5.

40. *DEG*, 1 June 1915, p. 5

41. K. Roberts, 'Gender, Class and Patriotism in Britain: Women's Paramilitary Units in First World War Britain', *International History Review* 19.1, 1997, pp. 52–65, p. 57.

42. Girlguiding, *The Guide Association Royal Charter and Bye-laws* <https://www.girlguiding.org.uk/globalassets/docs-and-resources/quality-and-compliance/royal-charter.pdf> [accessed 5 December 2019].

43. The designation 'troops' was later dropped in favour of 'companies' which sounded less militaristic.

44. *WT*, 11 July 1916, p. 2.

45. *WMN*, 8 May 1917, p. 5.

46. *WT*, 19 October 1917, p. 5; *DEG*, 25 October 1917, p. 4; *WT*, 4 February 1918, p. 3; *DEG*, 21 October 1918, p. 3.

daughters of the men she knew, socially or because of their office, in the county. Her style of recruitment was very much favoured by the future Chief Guide (and wife of Sir Robert Baden-Powell) who explained that she used the 'many friends she had made' to help her find commissioners, 'organizing, coaxing, enthusing, spreading the word'.[47]

By May 1918 when the new Chief Guide, Lady Baden-Powell, came to inspect the Guides in Exeter, there were eighty Devon companies.[48] At a rally later in the year Clinton reflected on how far the movement had come. She considered that this was because it responded to the needs of the day. It was entirely voluntary, and so benefited from enthusiasm and esprit de corps. The Government had pronounced it 'important war work'. Educational and religious bodies considered it met the needs of young people, 'helping as it did to build up finer women to take their place in national life, to exercise such responsibilities as the vote, and to become better helpmeets and comrades to their menfolk'. The movement 'was inter-denominational and non-political and offered a field where people could drop their differences and unite for the good of the girls'. It was 'an inspiring thought' to consider that the movement spread over 'Canada, South Africa, Australia and all our Colonies'.[49]

The Women's Institute Movement

Lord Clinton resigned his commission in 1917 and took up a government appointment as Joint Parliamentary Secretary to the Department of Agriculture. Lady Clinton was amongst the landowners' wives on the platform when the Minister for Food Production spoke in Exeter in June 1917.[50] She was not, however, a member of the Devon Women's War Agricultural Committee, local sponsors of Women's Institute (WI) development, and it seems that, rather as with the Girl Guides, her interest in the novel idea of WIs was initially aroused by women in Exmouth rather than at county or national level. Miss Agnes Prichard, with whom she had worked over the Girl Guides, and other Exmouth women were interested in the idea of a WI, and they persuaded Clinton to chair a 'representative' meeting of Exmouth women in May 1919. A Mrs Martin of Truro explained the idea of WIs to them. As a result of the

---

47. Quoted in R. Howell, *Splendid Fun: The Story of One Hundred Years of Devon Girl Guides* (Ivybridge, Howell, 2019), p. 12.
48. *WT*, 23 May 1918, p. 3.
49. Ibid.
50. *WT*, 23 June 1917, p. 2.

address it was agreed to establish a committee to set up a WI in Exmouth. Lady Clinton was elected a member of the committee.[51]

It was at almost the same time, on 26 April 1919, that, as described in the chapter in this collection about Sylvia Calmady-Hamlyn, the Devon Women's branch of the County Agricultural Committee was being addressed by Mrs Clowes, Chief Organiser of WIs for the Department of Agriculture. The Department was actively promoting the creation of WIs, an idea brought to the UK from Canada.[52] WIs were perceived nationally as one way in which the rural development priority of the Ministry of Reconstruction could be achieved.[53] Mrs Clowes described their functions. They were

> a very definite form of rural development and the encouragement of social intercourse in the country districts. They were non-sectarian and non-party. Their first object was to stimulate interest in the agricultural industry and in intensive agriculture. If women could be interested equally with men in agricultural enterprise they would be a great and valuable asset. Another object was the development of co-operative enterprise, in regard to which Mrs Clowes gave illustrations of the success which had attended experiments in canning blackberries and in jam-making on co-operative principles. Pig food and honey had been obtained by co-operation to the advantages of the village communities, and co-operation had done much to develop home industries such as toy-making, baskets and other handicrafts which had been greatly stimulated by the women's institutes.[54]

The group resolved to set up a committee to take forward the WI movement in Devon and 'Lady Clinton ... consented to serve on the committee.'[55] In 1920 the Devon Federation of WIs was formed, and Lady Clinton, representing the East Devon group of WIs, was elected its President.[56] Her election signified a principal difference between this movement and that of the Girl Guides, where her appointment as County Commissioner had been made, without consultation, by the central committee at Guide Headquarters.

51. *DEG*, 14 May 1919, p. 3.
52. M. Andrews, *The Acceptable Face of Feminism* (London: Lawrence and Wishart, 1997), pp. 17–40.
53. Ministry of Reconstruction, *The Aims of Reconstruction* (London, HMSO, 1918), p. 13.
54. *WT*, 26 April 1919, p. 4.
55. *WT*, 21 June 1919, p. 2.
56. *DEG*, 12 June 1920, p. 1.

During her first few years at the head of the WI movement in Devon, Lady Clinton confined her activities with local Institutes to those in the East Devon area, supporting new Institutes as they formed and joining in the activities of others. She chaired the meetings of the Federation and supported programmes such as the establishment of the annual exhibition of produce and handicrafts, the first of which was held in Exmouth in June 1919.[57] It was not until the end of 1923 that she began to visit Institutes elsewhere in the county, which she then did as diligently as she attended Guide events. In the first six months of 1924 she went to Chulmleigh, Honiton, Halwill and Beaworthy, Bickington, Tamerton Foliot, and Thorverton, in addition to Institutes around her home at Bicton. Her addresses focused on the aims of WIs, which she defined as Helpfulness, Cheerfulness, Loyalty and Perseverance.[58] This change in her practice seems to have been linked to two developments.

The principal factor that determined her assumption of a more visible role in leading the development of the movement was the resignation of Miss Calmady-Hamlyn as WI Organiser in March 1924. Calmady-Hamlyn's actions are discussed at greater length in a separate chapter, but her main criticism of the Devon Federation of WIs was the lack of democracy within the movement. It would be easy to accuse Clinton, an archetypal Tory member of the local aristocracy, of being one of those who assumed that local 'ladies' should automatically be elected to positions within each Institute. In fact she herself tried hard, possibly recognizing the justice of Calmady-Hamlyn's criticisms, to persuade Exmouth WI that, after she had been President for five years, it was time for someone else to be elected. '[T]here was a risk', she said, 'that after a thing had gone on for five years or so it would tend to get a bit flat. Fresh people with new ideas were wanted to prevent that, and the members must all take their share ... or they could not really call it a Women's institute.'[59] To no avail, however, as she was re-elected. The Federation's Executive Committee continued to show a predominance of county ladies.[60] Clinton's tours of WI branches demonstrate her understanding of the importance of engagement with the main body of the membership.

---

57. *WT*, 6 June 1919, p. 9.

58. Summarized in the account of the inaugural meeting of the Halwill and Beaworthy WI, *DEG*, 17 April 1924, p. 14.

59. *DEG*, 7 May 1924, p. 5.

60. The members of the committee elected in January 1925 contain a number of women such as Miss Dickinson and Mrs Luttrell who had been members of the Women's War Agricultural Committee. Newcomers such as Eleanor Acland and Juanita Phillips were similarly well-known figures in community life (*WMN*, 17 January 1925, p. 3).

The second factor that may have influenced Clinton was the political situation. The election called at the end of 1923 resulted in the first Labour Government, a minority government, which took office in January 1924. Clinton dreaded what she considered to be the extreme views held by the Labour Party, and her increased personal engagement with her members was probably in part intended to defuse potential class hostility and secure the re-election of a Conservative Government.

Clinton in the Political Climate of the 1920s

In 1922 the postwar Coalition Government had come to an end. It was succeeded by a decade of political turbulence in which a Conservative Government was on two occasions disrupted by short-lived Labour governments (1924 and 1929–1931). Clinton was fearful of the potential implications of a Labour Party in thrall to Soviet Russia taking office. 'People', she said in a speech to the Primrose League in 1924, 'did not want to see Britain reduced to the same conditions as Russia', and if 'the present [Labour] government was a very mild-looking animal it nonetheless possessed a fiery tail which would probably wag the dog before long'.[61] She was, however, careful to distinguish the Russian government, which she referred to as 'the small gang at headquarters' from 'the Russian people generally'.[62] Her instincts were that 'Socialists were for revolution, irreligion and ruination', whilst Conservatives were for 'Patriotism, Progress, Peace and Prosperity'.[63] She was for a while President of the Women's Council of the Honiton Division of the Conservative Party and elected a Vice-President of the Devon Division in 1924 when, as her proposer said, they wanted someone 'to put their back into the work'.[64]

One of her political speeches at the November 1924 election, made in North Tawton, shows her advocating a vote for the Party for its policies on colonial preference, education, more generous pensions and improvements to agriculture.[65] She was a great admirer of Mr Baldwin, the party leader, and spoke in support of his handling of the miners' dispute both before and after the General Strike.[66] When the bill for the extension of the franchise to all women over the age of 21 was passed she advocated the importance of

---

61. *DEG*, 27 May 1924, p. 8.
62. *DEG*, 21 October 1924, p. 7.
63. Ibid.; *DEG*, 16 December 1926, p. 3.
64. *DEG*, 19 November 1923, p. 5; *WMN*, 14 March 1924, p. 6.
65. *DEG*, 21 October 1924, p. 7.
66. *DEG*, 30 November 1925, p. 5; 16 December 1926, p. 3.

continuing work in the party to provide 'truth and not misrepresentation' about their policies.[67] She acknowledged that she was only 'a convert to the enfranchisement of women', but she had now been 'convinced of women's great part in the political work of today'.[68] Her contribution in the run-up to the 1929 General Election attracted the hostility of the *Daily Herald*, which sneered at her as 'honest Lady Clinton', picking up her claim that Conservative policies were to strengthen 'home life, religion and all that women held dear', and reminding its readers that 'what women hold dear' tends to be '[d]ecent homes, security from want and equality of opportunity for their children'. That, it claimed, was 'just what they don't get'.[69]

Two Thriving Movements

The Guiding movement continued to expand in Devon, with numbers reaching 2,000 by 1924, when the Chief Guide, Lady Baden-Powell, visited the county on a tour of inspection. Clinton claimed in her speech that the numbers of Guides and Brownies had doubled in one year.[70] Clinton was proud of her status as 'the senior county commissioner of Girl Guides in the world', the first to be given her warrant.[71] She presided at training days for Guiders in the South-West, lamenting that not enough women were coming forward to lead the girls: 'This was very sad when they thought of the number of idle girls there were spending their time in dancing and lawn tennis.'[72]

Clinton regularly attended Guide events throughout the county, advocating the movement to parents and potential well-wishers. In one address in Newton Abbot in 1925 she responded to criticisms that Guiding was a military movement, with salutes and uniform, and that they carried out drill and played too many games. She explained the salute as a courteous greeting, and the uniforms as ensuring that 'a princess and a girl from a cottage should wear the same dress as there was no distinction in their Guide movement', and 'girls realised they were members of a world-wide sisterhood'. The drill and games taught discipline and how to play 'for the side and not for self' as 'at

---

67. *DEG*, 23 April 1927, p. 5.
68. *WMN*, 12 April 1930, p. 9.
69. *Daily Herald*, 26 April 1929, p. 4.
70. *WT*, 20 October 1924, p. 9.
71. *WMN*, 23 March 1925, p. 3. She later modified this to having been one of the first pair appointed.
72. *WMN*, 22 October 1923. Clinton did not disapprove of all forms of dancing. She was President of the Devon Branch of the English Folk Dance Society. She regarded modern dances as 'dismal', however; a quotation *The People* published with relish, 21 December 1924.

the foundation of the movement ... was the ideal of unselfishness'. The Guides were 'beacons in dark days ... in these times of selfishness'[73]

Within the Federation of WIs growth in Devon mirrored the growth elsewhere, and Devon WIs were keen to see themselves as part of a national movement. By 1923 there were sixty-six institutes, and the expansion continued, reaching seventy-nine institutes in 1925, one hundred and eleven in 1927 and two hundred by 1936.[74] In 1924 83% of branches sent representatives to the National Federation Annual Meeting.[75] Clinton maintained her programme of visiting and encouragement: she was able to say in January 1925 that she had visited sixty of the seventy-nine institutes, and was pleased that some institutes were being founded in 'out of the way places', instancing one that was 'nine miles from a railway station'.[76] She acknowledged that these institutes needed extra help in order to pay travel costs for demonstrators and monthly lecturers. (This was something that the Devon Federation sought to help with financially.)

On her visits she would provide an address, often related to the values of the WI, such as the one on 'Citizenship' in which she emphasized her hearers' privileges and responsibilities as Englishwomen, and their need to make themselves acquainted with the important issues of the day. Her definition of citizenship, she said, was 'in small things, liberty; in great things unity; and in all things charity'.[77] She would then happily take part in the tea, listen to the dramatic sketches, try out a game or some singing and country dancing.[78] Another address she gave to help with values was her address on 'Jerusalem', the setting of William Blake's words used as a closing song at meetings by WIs from 1924 onwards. Clinton took the word and expounded that 'Jerusalem was a city of unity. They wanted peace, and they were helping to bring peace to the villages. Peace meant joyousness, and joyousness meant love. That was the real spirit of the Institute, to promote a spirit of comradeship and friendliness and to help to broaden their outlook.'[79]

---

73. *WT*, 29 May 1925.
74. *WMN*, 19 January 1924, p. 6; 17 January 1925, p. 3; *DEG*, 19 November 1927, p. 5; *WMN*, 27 November 1936, p. 10.
75. *WMN*, 17 January 1925, p. 3.
76. Ibid.
77. *DEG*, 24 June 1927, p. 15. She also used this when asked to address school children on Empire Day as an illustration of how to strengthen the Empire, see *DEG*, 23 May 1931, p. 8.
78. *DEG*, 24 June 1927, p. 15, using the report of Clinton's visit to celebrate the fifth birthday of her home WI in East Budleigh as an example.
79. *DEG*, 19 November 1927, p. 5, first delivered to the Annual Meeting of the Devon Federation Council.

One particular mission of the Devon Federation in which Clinton became involved was the establishment of a close relationship with the County Council over the development of agricultural and horticultural training and education for women. Clinton wrote a letter, published in local papers in April 1925, drawing attention to the availability of scholarships to women and girls for places on the Ministry of Agriculture scheme which, she said, had so far not been taken up.[80] Lack of take-up prompted further discussion in the Federation and Clinton wrote to members of the County Agricultural Committee, simultaneously (rather to the annoyance of the Committee) releasing the letter to local newspapers. The letter made the case for the needs of women for agricultural education to be given greater consideration. There were, as official statistics showed, 3,138 women employed in agriculture in the county but this did not include 'women occupiers, wives of farmers, small holders and farm domestic servants' who also had an entitlement to agricultural education. She wrote:

In these circumstances the comparative neglect of women's interests in the County scheme of agricultural education is much to be deplored. Within the last few years the assistance extended to men has sensibly increased. Recent appointments include those four district lecturers in agriculture (all men). But the facilities in agriculture of most concern to women, horticulture, poultry keeping and dairying, remain as before. The work of the two dairy instructresses is much appreciated and the invaluable work of the horticultural superintendent has greatly stimulated women's part in rural life. The steady growth of the WI movement has created a new demand among country women for further education in the women's branches of agricultural education. Although Seale-Hayne was apparently intended for residents in Devon, without distinction of sex, it is of no service to women, with the exception of occasional short courses. In short, women are not receiving their due share of the expenditure on agricultural education, and, therefore have a grievance both as members of the agricultural community and as ratepayers and taxpayers. They look particularly to their elected representatives to remedy this state of affairs.[81]

---

80. *WT*, 15 May 1925, p. 6.
81. *WT*, 15 May 1925, p. 6.

Public support for this approach was immediately forthcoming from a band of fruit and bulb growers in and around the Bicton estate.[82]

The members of the County Agricultural Committee were rather embarrassed. Fortunately at their next meeting they were able to announce that four scholarships had been granted to women for tuition in Somerset. However, Francis Acland (husband of Eleanor Acland, subject of another chapter in this collection), who was a member of the committee, stated that 'the Committee was anxious that women should have the same facilities as men whenever possible, and he hoped the members of the WI would not feel it was otherwise'.[83] His remarks were endorsed by both the Chairman of the Committee and the Chairman of the County Council. The committee agreed to write back to Lady Clinton asking for practical suggestions.

Calmady-Hamlyn, a member of the County Agricultural Committee co-opted for her long-standing interest in women in agriculture, did not believe Seale-Hayne was the right place to educate women, but proposed a new institute for women across the south-west counties. Clinton and the Federation did not agree with this, and their proposals to the committee, submitted in August, covered the need to provide a hostel for women students at Seale-Hayne to encourage the admission of women to courses there. They also advocated additional appointments of more women as chief horticultural officer; lecturer in dairying, to supplement the work of the dairy instructresses and to focus on instruction in clean milk production; and as an additional instructress in poultry and dairying. Finally they suggested that the County Agricultural Committee should offer prizes at a range of shows in horticulture, especially 'small fruit growing, poultry, dairy and bee-keeping'.[84] The Committee formally received the correspondence, but, as the *Western Times* commented, '[c]uriously they drew no comment whatsoever. Perhaps members were thinking too deeply to talk. In that formal reading of a letter they must have heard Woman knocking at the door of agriculture. Sooner or later that door will have to burst wide open.'[85]

The Devon Federation was frustrated by the lack of a positive response. One way of promoting change, they believed, was greater representation of women on the county agriculture and county education committees. (The County Council appointed thirty members of the agricultural committee and

---

82. *DEG*, 22 May 1925, p. 9.
83. *DEG*, 29 May 1925, p.3.
84. *WMN*, 25 August 1925, p. 6.
85. *WT*, 28 August 1925, p. 6.

the Ministry eighteen.) At this time there were no women county councillors in Devon so women representatives would have to be identified from outside that circle. The Federation tried to hijack a resolution being considered at the National Federation of Women's Institutes Annual Meeting in 1926. The resolution proposed the increase of countrywomen on district wages committees, and the Devon amendment proposed that representation for women on County Council committees should also be included. Clinton herself proposed the amendment, but it was defeated.[86]

The Federation persevered with Devon County Council, assisted by the advocacy of Francis Acland, not merely a county councillor but the Ministry of Agriculture's representative on the board of Seale-Hayne College. He and Clinton publicized in local papers in April 1927 the 130 Junior Scholarships funded by the Ministry of Agriculture, open both to girls and boys wishing to take up farm, garden, orchard or dairy work.[87] Clinton's letter mentioned with pride that the highest of the nine Ministry of Agriculture Scholarships won in Devon the previous year had been won by a woman.[88]

The WIs continued to press for additional support. In September 1929 Clinton wrote asking for more classes and an assistant to the horticultural officer, Miss Gunnell, or the dedication of Miss Gunnell full-time to WI work.[89] The joint sub-committee of the Agricultural and Education Committees deliberated and proposed that Miss Gunnell be released from her school garden work to allow her to do this. The recommendation was implemented in November 1929.[90] In 1930 the County Agricultural Committee appointed Clinton herself first to the Scholarships sub-committee, and then to the Joint Agricultural and Education Committee.[91] Clinton paid tribute to the County Council's positive approach to collaboration, saying that 'she did not think there was any county authority ... that rendered more help than Devon'.[92] Unfortunately these appointments were to be short-lived, as the Ministry of Agriculture's appointments in 1931 saw Clinton ousted in the name of diversifying representation (though the new nominees were exclusively male).[93] The College finally accepted

86. *WMN*, 18 June 1926, p. 3.
87. *WT*, 1 April 1927, p. 3.
88. Ibid.
89. *WT*, 13 September 1929, p. 14.
90. *DEG*, 21 November 1929, p. 6.
91. *DEG*, 11 September 1930, p. 3; *WMN*, 12 February 1931, p. 11.
92. *DEG*, 14 November 1930, p. 9.
93. *WMN*, 21 May 1931, p. 8.

women on full-time courses, accommodating them in their own hostel, in the academic year 1934–1935.[94]

Clinton in the 1930s

Both the Clintons experienced episodes of poor health at the beginning of the 1930s and took to spending more time abroad in the winter. They gave up some of their political commitments. Lady Clinton resigned her office as Vice-President of the Devon Conservative and Unionist Association in 1931.[95] As an alternative occupation, she enjoyed producing a small book, *Stories to Tell*, which contains many of the brief anecdotes and folktales with which she had entertained Guides and WI members.[96] In 1933 Lord Clinton, who had been appointed as a Privy Councillor in 1926, retired from most of his public offices. He had been Keeper of the Privy Seal to the Duke of Cornwall and Chairman of the Forestry Commission. Lady Clinton, however, did not retire. She evidently felt a strong patriotic need to support the National Government, urged upon the country, as she saw it, by King George V and Mr Baldwin. The Girl Guide and Women's Institute movements provided stability in a changing world and prepared their members to tackle change. She not only continued with her work within those organizations, but took on additional responsibilities, in spite of attaining her seventieth birthday in 1933.

In the early 1930s the Personal Service League was formed. Women became involved in making garments to send to the residents in the 'distressed areas' in Wales and the North-East, and indeed to local unemployed families, particularly, in Devon, in Plymouth and Exeter. Clinton was asked by the county President, Countess Fortescue, to chair the League's Devon-wide organization. The *Western Morning News* woman columnist, Devonia, seemed surprised that Clinton ('easily the busiest woman in Devon') had taken this on.[97] No doubt Fortescue was mindful of what Devonia was later to describe as the 'exemplary thoroughness' with which Clinton performed her duties.[98]

This was not the only additional responsibility Clinton assumed. She also increased her commitment to the Devon Nursing Association (DNA). As detailed earlier (p. 181) the provision of community nursing services was

---

94. *WMN*, 28 March 1935, p. 13.

95. *DEG*, 9 May 1931, p. 2.

96. J. Grey Hepburn-Stuart-Forbes-Trefusis, *Stories to Tell: Written or Remembered* (London: Robert Scott, 1930).

97. *WMN*, 8 July 1933, p. 3.

98. *WMN*, 30 May 1936, p. 15.

something in which she had long taken an interest, and she had been a Council member since 1915. Her anxiety about the future of the Association grew during the 1920s, when subscriptions started to fall, allegedly, she was told at the Queen's Jubilee Nursing Association 1924 Annual Meeting, because of the growth of Hospital Aid Societies. Some Aid Societies provided district nursing as part of their member benefits, but even where they did not individuals often felt that they could not afford two subscriptions and so they would pay the hospital aid one, as hospital treatment was the more expensive. She had passed on to the Budleigh Salterton Nursing Association the warning that hospital aid society schemes were 'crippling' Nursing Associations and recommended that the Association should try to safeguard its future by getting together a substantial sum as capital.[99] She repeated her warning in 1931.[100] By that time the DNA committee was itself being warned by the Treasurer that unless urgent action was taken they would be bankrupt within six years.[101] Lack of action, apart from Clinton's effort producing a calendar which raised £50, did indeed draw them into the position of overspending the following year by £1,330. At that point they obtained about a sixth of their funding from public authorities (the local authorities in their Poor Law capacity) and the remainder as subscriptions and donations.[102] It seems that it was Clinton herself who forced the issue of the need for additional fundraising at the 1932 meeting. The Association set a target of raising £10,000 as an investment fund.[103]

Clinton's principal idea for raising funds was a classic county bazaar or 'Olde Englishe Fayre' to be held in Exeter, as the county town and centre of railway and road networks, which she organized with two assistants and a Fayre Committee. She was inherently cautious about over-ambitious schemes, as she was to demonstrate in 1934 when she, perhaps unintentionally, scuppered the proposal for there to be a county pageant to raise funds for local hospitals. She felt from experience elsewhere that a venture which would cost at least £3,500 to put on would be likely to run at a loss, and cited experience elsewhere of similar loss-making fundraising ventures.[104] She probably considered that a straightforward county fayre would be much more likely to deliver a substantial sum of money and infinitely easier to manage.

99. *DEG*, 26 April 1924, p. 4.
100. *WT*, 18 July 1930, p. 9; *DEG*, 12 May 1931, p. 6.
101. *DEG*, 4 July 1931, p. 4.
102. *WMN*, 20 October 1932, p. 4.
103. *WMN*, 22 January 1932, p. 5.
104. *WMN*, 8 December 1934, p. 4; 14 December 1934, p. 2.

Clinton was advised on the organization of the Fayre by Dame Georgiana Buller (subject of another chapter in this collection), who was able to draw on her own wide experience of fundraising for the Red Cross and for the Princess Elizabeth Orthopaedic Hospital.[105] The Fayre was complemented by other initiatives, such as a separately organized café chantant and dance, and appeals in the newspapers, signed by Clinton and placed even outside the county in order to attract the sympathy of visitors to the county.[106] Events were also organized by local associations such as the Totnes and Bideford Nursing Associations' 'American teas'.[107] Clinton also seems to have been one of the pioneers of the now commonplace fundraiser, the recipe book containing a collection of recipes from distinguished and mainly titled contributors. She collected and collated these herself in a 'miniature newspaper', the *Cookery Chronicle*, which was sold at the fair and elsewhere.[108] The Fayre itself raised almost £2,500, a quarter of the overall target and by the beginning of 1933 over £4,000 had been raised.[109] The income this would raise when invested, however, was not enough to offset the continuing fall in subscriptions.[110] Subscribers, it seemed, continued to put Hospital Aid schemes ahead of district nursing when they could not afford both subscriptions.[111]

In 1935 Clinton had become a Vice-President of the DNA.[112] It was not surprising therefore that when at the end of 1936 Lady Amory, President and Committee Chairman of the Association, retired, Clinton was asked to succeed her.[113] What perhaps is surprising is that Clinton, then in her mid-seventies, agreed. It seems that a separate chair of Committee was appointed, but Clinton was no absentee President, and had to meet the demands of the role in addition to her continuing work with the Girl Guides and WIs.

Over the next twelve years her period as DNA President was to include the implementation of the new Midwives Act (1936), which Devon County Council commissioned the DNA to implement on their behalf; the trials and tribulations of a Second World War in which she represented the DNA on the County Council's Maternity and Child Welfare Committee; and finally after the war the handing over of the service to local councils as the new agents

105. *WMN*, 19 November 1932, p. 11.
106. *Western Mail*, 21 October 1932, p. 2.
107. *WMN*, 1 November 1932, p. 4; *NDJ*, 3 November 1932, p. 5.
108. *WMN*, 12 November 1932, p. 13.
109. *WT*, 2 December 1932, p. 11.
110. *WMN*, 21 June 1933, p. 8.
111. *DEG*, 15 June 1934, p. 7.
112. *WMN*, 6 July 1935, p. 7.
113. *NDJ*, 14 January 1937, p. 5.

for universal community healthcare under the NHS Act. It was an amazing contribution by someone who was to be 85 when the Labour Government's plans for local authority health care came to fruition.

That particular scheme was one about which she must have had reservations. She had argued as late as 1937 that 'if the hospitals and nursing associations were to be taken over by the State they would lose some of the finest of our national characteristics'.[114] Now this transfer was inevitable. One of her final actions before handing over the service was to raise funds for a pension fund for those nurses who would not be eligible for pensions under the new County Council scheme.[115] The other was to seek to establish a voluntary service for visiting 'aged and lonely persons in their own homes', to complement the work of the district nurses.[116] Her values and sense of what was 'right' had remained steadfast since her days as a young married woman visiting the sick and making proper provision for dependent servants.

In 1936 Clinton did seek to divest herself of her commitment to the WIs. She offered her resignation as President, which was received with immense regret. Juanita Phillips, the chairman, said: 'I feel we have been rather selfish in the demands we have made on her, but we have sought her presence with us in our groups and institutes out of a very real and genuine affection.'[117] No successor emerged, however, and the following year she agreed to resume the Presidency, so long as the calls on her were 'kept within reasonable bounds', and that she was not expected to 'visit so many evening meetings in the winter or travel long distances'.[118] She continued her commitment to the WIs and to Guiding well into the 1940s.

The Clinton Family

In recent years, the Royal Family have come under criticism for the way in which the family committed some of their Bowes-Lyon relatives to be cared for in the institution known in the mid-twentieth century as the Royal Earlswood Hospital for mental defectives. The women concerned were Katherine and Nerissa Bowes-Lyon, who were also two of the Clintons' granddaughters. Their admission was arranged in 1941, along with three of the Clintons' Fane granddaughters, Idonea, Ethelreda and Rosemary. A genetic

---

114. *DEG*, 20 January 1933, p. 7.
115. *DEG*, 30 April 1948, p. 2.
116. *WMN*, 9 April 1949, p. 2.
117. *WMN*, 27 November 1936, p. 10.
118. *DEG*, 11 June 1937, p. 10; *WT*, 18 June 1937, p. 6.

disorder seems the most likely explanation for the number of the cousins affected. This family tragedy needs to be understood in the context of the best medical advice of the day, which was that such young women needed the care of a specialist institution. The Clintons' son-in-law, John Bowes-Lyon, Fenella's husband, had died in 1930; Harriet had divorced Henry Fane in 1935 and her eldest son Charles was killed in action in 1940. The loss of the girls' eldest brother seems to have triggered an agreement to provide a secure future for the girls away from their family homes. The family agreed to pay for the girls to be cared for in an institution that would have been seen at the time as the place that best met their needs. The family would probably also have been advised that they should refrain from any further contact as it was considered that it would be distressing for patients to have past memories reawakened. Like many grandmothers of children with learning disabilities, Clinton might have grieved deeply at the loss of contact with her grandchildren, but would have supported a decision based on medical advice.

Clinton died in 1953, not long after her ninetieth birthday. Her coffin travelled from Fettercairn to Huish where it was draped in a Girl Guide banner and attended at an all-night vigil by staff from the Clinton estates. *The Times* provided her with an obituary in which the first sentence referred to her father, the second to her husband, describing his pedigree and his estates. Lord Clinton was also the subject of the third and final sentence which referred to the 'happiness of the whole-hearted support of Lady Clinton during an exceptional long period of married life'.[119] There was no word about her own work for the Girl Guides; the Women's Institutes; or the Devonshire Nursing Association, organizations perhaps beneath the dignity of *The Times* to notice. It was left to local papers, such as the *Brechin Advertiser* in her Scottish homeland, to pay tribute to her 'practical support to all movements having for their object philanthropy and general improvement of community conditions'.[120]

The only formal honour accorded to Clinton was that of appointment as a Commander of the Order of St John, made by the sovereign in recognition of her work in support of its mission 'to prevent and relieve sickness and injury, and to act to enhance the health and well-being of people anywhere in the world' and probably related to her role as County President of St John Ambulance, which she became in the 1940s. Yet her contribution to the voluntary sector in Devon during the 1920s and 1930s was substantial. Her lifetime had seen unprecedented change politically, socially and technologically.

---

119. *The Times*, 29 August 1953, p. 8.
120. *Brechin Advertiser*, 15 September 1953, p. 6.

Her combination of great social status and an unaffected natural manner enabled her to help new organizations, like the WI and the Guides, find widespread acceptance within socially conservative communities. For the nursing associations, the charitable service providers she had supported since her youth, she retained a commitment born of the belief that a service funded by donations was intrinsically better than one funded by taxation. Although the arrival of the National Health Service removed the purpose of nursing associations she sought to retain an element of voluntarism with her proposal for after-care community committees, and to make sure that the 'old servants', the nurses, were given a reasonable sum to live on.

In 1927 Lord Mildmay of Flete, who knew Clinton well both through his own role in the Conservative and Unionist Party and through her work with his wife in the Guiding movement, referred to the fact that her association with the WI and Girl Guiding movements meant that she had 'won her way to the hearts of Devonshire people'.[121] It does indeed seem that her assiduous efforts to travel the length and breadth of Devon visiting and encouraging the smallest of organizations made her well-known and respected throughout the county. Her gifts were not necessarily strategic, but she was diligent, thorough and approachable. At a time when the emphasis was on an egalitarianism in new organizations such as the Girl Guides and the WIs, she was able to keep together county-wide movements in the second largest county in the country.

121. *DEG*, 23 April 1927, p. 5

CHAPTER EIGHT

Mary Sylvia Calmady-Hamlyn (1881–1962)

JULIA NEVILLE

Sylvia Calmady-Hamlyn, photographed with Queen Elizabeth II at the Royal
Agricultural Show in Newton Abbot, 1952

In May 1920, the Devon County Agricultural Association held the Devon County
Show for the first time since the spring of 1914. Exeter was the host city, and
the city council made available as a showground the land they had just bought
for the first of the decade's new council houses, on Buddle Lane. Among those
present was the only woman member on the Council of the Association, Miss
Sylvia Calmady-Hamlyn,[1] who acted as one of the stewards.[2] As an exhibitor in

---

1. An earlier version of the section of this chapter dealing with Miss Calmady-Hamlyn's service
   during the First World War was published as J. Neville, '"They Women Have Done Well": Sylvia
   Calmady-Hamlyn and Women Working on the Land', in *Food, Farming and Fishing in Devon during
   the First World War* (Exeter: Short Run Press, 2016), pp. 129–33. Also available at <http://www.
   devonhistorysociety.org.uk/research/food-farming-fishing-devon-first-world-war>.
2. *Devon and Exeter Gazette (DEG)*, 13 May 1920, p. 1.

Julia Neville, 'Chapter Eight: Mary Sylvia Calmady-Hamlyn (1881–1962)' in: *Devon Women in
Public and Professional Life 1900–1950: Votes, Voices and Vocations*. University of Exeter Press
(2021). © Julia Neville DOI: 10.47788/BYWJ9009

her own right, Calmady-Hamlyn had a good show. In the Mountain and Moorland pony class she took third place in one class, and she won the class for pony mares (in foal or with foal at foot) with Thyrza, a 'beautiful little pure Dartmoor pony … and its diminutive foal' which were 'surrounded by admirers as soon as they left the ring'.[3] Thyrza had already been placed third in the London Spring Show of the National Pony Club; and Calmady-Hamlyn was also to win a national prize later that year at the Royal Show at Darlington while a Dartmoor mare she had bred took first place at the Royal Richmond Show.[4] She also won prizes at local shows at Holsworthy, Launceston, Lydford and Okehampton.[5]

Her show awards, however, were not her only successes that year. In March she was made a Member of the Order of the British Empire for her war work as secretary and organizer for the Devon Women's War Agricultural Committee.[6] In August she was appointed as one of the first women JPs in the county (and indeed in the country).[7] She had earlier become the only woman Governor at Seale-Hayne, the county's agricultural college, which was now accepting its first intake of students.[8] She was also embarking on another project, equal in scope to her work for women in agriculture during the war: the task of establishing the Women's Institute movement in Devon. Her talent for organization had been honed by her First World War experiences, and she was excited by the prospect of helping to improve life in Devon's rural communities, for she was a true countrywoman and had seen with regret how isolated many of those living in Devon farms and villages were from one another and from everyday social life.

The Calmady-Hamlyn Stud

Miss Mary Sylvia Calmady-Hamlyn, always known as Sylvia, was born in 1881, a member of the Calmady-Hamlyn family of Bridestowe. Her father was Vincent Calmady-Hamlyn of Leawood and Paschoe, and the principal landowner in Bridestowe, not far from Okehampton, on the edge of Dartmoor. Her mother Emma was the daughter of Joseph Pease, a wealthy industrialist

3. *Western Times (WT)*, 13 May 1920, p. 3.
4. Ibid.; *DEG*, 5 July 1920, p. 6; 18 June 1920, p. 7.
5. *DEG*, 11 June 1920, p. 10; *WT*, 16 July 1920, p. 6; *WT*, 3 August 1920, p. 8; *WMN*, 10 September 1920, p. 7.
6. *London Gazette, Supplement*, 30 March 1920, p. 3835.
7. *WT*, 6 August 1920, p. 6.
8. *The Times*, 12 June 1962, p. 15.

and Quaker, and Sylvia was actually born in her mother's family home in Guisborough in Yorkshire. Her mother died in 1888 when Sylvia was only a child, and her father when she was 16. She was left in the guardianship of her grandfather and aunts, who sent her to the newly founded Wycombe Abbey School, a boarding school offering a curriculum like that of boys' public schools. It taught academic subjects and organized games rather than merely fashionable accomplishments. Here she acquired a taste for hockey and cricket that continued into adult life. Her family ensured that she was presented at court by her aunt when she was 21, but Sylvia was not interested in London society.[9]

When her father died in 1898 she did not succeed to the family estates in Bridestowe, but she had inherited enough money from her mother's family to allow her in her twenties to set up an independent establishment in the village, at Bidlake Vean. Here she employed a cowman-gardener ('with experience of Jerseys'), a chauffeur for her Siddeley car, and, as the 1911 census noted, a cook, a parlourmaid and a groom.[10] Also recorded on the 1911 census was a visitor, Grace Retallack. Both Grace and her sister Joan, whose family lived in Exmouth, seem to have been long-standing friends.

Sylvia's father's family were practising Anglicans and stalwart supporters of the parish church, and her mother, as noted above, had been brought up as a Quaker, but she herself converted to Roman Catholicism in her twenties. She gave money for the establishment of the Roman Catholic Mission at Okehampton in 1906, and by 1909 a monthly mass was being held at an oratory in her house at Bidlake Vean.[11] To become a Roman Catholic in the 1900s was unusual. Although legal discrimination against Catholics had been abolished in the nineteenth century, Catholics would still have been regarded as 'different' in Devon's traditional rural communities.

Whilst there were Black Orpington hens and pedigree Jersey cows at Bidlake Vean, Calmady-Hamlyn's main occupation was a pony-breeding business, for which she gained a national reputation.[12] As the *Western Times* reported in 1913:

---

9. Family history information from <www.ancestry.co.uk>; *DEG*, 3 September 1897, p. 12; *Morning Post*, 29 March 1898, p. 3; *DEG*, 18 June 1902, p. 3; *Who's Who in Devonshire* (Hereford: Wilson & Phillips, 1934), p. 54.

10. *DEG*, 26 September 1908, p. 2; 11 March 1910, p. 4; 15 July 1912, p. 2; 10 December 1909, p. 1; <www.ancestry.co.uk> (entry in the 1911 census for Bidlake Vean).

11. *WT*, 8 June 1906, p. 5; *London Monitor and New Era*, 23 January 1909, p. 3.

12. *DEG*, 10 December 1909, p. 1; *WT*, 11 May 1912, p. 3.

'Miss Calmady-Hamlyn started her stud in 1903, and has since won 250 prizes. Her stud comprises a select lot of Polo Pony, young stock, and pure Dartmoor ponies, also a few miniature Polo-type-blood riding ponies.'[13] Pony-breeding was a suitable, if mildly eccentric, occupation for an Edwardian country gentlewoman: at local shows in 1907–1908 Calmady-Hamlyn was competing against the Hon Mrs Jervoise Smith of Harberton, Miss Imogen Collier of Horrabridge, Mrs Clarence Spooner of Yelverton and Miss Dorothy Bainbridge, as well as all the men.[14]

Her stud took time to establish: the first show at which she is recorded as winning a prize was her local show, the Okehampton and District Agricultural Association annual show, in 1906.[15] She toured the local shows: South Brent, Lydford, Tavistock and Holsworthy, first won a first prize at the Devon County Show in May 1907, and then took second and fourth in the brood mare class at the National Polo and Riding Pony Society's annual show in Islington in 1908.[16] Although her first awards were not specifically related to Dartmoor ponies, this was a breed whose development she came to support. The records of Foxhams Stud at Horrabridge, for example, list amongst the forebears of their present horses Heather Mixture, a filly foaled in 1910 and winner of the First Prize (Dartmoor Brood Mares) at the National Pony Society show in 1904.[17] Calmady-Hamlyn had bought her from the Tavistock breeder who won the prize, and entered her in Volume 12 (1911–1912) of the Polo and Riding Pony Society's Stud Book. The following year, she sold her on, already in foal, to Miss Collier of Foxhams Stud.[18]

As her reputation grew, Calmady-Hamlyn was asked to take on wider roles. She spoke about her experience of pony farming nationally in 1910 at the 'practical' agricultural session of the Women's Congress held at the Japan–British Exhibition.[19] In 1912 she became the first woman President of the Okehampton Agricultural Society at a time when it was unusual for a woman even to be on the committee of an Agricultural Society.[20]

---

13. *WT*, 8 July 1913, p. 7.
14. *WT*, 25 September 1906, p. 6; 7 June 1907, p. 3; 6 August 1907, p. 6.
15. *DEG*, 14 September 1906, p. 12.
16. *WT*, 23 May 1907, p. 3.
17. Foxhams Stud was founded by Imogen Collier (later Mrs Joseph Muntz), referred to above as one of Sylvia Calmady-Hamlyn's competitors. Her interest in horse and pony breeding paralleled that of Calmady-Hamlyn. The stud is still in existence.
18. See <www.foxhamsstud.co.uk/horses/heather-mixture> [accessed 12 June 2019].
19. *The Times*, 21 May 1910, p. 4.
20. *WT*, 20 May 1913, p. 2.

There is no evidence that she was involved in the women's suffrage movement. Her area of mid-Devon in fact received little attention from either
the constitutional or the militant suffragists. She did take on one of the
traditional roles of county ladies when she was elected in 1912 as the representative for Bridestowe and Sourton on the committee of the Devonshire
Nursing Association, which supervised the appointment and training of
District Nurses.[21] These opportunities offered her experience in committee
work and public speaking, which would be of great assistance to her in her
later career.

The First World War

In 1915 Calmady-Hamlyn, who seems to have been a Liberal Party supporter
and a firm patriot, joined the Okehampton and District Parliamentary
Recruiting Committee, formed to encourage young men to volunteer under
Lord Derby's recruiting scheme. She became the member responsible for
recruitment in Bridestowe.[22] She and Miss Retallack also took on the work
of collecting local subscriptions for the Belgian refugee family housed in
Bridestowe.[23] In August 1915, when sending apologies for not being able to
attend the opening of the Okehampton Liberal Club, she wrote that she
hoped that 'Okehampton Liberals, following Mr Lloyd George's inspiring
example, would be foremost among patriots in the deadly struggle for
freedom with which the country is confronted'.[24] She saw it as the duty of
women to fill the places left by the men who joined up and, using her
knowledge and expertise in animal husbandry and farming, she became
involved in the wartime efforts to encourage women to work on farms in
Devon.[25]

Her war work fell into three phases. Between November 1915 and January
1917 she worked through the Devon Women's War Service Committee to
develop registers of women workers available for farm labour. In January 1917
she was appointed (on an unpaid basis) as travelling inspector for the Ministry
of Agriculture and Fisheries in the South West. In May 1918 she was appointed

---

21. Devon Heritage Centre (DHC), 367G/B/1, *Devonshire Nursing Association Annual Report*, 1913,
     p. 2; *DEG*, 1 March 1912, p. 9. Calmady-Hamlyn appears to have given up this representative
     role when other work took her away from the area.
22. *WT*, 5 November 1915, p. 2.
23. *DEG*, 13 November 1914, p. 8.
24. *WT*, 3 August 1915, p. 5.
25. *DEG*, 14 July 1919, p. 4.

County Organizer for the Devon Women's War Agricultural Committee (WWAC), a post she held until April 1919.

Calmady-Hamlyn's expertise had already been recognized in her own district by co-option to the Okehampton and District War Agricultural Committee in August 1915.[26] She was also co-opted as a woman member of the Devon County War Agricultural Committee (WAC) and subsequently approached to serve on the Devon Women's War Service Committee (WWSC), a committee established by the Lord Lieutenant's wife, Countess Fortescue, to encourage and enable women to join the war effort.[27] Calmady-Hamlyn's task was to establish village registrars in West and North Devon. Their role was to be to identify women willing to work on farms, and provide their names to farmers seeking help. She spoke at public meetings to encourage women to come forward to register not only in Okehampton but in Barnstaple, Morchard Bishop, Tavistock, Ilfracombe, Frithelstock, and South Molton.[28] In Barnstaple she shared a platform with the National Farmers' Union chair and the 'agri-culturists' present passed a motion to support the employment of women.[29] By June 1916 the county reported 2,472 women registered in all categories (full-time, part-time, milking only) of whom 608 (25%) had worked during the previous quarter.[30]

In January 1917, Calmady-Hamlyn was appointed as a Board of Agriculture Inspector specifically to develop the new initiative to create a Women's Land Army (WLA). Her work covered the area between London and Land's End. It involved travelling six days a week on 'any available trains', clad in 'a Land Army overall, thick topcoat, and heavy boots', thus causing 'consternation' amongst the other 'important officials' travelling in the first-class coaches.[31] She recalled that food was hard to come by and she usually left home with a good supply of hard-boiled eggs as she often reached her destination too late to obtain rations. 'On Mondays the hard-boiled eggs were appreciated. By

---

26. Local War Agricultural Committees were established to ensure continuity of, and indeed an increase to, food production despite the loss of the labour of the men who left to serve in the armed forces.

27. WT, 5 November 1915, p. 15. The WWSC appears to have been intended to co-ordinate activities across a range of sectors, but its role in relation to farm work was taken over by the WWAC, whose formation and relationship to the main WAC were increasingly prescribed by the Government.

28. WT, 3 January 1916, p. 4; 18 February, p. 5; 11 March 1916, p. 3; North Devon Journal (NDJ), 10 February 1916, p. 7, 6 April 1916, p. 7, 18 May 1916, p. 6.

29. NDJ, 10 February 1916, p. 7.

30. DHC 1262M/L/141, report to Devon Women's War Service Committee, June 1916.

31. WMN, 17 February 1939, p. 4. In an interview Calmady-Hamlyn reminisced about her time as an inspector.

Wednesday their flavour began to pall. When Thursday arrived I felt I never wanted to see an egg again as long as I lived.'[32] The WLA scheme, as she explained to the WWAC, 'did not really touch on the kind of work the committee had been doing', which would be continuing. She meant that the WLA initiative trained women to undertake full-time agricultural employment rather than merely to match local volunteers, who were often only available part-time, to local needs.[33]

The scheme for full-time paid women workers was never as successful in Devon, in terms of numbers, as the recruitment of local women in their own communities but Calmady-Hamlyn made strenuous efforts to make it work. The Treasury funded formal training courses for women, and initially the Devon course was based at Seale-Hayne College, the new agricultural college for Devon that had been on the point of opening as war broke out.[34] Even before the creation of the WLA, Seale-Hayne had been providing some training for women, as the WWAC chair reported in March 1917 that there were twenty-seven girls being trained and a waiting list of eighteen.[35]

There was some hostility amongst Devon farmers to the idea of full-time employment of women farmworkers. Even at the time, the Director of the Women's Branch of the national Food Production Department told colleagues that 'the Women's Committee works ... in spite of opposition'.[36] The modern historian of the Land Army, Bonnie White, states that 'not a single Devon farmer offered his farm for training'; and when demonstrations were arranged, 'few women came forward'.[37] The climate appears to have been more hostile in South Devon, on which White bases her argument, than in Mid- and North Devon. Calmady-Hamlyn drew attention to the 'scandalous wages' offered by South Devon farmers to women: only 6d (sixpence) an acre for weed-cutting, while in her own district it was at least 1s (one shilling) an acre. Whilst South Devon only offered 7s 6d per acre for pulling mangolds, the rates was 12s per acre in Bridestowe.[38] Calmady-Hamlyn was well-supported in North Devon by members of the Barnstaple branch of the Devon Farmers' Union, whose leading members recalled how much more women had been involved in farm

32. Ibid.
33. *WT*, 17 March 1917, p. 2.
34. *WT*, 2 November 1916, p. 2.
35. *WT*, 20 October 1917, p. 3.
36. The National Archives (TNA) MAF 59/1. Referred to in a report of 4 October 1916.
37. B. White, *The Women's Land Army in First World War Britain* (Basingstoke: Palgrave-Macmillan, 2014), pp. 37, 59. See also her article, 'Sowing the seeds of patriotism? The Women's Land Army in Devon, 1916–1918', *The Local Historian*, 41.1 (2011), pp. 13–27.
38. *WT*, 21 October 1916, p. 2.

work in earlier generations.[39] Mid- and North Devon were very much the areas of the county where her family were respected and influential and where her advocacy carried a weight that it would not have done in South Devon. The Lord Lieutenant, himself a North Devon man, appreciated her support and advice. He discussed farming issues with her and on at least one occasion stayed at her home at Bidlake Vean where, he recorded in his diary, they had 'much useful talk'.[40] It was probably at his instigation that she became a member of the Devon Appeal Tribunal, hearing cases made against conscription.[41] Perhaps he hoped that she would be firm in stating what farm work could be undertaken by women working in place of the appellants. Her initial experience led her to write to *The Times*, quoting what the wife of a smallholder had told her: not to expect that the farmers would ever employ women while they could keep back their sons. Her letter was optimistic in tone, however. 'It is obvious', she said, 'that there must be difficulties in any new scheme that involves the breaking down of traditions and prejudice, but given a little time to accustom all parties to the new idea there is every prospect that the success of women's farm work will be assured. Chi va piano, va sano.'[42]

As one way of tackling the scepticism of farmers, she was prompted to suggest what seems to have been an idea unique to Devon, the 'women-only farm'. This was to be a way of convincing sceptics that women could manage a farm and undertake all the tasks associated with it. The 130-acre farm was at Great Bidlake, close to Calmady-Hamlyn's home, and at her suggestion, with its owner's consent, it was taken over by the Devon WAC in October 1917.[43] With advice and support from a local farmer, ploughing began and a small dairy was established. The farm was staffed by a forewoman and three girls. Calmady-Hamlyn wrote about the efforts and successes of the first year of the experiment in the *Journal of the Board of Agriculture*.[44]

Calmady-Hamlyn also worked to extend the opportunities for women, partly by developing specialisms such as forestry and hay-baling. She reported in September 1917 to the WWAC on the timber-cutting and forestry that

---

39. *WT*, 5 February 1916, p. 3.
40. R. Batten, ed., *A Lord Lieutenant in Wartime: The Experiences of the Fourth Earl Fortescue during the First World War*, Devon and Cornwall Record Society, new series 61 (Woodbridge: Boydell, 2018), p. 165.
41. *London Gazette*, 3 March 1916, p. 2344.
42. *The Times*, 28 April 1916, p. 7.
43. *DEG*, 17 November 1917, p. 3.
44. DHC 1262 M/O/LD/142, 21–50, Devon County Council Agricultural Executive Committee Minutes, September 1917–January 1918; Calmady-Hamlyn, 'A Woman's Farm in Devon', *Journal of the Board of Agriculture*, 25.7 (1918), pp. 834–39.

women volunteers were undertaking on the Duke of Bedford's West Devon estates at Endsleigh, where the success of the twelve girls initially placed there had led to a request for a further twenty-four. Eventually a gang of over seventy women was employed there.[45]

In May 1918 Calmady-Hamlyn took on her third wartime role. She agreed to step into the role of County Organizer for the Devon WWAC.[46] She organized recruiting rallies to keep up the supply of recruits, but acknowledged that the numbers enrolled were not large. There were no more than 178 girls placed and twenty-nine in training in September 1918.[47] By contrast, 4,300 women were in part-time work, which meant that Devon had done 'uncommonly well', as she reported to the WWAC.[48] Great Bidlake Farm was no longer just a 'women-only' working farm, but had replaced Seale-Hayne as a training centre when the college buildings were taken over as a hospital. Although the farm's first year's balance sheet showed a deficit, this was due primarily to the inclusion of the setting-up costs as expenditure. Nonetheless, the end of the war was the end of the Great Bidlake Farm experiment too. A suggestion that it should become a 'women's profit-sharing farm' was rejected.[49] The County Council closed and sold it along with other farms acquired under Defence of the Realm Act powers.[50]

The end of the war also signalled the end of the initiative to attract women into farming. By 1920 the 178 girls working as farm employees had dwindled to forty.[51] The Land Army was demobilized completely by December 1919. Calmady-Hamlyn had always believed that their work was designed only to fill the gap till the men came home, when they were 'longing to hand back the charge to the men'.[52] She retired from her own position, receiving the MBE for her wartime work.[53]

45. *DEG*, 22 September 1917, p. 3; 1 February 1919, p. 4. See also 'Miss Sylvia Calmady-Hamlyn and Timber Girls in Devon', published by Courage Copse Creatives, *The Timber Girls Heritage Project* <http://www.local-devon-biochar-charcoal.co.uk/project/timber-girls-heritage-project> [accessed 17 May 2020].
46. *DEG*, 18 May 1918, p. 4.
47. *WT*, 21 September 1918, p. 2.
48. *WT*, 21 January 1919, p. 2
49. *DEG*, 20 September 1919, p. 6.
50. *WT*, 20 September 1919, p. 2.
51. *WT*, 28 May 1920, p. 4.
52. *DEG*, 14 July 1919, p. 4.
53. *London Gazette* (Supplement), 30 March 1920, p. 3835.

The Reconstruction of Rural Life After the War

After the war, Calmady-Hamlyn went back to her pony-breeding business and continued her successes at district, county and national shows. In the first Devon County Show after the war she won a first with Thyrza and her foal in the Mountain and Moorland Pony Mare class, and a month later won the 14.2 hand hack class at the Royal Richmond Show with Syllabub.[54] One of her riding horses, a 1922 national prize winner, was presented by its purchaser to King George V when he was looking for a saddle horse.[55] Her reputation was firmly established and she was soon asked to judge moorland and polo pony classes, first at the Devon County Show in May 1921, and then at the National Pony Society show in March 1922.[56] This meant she showed her own stock at other events or in other classes: at the Bath and West Show in 1921 and in the Children's Riding Class at the National Pony Show, for example.[57] Schooling the ponies for child riders was one of her particular areas of expertise. She supplied many local young people including members of the county gentry families with their first mounts.[58] By 1931, her national reputation led the Council of the National Pony Society to elect her to a seat on the Mountain and Moorland Pony Committee and she thus became the first woman member of the National Pony Society Council.[59]

She was not allowed simply to retreat to the stables and the showring, however. This was a time when public service organizations, learning from wartime experience of the benefits of engaging women, were urgently looking for women to accept positions. During 1919–1920, Calmady-Hamlyn was almost immediately appointed or co-opted onto the Devon War Memorial Committee, the Plymouth Profiteering Appeal Tribunal, the Landswomen's Association, the new Devon County Agricultural Committee (and its women's sub-committee), and she continued as a member of the Devon County Agricultural Association.[60] She also became involved in the development of

---

54. *WT*, 13 May 1920, p. 14; *DEG*, 14 June 1920, p. 1.
55. *WMN*, 23 November 1933, p. 3, published with a picture of the King riding the horse in 'the Row'. Calmady-Hamlyn must have been proud of this as, according to the *WMN*, the details were written up in the *Buckfast Abbey Chronicle*..
56. *WT*, 11 December 1920, p. 4; 17 December 1921, p. 3.
57. *DEG*, 6 June 1922, p. 6; *WT*, 9 March 1923, p. 7.
58. *WMN*, 17 February 1939, p. 4, mentions Anthony Mildmay of Flete, the Duke of Northumberland, Lord Clydesdale and Lord Delaware.
59. *WMN*, 29 April 1931, p. 29. She was soon followed by Miss Collier of the Foxhams Stud.
60. *WT*, 7 June 1919; p. 2; *DEG*, 15 November 1919, p. 4; 13 December 1919, p. 2; DHC Devon County Council, Minutes and Reports, 19 June 1920.

Women's Institutes (WIs) and this, in particular, was to consume a great deal of her time and effort.

Even during the war, the government had recognized the need to respond to the sacrifices they had demanded from the people by taking action for the improvement of everyday life. A Ministry of Reconstruction had been created in 1917 and by early 1918 the Ministry had placed on county councils the duty of making practical suggestions for the development of rural districts after the war. Devon County Council delegated this responsibility to the WAC, of which Calmady-Hamlyn was a member.[61] The brief was wide-ranging: it covered 'the improvement of agriculture, horticulture, forestry and rural industries as well as the amelioration of the social conditions and general welfare of rural communities' and the provision of the 'necessities, comforts and amenities of country life'.[62] By June 1918 the committee had determined that 'village reconstruction' was key to the future of the countryside and proposed 'the development of village industries and the formation of women's institutes'.[63]

The WI movement had begun in the UK during the war. Its history has been outlined by Jenkins and most recently by Robinson.[64] They demonstrate how the Institutes were started in Canada, sponsored in the UK during the war by the Agricultural Organization Society, then taken up by the Food Production Department with the aim of stimulating a greater contribution by women towards the war effort. WIs set up War Savings Associations, organized knitting groups, opened soup kitchens, collected moss and herbs for dressings, jammed and bottled fruit, conserved and stored vegetables, marketed produce, and began to cultivate waste ground.[65] The Ministry of Reconstruction recognized that, beyond the war effort, they had the potential to play a part in 'educating country women in citizenship and self-reliance'.[66]

In April 1919, Mrs Clowes, a WI regional organizer, came to speak to the Devon WWAC. She drew attention to the fact that there were already over 1,000 Institutes in England, including several in Devon. She emphasized that the first object of the movement was to 'stimulate interest in the agricultural

61. DHC DCC Minutes and Papers, 15 March 1918.

62. Letter from the Minister, quoted in *WT*, 18 May 1918, p. 4.

63. *WT*, 21 June 1918, p. 2.

64. I. Jenkins, *The History of the Women's Institute Movement of England and Wales* (Oxford: Oxford University Press, 1953); J. Robinson, *A Force to be Reckoned With: A History of the Women's Institute* (London: Virago Press, 2018).

65. Jenkins, *History of the WI Movement*, p. 22.

66. Ministry of Reconstruction, Adult Education Committee, *Final Report*, Cmd. 321 (London: HMSO, 1919), pp. 143–44.

industry and in intensive agriculture', to carry on the work to increase food production at home that had begun during the war. New ideas were to be tried out, such as the development of cooperative enterprise in areas such as pig-keeping and the opening up of marketing opportunities for the products of home industries such as toy or basket-making. Calmady-Hamlyn was asked by the WWAC (as she was agricultural organizer at the time) to chair a group to take forward the development of WIs in Devon and she thus effectively became the Voluntary County Organizer.[67]

Calmady-Hamlyn would have been familiar with the idea of WIs from her involvement with the Board of Agriculture. In Devon, her role identifying village registrars had brought her into contact with a wide range of village communities and this had extended to contact with individual farms, as the travelling inspector for the Board of Agriculture. She learned how isolated farm workers and farming families could be.[68] When the idea was formulated that part of postwar reconstruction should be to reinvigorate rural life by the development of clubs and societies at village level, she could see how the WI movement could play a significant part. She threw herself into the development of Institutes, recruiting able lieutenants and speakers; organizing a four-day WI 'school' to help possible advocates understand the potential of the movement; working with the Village Clubs movement over possible collaboration; and travelling around the county herself to speak in innumerable villages, seeking to persuade them to set up an Institute.[69] The numbers of Institutes in the county grew from thirteen in 1919 to sixty-six in 1924.

The sessions at the WI school included reports from the county's existing Institutes on activities such as fruit-bottling, pig-rearing, blouse-making and millinery as well as community service projects such as providing a hot meal for schoolchildren who lived too far away to go home to lunch. New ideas were introduced by the speakers, such as drama and curing animal skins for gloves. The importance of introducing women to the share they now had in the 'government of this great Empire' and the 'great questions of the day' was emphasized.[70] The organizers whom Calmady-Hamlyn recruited to assist her

---

67. WT, 28 April 1919. The role of the Voluntary County Organizer is described in Jenkins, *History of the WI Movement*, p. 24.

68. DEG, 17 November 1917, p. 3.

69. The idea of co-locating men's and women's organizations in the same village club premises received general support in Devon, where Calmady-Hamlyn organized a parish enquiry, but was rejected nationally, see Jenkins, *History of the WI Movement*, p. 56.

70. WT, 5 November 1919, p. 4; 6 November, p. 2; 8 November, p. 2.

were three women who had worked with her on the WWAC, and Miss Hepburn, one of the women appointed to the County Education Committee.[71]

A Justice of the Peace

Calmady-Hamlyn was one of the first women magistrates in Devon. The Sex Disqualification (Removal) Act 1919 provided, amongst other things, for women to be eligible to serve both as jurors and as magistrates. In August 1920 Calmady-Hamlyn was appointed to the Okehampton Bench.[72] The Lord Chancellor's appointments to the County Commission of the Peace were made on the basis of recommendations by the Lord Lieutenant. In Devon this was still Earl Fortescue, who, as noted above, knew Calmady-Hamlyn well through her war agricultural work and who had already nominated her as a member of the Devon County Profiteering Appeal Tribunal.[73] She was sworn in as Justice of the Peace at the Assizes at Exeter in October 1920 along with four other women, including Eleanor Acland (subject of another chapter in this collection).[74] She made her first appearance at the Okehampton magistrates' court on 8 December and thereafter sat regularly as a member of the Okehampton Bench, hearing cases such as those for desertion, petty theft or animal cruelty, and private prosecutions such as that for trespassing in search of game on land belonging to the Prince of Wales.[75]

As part of her role as a Justice of the Peace, Calmady-Hamlyn also became a member of the Prison Visiting Committee for Plymouth Prison, with fellow magistrate Eva Trefusis serving in a similar role for Exeter Prison.[76] She favoured a more rehabilitative approach than was at that time favoured in the Plymouth prison. She condemned the 'eternal laundry', the only task allotted to women prisoners. As she suggested when addressing a Plymouth Women's Citizens' Association conference in 1923, some women at least would be better able to 'save their souls' if allowed to do work that interested them, such as agricultural work. She proposed that a form of agricultural colony might be set up to help break the cycle of 'girls who find themselves in prison

---

71. *WT*, 8 November 1919, p. 2.
72. *WT*, 6 August 1920, p. 6.
73. *DEG*, 15 November 1919, p. 2.
74. *WT*, 8 October 1920, p. 7.
75. *WT*, 9 December 1920, p. 3; 13 January 1921, p. 3; *DEG* 10 February 1921, p. 6; 14 October 1921, p. 5.
76. *WT*, 6 January 1921, p. 2.

over and over again'.[77] This does not appear to have been directly followed up, although the Exeter branch of the Brabazon Employment Society, which promoted recreative work for those in institutions such as the workhouses, had in 1922 initiated work for women prisoners in Exeter, believed to be the first provincial prison to receive this service.[78] It was perhaps the initiation of this service that sparked Calmady-Hamlyn's interest in other opportunities for women prisoners.

Her role as a magistrate led to involvement in a new organization set up for women in the county who held public positions, as JPs, as local council-lors or co-optees, or as Poor Law guardians. The Devon Council of Women on Public Authorities (DCW) was a society founded in 1923, affiliated to the National Council of Women. The council met two or three times a year throughout the 1920s and 1930s to hear invited speakers on topics of relevance to the laws they had to administer and to discuss current issues such as censor-ship or eugenics.[79] Calmady-Hamlyn attended the first meeting, when the whole idea of such a body was criticized in a letter from Eleanor Acland who felt that 'as there was already a branch of the Equal Citizenship Association (ECA) locally, there was no need for yet another Society, which would only draw women away from the ECA'.[80] Calmady-Hamlyn asked what lay behind this objection. The chair explained that she understood that Acland did not want to dilute the campaigning work of the ECA, but that in fact the purpose of the proposed DCW was self-education, aiming to fit its members for their new responsibili-ties, rather than campaigning. 'You have entirely satisfied me', replied Calmady-Hamlyn. 'Mrs Acland has no absolute right to say we shall not go to school if we choose.'[81] She became a member of the DCW Executive Committee.[82]

The Mid-1920s

In 1922, Calmady-Hamlyn sold her bungalow and farm at Bidlake Vean, gave up her seat as governor at Okehampton Grammar School, and moved to Buckfast, initially to the Abbey Farm, then to Pearroc Vean.[83] It is not clear

77. *WMN*, 5 May 1923, p. 3.
78. *WMN*, 25 November 1922, p. 3.
79. Report of inaugural meeting, *DEG*, 6 October 1923, p. 3.
80. Exeter's Society for Equal Citizenship had been formed in 1922. Acland was elected President at the first annual meeting (*DEG*, 29 May 1923, p. 5).
81. Its full title was 'The Devon Council of Women on Public Authorities'.
82. *WT*, 31 July 1925, p. 4.
83. *WMN*, 18 October 1922, p. 4.

why she chose to do this. In many ways her life continued on the same course: she continued to run her pony-breeding business in its new location; she sat as a magistrate in Totnes rather than in Okehampton; and she continued initially to be engaged with the WI movement.

A possible clue is that Buckfast Abbey has been a stronghold of Roman Catholicism in Devon since its refoundation in 1882. By the 1920s the long slow process of building its new church was well under way. It perhaps provided more support to Calmady-Hamlyn in the practice of her faith than she had found in the little oratory at Bidlake Vean or the Mission Church in Okehampton. Her faith was important to her. Her appointment as magistrate was noted by the Roman Catholic weekly *The Tablet* as exceptional, not because she was a woman but because she was 'the only Catholic magistrate in Devonshire'.[84] Moving closer to other members of her faith community may have provided her with more support from like-minded people. The period 1922–1924 seems to have been a turbulent time in her personal life generally. Her health was not good and she took several months off from her WI work during the autumn and spring of 1921–1922. She also resigned from the Cultivation Sub-Committee of the Devon Agricultural Committee.[85] Her political allegiance was shifting too, away from support for the Coalition Liberals towards support for the Labour Party.[86]

Gradually she became disillusioned with the policy that the Devon County Federation of Women's Institutes was adopting towards the development of wider participation in Institute business. She had emphasized in her annual report in 1923 that she felt there was a need to make the movement 'more and more representative of everyone without exception', but she felt unsupported in her efforts to achieve this, and in 1924 she resigned her post as Chairman of the Devon Federation of WIs.[87]

Her resignation was not immediately made public but featured, without comment, at the Federation's meeting in June. It appears that she had asked to have the opportunity to explain her decision there, and that this had been

---

84. *The Tablet*, 16 October 1920, p. 36.

85. *WMN*, 20 May 1921, p. 3.

86. The 'Coalition Liberals' were the party members who remained loyal to former Prime Minister Lloyd George, after the break-up of the wartime coalition. The party was known as the National Liberal Party, to distinguish it from the Liberal Party led by Herbert Asquith. *WT*, 10 June 1921, p. 4, reports that she had been invited to a meeting to form a council of the Coalition Liberals in Devon (although she did not attend). By 1924 she is being discussed as a prospective Labour Party parliamentary candidate for Tavistock (*WT*, 17 October 1924, p. 2).

87. *WMN*, 23 January 1923, p. 3; *DEG*, 5 July 1924, p. 10 reported on the half-yearly report to the Federation which referred to her resignation in March 1924.

refused. At the end of July, therefore, she wrote an open letter to members of the movement, which was published in the local press.[88] In this she stated that her commitment to establishing WIs as a vehicle for rural development 'along healthy and democratic lines' had proved impossible because her proposals as Chairman lacked support from the rest of the Executive, and 'in honesty' she could only offer her resignation.

The *Western Times*, a Liberal paper, reported that she had resigned because the movement, and specifically the Executive Council of the Devon Federation, was too much in the hands of the 'county lady', nine-tenths of whom, it was claimed, were Unionists.[89] Calmady-Hamlyn added that she had been 'doing her best to get direct representation of the classes who are concerned with the WI movement' but that 'she felt that she had no backing', even though, aware of the difficulty of 'getting the country woman to elect any but their leading ladies' she had suggested co-option to make the committee more representative of its membership. The fourteen-strong Executive Committee elected in January 1924 demonstrated exactly what she meant. It was headed by the wife of one of Devon's premier peers, Lady Clinton (subject of a separate chapter in this collection) and included women from county gentry families such as the Fulfords, the Luttrells and the Peeks, the class from which Calmady-Hamlyn herself was drawn.[90]

The Executive Committee made no direct comment on her views, although Lady Clinton alluded to it obliquely in her July address to the half-yearly meeting of the Federation, saying that theirs was 'a democratic movement ... shown by the resolutions the Institutes had brought forward'.[91] Clinton had recruited Calmady-Hamlyn as a District Girl Guide commissioner at the end of the war, which indicated a general level of approval and trust, and no doubt she was sorry to lose her from the WI movement.[92] It seems likely that Calmady-Hamlyn resigned her position in the Guiding movement at the same time as there are no further references to her involvement.

The publication of Calmady-Hamlyn's open letter generated three responses in the press, which may be taken as typical of the overall views

88. *DEG*, 1 August 1924, p. 2.
89. *WMN*, 30 July 1924, p. 5; *WT*, 1 August 1924, p. 11.
90. *DEG*, 19 January 1924, p. 4.
91. *DEG*, 5 July 1924, p. 5.
92. Calmady-Hamlyn is referred to as a District Commissioner in *WT*, 20 May 1921. For Clinton's appointment of Guide Commissioners, see Chapter 7 on Jane Grey Clinton, pp. 184–85.

on her action. The first felt that her overall goals were right, but that it was 'not usefully attainable at the moment' and asked her to use her skills in future to further the creation of local industries.[93] The second, from 'a working woman', pointed out that Institute members were often grateful that those who could spare the time volunteered to undertake commitments in the daytime which people like her could not do.[94] The third defended her action, saying that the WI movement had been 'exploited for political purposes ... by the rabid section of the Primrose League'.[95] It appears that this was one example of a national division of opinion that, as Robinson summarizes, meant that '[l]eft-wing politicians labelled it a hot-bed of Toryism, while Conservatives claimed it was all part of the Labour propaganda machine'.[96]

Calmady-Hamlyn had burnt her boats, however. She took no further part in the development of the movement, confining herself chiefly to her agricultural interests and her duties as a magistrate. She did volunteer in 1923 to become a member of the management committee of the Ashburton Cottage Hospital, but she did not remain for long on the committee, although she regularly paid an annual subscription.[97] A new commitment, which was to become a large part of her life, was the creation of the Dartmoor Pony Society.

The breeding of Dartmoor ponies was a particular interest of another local woman, Norah Dawson. After Calmady-Hamlyn moved her stud from Bridestowe to Buckfast she met or resumed acquaintance with Dawson. Norah Dawson's father had bought Holne Park near Ashburton at the end of the 1880s, but after his death, and that of Dawson's brother in 1914, her mother had let the house. She and her daughter returned to it in the spring of 1924 and Dawson, who had worked with Calmady-Hamlyn during the war, evidently soon re-established contact with her.[98] They are mentioned together in a court case resulting from an episode that occurred in October 1924.[99] The two eventually decided to go into partnership at Pearroc Vean rather than to

---

93. *WT*, 8 August 1924, p. 6.

94. *WT*, 15 August 1924, p. 6.

95. *WT*, 29 August 1924, p. 6. The 'Primrose League' was a women-led fundraising movement for the Conservative and Unionist party. Its branches or 'habitations' were generally led by aristocratic and gentry women.

96. Robinson, *A Force to be Reckoned With*, p. 121.

97. *WT*, 16 February 1923, p. 10.

98. *WT*, 14 March 1918, p. 3. Dawson conducted skills tests for women farm workers.

99. *WMN*, 14 October 1924, p. 8.

compete against each other, and prizes from 1928 onwards are awarded to the Misses Calmady-Hamlyn and Dawson of Buckfast.[100]

Calmady-Hamlyn had herself long been interested in the breeding of ponies with Dartmoor pony stock. Just after the war she had purchased a part-bred Arab, part-bred Dartmoor colt foal called The Leat, which became progenitor to many successful Dartmoor ponies.[101] She expressed her views about the breed in 1930 when she became secretary to the society, a post that she was to hold until 1960.[102]

> It is a great pity that Westcountry breeders no longer produce such a cross [of a Dartmoor mare and a thoroughbred], as it is of great value. In the five years before the Great War I was able to supply such ponies to win several years in succession the pony championships at Olympia and Richmond, ponies which were bought from Devon farmers and small holders. I have been asked repeatedly nowadays for such ponies, and have always to reply that there are no longer such ponies in Devonshire. This is a very short-sighted policy on the part of Devon breeders ... Personally I think the chief value of Dartmoor blood is as foundation stock for riding ponies. There is clearly no use at all for the bulk of the ponies that now remain on the moor, and the best work of the Dartmoor Pony Society will be accomplished in preserving the best of the ponies.[103]

In 1924, with Dawson and Calmady-Hamlyn as principal supporters, the Dartmoor Pony Society was formed as a breed society with its own studbook. (These are Dartmoor pedigree ponies, with a strain of Arab blood, not the Dartmoor hill ponies.) Calmady-Hamlyn became a member of the Dartmoor Pony Society Council, on which she was to remain for many years.[104] Dawson, also a member of the Council, donated a Challenge Cup to the Devon County Show for the best Dartmoor or Exmoor pony, which Calmady-Hamlyn won at the 1925 show with Judy V.[105]

---

100. The first occasion on which a prize is awarded to the partnership was at the Okehampton Show in 1928, *WMN*, 7 September 1928, p. 10.
101. Described at <http://www.foxhamsstud.co.uk/other-stallions/the-leat> [accessed 1 October 2020].
102. *The Times*, 12 June 1962, p. 15.
103. *WMN*, 19 March 1930, p. 19.
104. *WMN*, 2 June 1926, p. 9.
105. *WMN*, 13 May 1925, p. 8.

Once Calmady-Hamlyn and Dawson were in charge they took action to promote the profitability of the breed, and thus to persuade breeders to improve their stock. A key part of this initiative was the annual Dartmoor Pony Show, first held at Brimpts, Dartmeet in 1931. The Prince of Wales, who bred Dartmoor ponies at his Duchy farm, provided a challenge cup for the best brood mare.[106] The show was designed to attract entries from 'moorland farmers, smallholders and working men', whose success the Society regarded as vital to the future of the breed. These were not people likely to go to London to show their ponies so a local specialist show offered them new opportunities for sales.[107]

Similarly, when the Bath and West Show was held in Plymouth in 1938 the Society persuaded the committee to put in a class exclusively for Dartmoors instead of linking them with other mountain and moorland ponies, and attracted thirty-seven entries. Calmady-Hamlyn contrasted it with the position in 1922 when she and the Prince of Wales were the only two breeders to enter Dartmoors.[108] Owners were encouraged to improve their stock by a system of grants. The Society offered three guineas for a colt accepted by the judges at Brimpts, and five guineas if the same colt made an appearance the following year.[109] Running the Society was hard work, however. There were disagreements over the policy about culling unsuitable stallions on the moor, friction with the National Pony Society over the studbook and a 'travelling stallion scheme', financial problems when the Customs and Excise Department imposed entertainment tax on the show; and concerns over unsuitable stock being approved.[110] This last led to the rule that the inspection of stallions should be undertaken by two inspectors and the secretary (Calmady-Hamlyn).[111]

Agricultural Education

One area where Calmady-Hamlyn maintained her interest was in agricultural development, and specifically agricultural education. Expertise such as hers was too good to waste. She became a member of the Devon District Agricultural Wages Committee, where she kept an eye on the wages of female agricultural

---

106. *WMN*, 25 July 1932, p. 6.
107. *DEG*, 12 August 1932, p. 12.
108. *WMN*, 28 May 1938, p. 6.
109. *WMN*, 23 June 1938, p. 6.
110. *WMN*, 24 March 1938, p. 2; 9 August 1937, p. 3.
111. *WMN*, 17 June 1937, p. 6.

workers.[112] She was also appointed as a member of the Devon County Council Agricultural Committee.[113] Even in 1923 she was still the only woman on the Council of the Devon County Agricultural Association.[114] She became involved in the efforts to expand and increase the popularity of the Devon County Show, which the Association wanted to encourage more young people to visit and participate in. In one particular initiative she encouraged elementary school children visiting the show to write an essay about their experience for prizes, for which she paid herself. In 1926 she received 150 essays, all of which she read in detail.[115]

Her work on the County Agricultural Committee complemented her role as a Governor of Seale-Hayne College, on which she served between 1920 and 1940. In spite of the potential of the courses offered there the college initially struggled to recruit boys, finding that potential applicants, who normally left school at 14, were not able to apply for a place at Seale-Hayne and a Ministry of Agriculture scholarship until they reached the age of 16. They took jobs and lost interest in education. Some of the committee felt that they should open courses for 14-year-olds, but Calmady-Hamlyn believed that Seale-Hayne 'was of the nature of a university, and it was hardly desirable that young boys should go there at an age when they naturally needed more discipline than would be possible at such an institution'.[116] The committee agreed instead to explore an additional Farm Institute for the training of younger boys. By the autumn of 1932 there were seventy-two students at the college, enrolled on a wide range of courses.[117] Whilst it was possible to take a course that led to a London University degree, it was also possible to study for a range of certificates, to take a one-year special course for farmers' sons, or a practical farming course for farm pupils.[118]

Calmady-Hamlyn was not an advocate for courses for women at the college. In 1925 the Devon Federation of Women's Institutes sought to enlist the support of the Governors in seeking to increase facilities for

112. *WT*, 28 May 1920, p. 4; *DEG*, 1 July 1920, p. 3, refer to her on a sub-committee looking into the matter of providing better facilities for the granting of permits. It is possible that this was a co-opted position as the constitution of the District Wages Committee under the regulations of the Corn Production Act refers to her appointment formally in December 1920 (*DEG*, 13 December 1920, p. 1).
113. DHC, *Devon County Council Minutes*, 19 June 1920.
114. *DEG*, 2 November 1923, p. 6.
115. *DEG*, 6 March 1926, p. 3; 14 May, p. 19; 17 June, p. 2.
116. *WT*, 25 April 1924, p. 6.
117. *WMN*, 8 July 1932, p. 3.
118. *WMN*, 7 August 1931, p. 3.

agricultural education for women. Sir Henry Lopes, who had been struck by the excellent produce displayed at the WI Exhibition in Exeter, supported this move. Calmady-Hamlyn, however, felt that it would be better to have an Institute dedicated to training women, perhaps for four counties in the South West, rather than simply to establish a course at Seale-Hayne. She always had an ambivalence about what jobs women should do. Her initial attitude towards women land workers during the war had been that they were 'filling in' while the men were away at the war and her speech at the demobilization of the Women's Land Army in Devon said that 'the last thing on their minds was to keep out the men when they came home'.[119] In 1922 she wrote to the papers after receiving seventy-five applications from unemployed men for the post of gardener/handyman. Many of the applications were from ex-servicemen, making 'heart-breaking reading', and she urged women holding 'men's jobs' to 'give them up for the sake of the men who fought'.[120] Yet in 1920 she was pleased to employ a woman in the position of a groom (traditionally a man's job) and wrote that '[h]orses are very partial to being handled by women'.[121] The boundaries between 'men's jobs' and 'women's jobs' were, for her, not fixed for all time.

Her idea did not receive support, probably on the grounds of cost, and the Committee invited further suggestions from the WI Federation.[122] It was not until a new principal arrived in 1933 that the admission of women was addressed seriously. The first women students were not admitted until the autumn of 1934.[123] Unlike women students, women instructors, particularly for the practical courses in dairying or poultry, were accepted. However, Calmady-Hamlyn made it clear that she did not believe that the committee should discuss whether a man or a woman should be appointed to any particular post in advance of the appointment. She did not like 'the idea of engaging a woman simply because they might get her at a cheaper salary'.[124]

Later Life

Calmady-Hamlyn continued to run Vean Stud at Buckfast with Norah Dawson until the late 1930s. They remained active in the Dartmoor Pony Society, with

---

119. *WT*, 14 July 1919, p. 2.
120. *WMN*, 10 February 1922, p. 5.
121. *Landswoman*, 1 July 1920, p. 23 & 1 February 1920, p. 6.
122. *WMN*, 28 May 1925, p. 3; *DEG*, 29 May 1925, p. 3.
123. *WMN*, 28 March 1935, p. 13.
124. *WT*, 26 February 1927, p. 12.

Calmady-Hamlyn as secretary and Norah Dawson as treasurer. In 1932 Norah's mother, the Hon Mrs Jane Dawson, died at Holne Park, where she and Norah had been living.[125] Mrs Dawson's will showed how hostile she was to her daughter's Roman Catholicism, and possibly also that she blamed Calmady-Hamlyn for encouraging her conversion. She left instructions that no women were to attend her funeral, and that Holne Park should not be sold to her daughter, but that the trustees should give especially favourable terms to a purchaser who was not a Roman Catholic. The trust was to give her daughter instead an income of £700 a year.[126] Evicted from her family home, Dawson moved into the house at Pearroc Vean.

In 1938 Calmady-Hamlyn and Dawson moved back to the Bridestowe area, to Little Bidlake, close to what had been the 'women-only farm'. They immediately agreed to provide funds for the purchase of a building for conversion and use as a village hall and made this over to the parish by deed of gift.[127] At its opening, Calmady-Hamlyn said that it was better to live in the country than the town, but 'rural life must be made attractive'. She envisaged the hall as the hub for village activity. In 1939 she stood as a candidate in the local county council by-election, opposing and losing to the candidate who represented the Conservative interest.[128]

During the Second World War she became again involved in the wartime agricultural effort through the Women's Land Army and was co-opted onto the National Pony Society's War Emergency Council to represent Dartmoor.[129] After the war she moved back to Buckfast and, when Norah Dawson died in 1945, she continued her work with the Dartmoor Pony Society. Her work included extending the membership of the society, attracting interest from America and royalty (Princess Margaret), the publication of a booklet about the breed, and an exhibition about the pony at the Festival of Britain.[130] In 1950 she acquired thirty-eight cottages at Buckfast, property released by the closure and sale of the mill, whose workers had lived in the cottages. She arranged to transfer the cottages to the local authority and for the residents to become their tenants.[131]

---

125. This is the address given for Dawson as Treasurer of the Dartmoor Pony Society up to 1932.
126. *Gloucester Citizen*, 26 April 1932, p. 11
127. *WT*, 2 December 1938, p. 8.
128. *WMN*, 14 January 1939, p. 6; *WT*, 3 February 1939, p. 6.
129. *WT*, 17 May 1940, p. 3.
130. *WMN*, 28 February 1950, p. 3; M.S. Calmady-Hamlyn, *The Dartmoor Pony* (London: British Horse Society & Buckfast, Dartmoor Pony Society, 1949); 4 August 1950, p. 3; 23 November 1950, p. 4.
131. *WMN*, 5 April 1950.

In 1960 she was awarded the British Horse Society's Gold Medal of Honour for her work for the Dartmoor pony breed. She died in 1962, receiving the distinction of an obituary in *The Times*, which described her work with horses, and particularly with the Dartmoor Pony Society, her work for the Board of Agriculture and in agricultural education, and her work as a magistrate.[132] She is buried in the private cemetery at Buckfast Abbey.[133]

---

132. *The Times*, 12 June 1962, p. 15.
133. Ibid.

Conclusion: Devon Women's Votes, Voices and Vocations

This collection of biographies set out to explore the ways in which women in Devon worked, particularly after the First World War, to create, increase and use opportunities for women and girls in family life, local communities, education and the professions. These opportunities, as described in the introduction, were partly the result of legislation fought for by the women's suffrage movement and partly the result of wider social change.

The decision to use biography as the lens through which to consider the roles of a group of local women in the first half of the twentieth century proved a fruitful one. It facilitated the recognition that the women concerned not only led change in their different fields but acted as supporters to other women leaders working on areas of shared concern. Their common membership of various voluntary organizations active in the county is detailed in the Appendix. This shows the range of their interests, both in the Devon branches of national movements, such as the Girl Guides and the Electrical Association for Women, and also in independent local organizations such as the Devonshire Association for Cripples Aid, the Devon League of Workfinders and the Plymouth Women's Hospital Fund.

As well as pursuing their own particular interests, the women were engaged in contributing, through a range of democratic opportunities such as electioneering and lobbying, to the achievement of more universal goals such as the reform of the legislative framework that had constrained the lives of earlier women. Deeply affected by their experience of the First World War, they also sought not only to mitigate its long-term effects but also to support efforts, such as the League of Nations, to make a world to which global warfare would never return. The identification of these shared motives and actions reinforces the point made by Caine, that biographies supply a rich context for the actions of the individual, and are therefore particularly suited to the understanding of women's roles and achievements. Women are more likely than men to

'Conclusion: Devon Women's Votes, Voices and Vocations' in: *Devon Women in Public and Professional Life 1900–1950: Votes, Voices and Vocations*. University of Exeter Press (2021). © Julia Neville, Mitzi Auchterlonie, Paul Auchterlonie and Ann Roberts DOI: 10.47788/NEID3481

perform a range of different roles; biography reveals this more effectively than studies of institutions, events or movements.[1]

The subjects, though not well known nationally, proved to be women of talent, commitment and a strong sense of values. As detailed in the introduction, they all, even Daymond, a working-class woman, came from the 'servant-keeping' strata of Devon society, which no doubt enabled them to dedicate more time to their chosen causes than would otherwise have been the case. This should not diminish appreciation of their achievements: many other women in similar positions chose less challenging lives. Indeed other women, as the correspondence prompted by Calmady-Hamlyn's resignation from the Devon Federation of Women's Institutes Executive Committee suggests (p. 215), were often grateful that there were others who were willing and able to attend meetings and serve on committees. The National Union of Women's Suffrage Societies had operated in a similar way within the county, with representatives to South West Federation meetings usually comprising those from these same classes. The women were themselves conscious of the need to broaden their representative base. In the 1920s, organizations such as the Mothers' Union sought to set aside places on their central committees for 'working women', but time for participation remained a problem. The Women's Institutes and the Electrical Association for Women were right to press for improvements that would lessen the time that most women were inevitably required to spend on housework and free them for other pursuits.

The origins of the Devon women in this study affected the social networks to which they initially had access. Some of the women could draw on family networks and influence at local and national level. Acland, Cecil and Clinton were well-connected politically. Buller and Calmady-Hamlyn were from county gentry families with a wide circle of local influence. Daymond had established a prominence in her local community through her background in the Women's Co-operative Guild and her husband's position as a Devonport councillor.

Four of the group were married, and their husbands supported their work; their own activities were often driven by interests similar to those of their wives, although conducted in different contexts. Husbands were also on occasion called on to defend their wives' actions: they were still held in law to be responsible for what their wives did, and both Bishop Cecil and Francis Acland

---

1. B. Caine, *Biography and History*, 2nd edition (London: Red Globe Press; Macmillan International, 2019), pp. 23–24.

found themselves named in court actions related to their wives' activities.[2] There is, however, no hint of any constraint being applied to these women's subsequent activities. Theirs seem to have been partnerships of equals. As Lord Clinton said on the occasion of his golden wedding, describing his marriage: 'There must be no question of obedience or mastery ... No two people can always concur, so they must agree to differ and practise mutual forbearance.'[3]

The women had different political allegiances and shifts from one party to another occurred as the complexion of the political parties changed over time. Acland remained a committed Liberal and Clinton a Conservative, but Daymond moved from Liberalism to Conservatism, and Calmady-Hamlyn from Liberalism to Socialism. Most of these women were members of the Church of England, though for some, such as Cecil and Headridge, it was more of a driving force than it was for others. Daymond was a committed Methodist and at one point a Salvationist, and Calmady-Hamlyn, unusually, left the Church of England for Roman Catholicism. Despite these differences, the women came to share a commitment to organizations that cut across boundaries of class, religion and politics, whether in the suffrage movement, the Women's Institutes or in educational and professional circles. Participation in those primary networks of family, religion and politics meant that these women had an expectation that their voices would be heard and their points of view given consideration.

Their experiences of education differed, as two of the group were born in the early 1860s, four in the 1870s and two in the 1880s. Educational opportunities in secondary and university education were more readily available to the younger women than to the older group, although class and gender also affected their access to high quality education. Both Cecil and Clinton lamented the poor quality of their education, undertaken at home by governesses at a time when aristocratic families would have been unlikely to permit their daughters to attend boarding school. Ramsay had to wait until her brother's education was complete before she was allowed to pursue a university course. They all sought to change the chances their successors had of full access to educational opportunities.

Headridge and Ramsay had professional qualifications to add to their general education and to give them a platform from which to speak. The younger women in the group had been involved in the movement for women's suffrage,

---

2. This was altered by the Law Reform (Married Women and Tortfeasors) Act 1935, another step on the road to equality.

3. *Western Morning News*, 2 June 1936, p. 4.

where their participation helped them learn to speak with confidence on the need for reform. Cecil and Clinton had had to learn to meet the expectations of those in their social position by speaking in public, even if on limited topics such as fund-raising for good causes.

The women were leaders in their own spheres of local activity. They kept closely in touch with national peers: Cecil was on the governing body of the Mothers' Union and one of the first women members of the national synod of the Church of England. Buller was a member of the Central Council for Cripples Aid. Daymond represented the Devonport Guardians at national conferences. Acland took a national role in the development of Liberal Party policy. Ramsay was at different times secretary and president of the Medical Women's Federation. They were then able to act as 'influencers', discussing and refining goals and aspirations for change by engagement with local groups. This could be slow and painstaking work in a county with over 500 parishes and more road miles than Belgium. The South West NUWSS Federation had earlier recognized the need for such work, with initiatives such as a caravan tour to foster interest across rural constituencies. In the 1920s, enabled by the motor car (as well as by an extensive rural rail network), women such as Calmady-Hamlyn, Cecil and Clinton were able to go to meetings of local groups in villages as well as market towns across the county. Such outreach work complemented the arrangements for central county-wide meetings involving elected representatives as provided for in the formal structures of the organizations involved. Structures with both county and local groups were seen as critical to effective engagement. Buller, for example, designed such a structure for local orthopaedic associations feeding into the Devonshire Association for Cripples Aid. At such central meetings, actions such as the taking of a resolution to a national conference, or the lobbying of MPs, or the writing of a letter to the County Council were agreed.

For the professional women in this study the challenges were rather different. Ramsay played a dual role, operating both within Plymouth Citizens' Association on a broad front, and in the world of medical politics, where she was active in seeking to secure for herself and for other women doctors the opportunities that came as a matter of course to men. For Headridge, on the other hand, many of the battles for acceptance had been won by head-mistresses from an earlier generation. She does not appear to have been involved in the work of professional associations and the engagement of women on the City Council's Higher Education Committee had already been pioneered by the redoubtable Jessie Montgomery. She was, however, fully alive to the need to prepare her students for new opportunities, and the fact that she engaged several of the subjects of these biographies to address the school on Speech Day demonstrates her commitment to opening doors to new expectations of the ways in which women could participate in social and civic life.

Some of the women were very conscious of their lack of background knowledge on topics with which their positions, as JPs for example, or as councillors, required them to deal. They lacked the opportunities their male peers had for discussion with like-minded individuals in gentlemen's clubs. Under the leadership of another local woman committed to change, Juanita Phillips,[4] they set up the Devon Council of Women (DCW) expressly as a learning community. The DCW, whose full title was the Devon Council of Women on Public Authorities, was a branch of the National Council of Women but, apparently uniquely, one whose membership was not open to all women. It was set up to enable women councillors, Guardians and JPs to hear experts and discuss issues relevant to their work. Acland disapproved of its formation, arguing that it would compete with the local Equal Citizenship Society, but the members involved saw it as a useful way of giving them access to the latest thinking, thus enabling them to better perform their roles.[5] Daymond, Calmady-Hamlyn and Buller all took part in this group, and Cecil also became involved on occasion.

The principal interests of the women in these studies lay in different fields: educational and professional; moral welfare; and the improvement of services and associational life within local communities. Whilst this work was partly undertaken, in Thane's words, 'to improve the relative position of women', a prime 'feminist' goal, it should more appropriately be seen as part of a broader 'women's movement', where the emphasis was on fostering women's development on a number of fronts.[6] These women did wish to help others to make the best of the new opportunities of democratic citizenship. However, they were also concerned with the practicalities of reducing domestic drudgery (through the Electrical Association for Women, for example, for which Daymond was a powerful local advocate) or mitigating some of the

---

4. Juanita Phillips was a borough councillor in Honiton and Devon County Council's first woman county councillor. For her career see J. Neville, 'Challenge, conformity and casework in interwar England: the first women councillors in Devon', *Women's History Review*, vol. 22, no. 6, 2013, pp. 971–94, DOI <https://doi.org/10.1080/09612025.2013.780846>.

5. Exeter's Society for Equal Citizenship had been formed in 1922. Acland was elected President at the first annual meeting (*DEG*, 29 May 1923).

6. P. Thane, 'Women, Liberalism and Citizenship, 1918–1930', in E.F. Biagini (ed.), *Citizenship and Community: Liberals, Radicals and Collective Identities in the British Isles, 1865–1931* (Cambridge: Cambridge University Press, 1996), pp. 76–77.

challenges of looking after disabled children (Devonshire Association for Cripples Aid, Diocesan Association for Friendless Girls). They were concerned too with enriching lives socially, culturally and spiritually. Women's Institute meetings encompassed education, performance arts and social time. Cecil felt it important that the spiritual dimension of Mothers' Union work should not be lost. Acland encouraged the Girl Guides to use Killerton for rallies and woodcraft. Headridge fostered drama and music outside the school curriculum.

When considering the period after the First World War, earlier historians assessed the women's movement initially as an intermission, particularly for working-class women. They suggested that this was the result of fragmentation within the movement between the 'old' feminists, who focused on parity for women in the domestic, civic and employment spheres, and the 'new' feminists, who considered that the award of the vote should be fulfilled by efforts to alleviate women's lives by securing greater control over their own lives and those of their children and by winning greater access to financial support. More recently this stark division has been called into question. Women, and those in the Devon study demonstrate this, did not necessarily choose to support one model rather than the other, but could maintain a pluralistic approach. They sought to take forward the cause of greater freedom and equality for women on multiple fronts. Some of their goals were attained: the 1928 grant of the Parliamentary franchise to women on the same terms as men, for example. Other goals took longer. The appointment of women police in Devon was not achieved until after the Second World War, but even on this issue some progress was made. The public promotion of the idea did succeed in winning over some individual councillors.[7] 'Nothing ever gets done unless you shout long and hard for it' was Buller's belief, and these women were willing and able to persevere in their quests for change.

This book calls into question whether the past focus in women's history on histories of institutions and causes is sufficient to enable a view to be taken about the success of feminists during the mid-twentieth century. Taken together, these biographies show how women who were otherwise 'hidden from history' worked individually and collaboratively to support one another to create change at the local level, while also influencing national organizations. They

---

7. DHC Westcountry Studies Collection, Special Collections F6, *Scrapbooks of Juanita Maxwell Phillips*, 4 Feb 1928 (Vol. Preliminary p. 4b). Cyril Tweed (East Devon coroner and Honiton Town Council member) said at one of the meetings about women in the County Police Force that 'having sat on the fence for so long he had now fallen off on the address of Miss Hartland' (Miss Hartland had spoken about the work of women police in Gloucestershire)

were neither 'old' nor 'new' feminists, in the terminology of previous studies. They were practical, incremental feminists.

Was Devon unique in having such a group of women interested and able to work on so many fronts in such a rural county? Progress in Devon seems to have been a 'zig-zag road', to borrow the phrase that Ramsay chose as the title of her memoir. There were failures, such as the campaign for the appointment of women police, but successes too, such as the opening up of agricultural courses at Seale-Hayne College to women. Similar studies in other regions, both rural and urban, particularly those that look at collaborative links between local women, may give a more rounded picture of the progress of the broader women's movement across the UK or indeed internationally.

Appendix

Voluntary Organizations in Devon Supported
by the Subjects of these Biographies

EA = Eleanor Acland, GB = Georgiana Buller, SCH = Sylvia Calmady-Hamlyn,
FC = Lady Florence Cecil, JC = Lady Clinton, CD = Clara Daymond,
JH = Jessie Headridge, MR = Mabel Ramsay.

This list excludes political and professional organizations to which the
women belonged, and also their religious affiliations.[1]

Organization	Women Involved
Alexandra Rose Day Committee (Exeter)	FC
Anglo-American Women's Crusade	EA, FC
Ashburton Cottage Hospital Management Committee	SCH
British Women's Temperance Association	FC, CD
Cancer Relief (Devon and Exeter Fund)	EA
Church Army Housing Project	GB, FC
Dartmoor Pony Society	SCH
Devonshire Association for Cripples Aid	EA, GB, FC, JC, JH (school)
Devon County Agricultural Association	SCH
Devon County Arts and Crafts Association	JH
Devon League of Workfinders	GB, FC
Devonshire Red Cross	GB
Devon Women's War Agricultural Committee	SCH

1 It is not always possible to determine whether the women were formal members of
an organization or merely supporters.

Devon Women's War Service Committee	SCH
Diocesan Association for the Care of Friendless Girls	FC
Electrical Association for Women	CD
Exeter Lying-in Charity	FC
Exeter Women's Welfare Association	EA
Exeter Workmen's Dwellings Company	FC
Friends of Exeter Cathedral	GB
Girl Guides	EA, JC, JH (school)
Girls' Friendly Society	FC
Good Templars (Temperance)	CD
League of Nations	EA, FC, MR, JH (school)
Medical Women's Federation (SW Association)	MR
Mothers' Union	FC
National Council of Women	
• Devon Council of Women on public authorities	GB, SCH, FC, CD
• Individual membership	EA
National Spinsters' Pension Association	CD
National Union of Societies for Equal Citizenship	
• Exeter and District Women Citizens' Association	EA, JH
• Plymouth Citizens' Association	CD, MR
National Union of Women Workers	
• Exeter branch	FC
National Union of Women's Suffrage Societies	
• Exeter branch	JH, GB
• Plymouth branch	CD, MR
• South West Federation	EA
Nursing Associations	
• Devonshire Nursing Association	FC, JC
• Local District Nursing Associations	SCH, FC, JC, CD
Okehampton Agricultural Society	SCH
Okehampton and District Recruiting Committee	SCH
Peacemakers' Pilgrimage	EA, FC
Personal Service League	JC
Plymouth Guild of Social Service	CD
Plymouth Venture Club (Soroptimists)	MR
Royal West of England Institution for Deaf and Dumb Children	FC
RSPCA (Ladies' Branch)	FC
Save the Children Fund (Exeter branch)	EA, FC

Seale-Hayne College Governors	SCH
Townswomen's Guild	CD
United Associations of Great Britain and France (Devonshire Branch)	EA, FC
Women Signallers' Territorial Corps	JC
Women's Co-operative Guild	CD
Women's Hospital Fund	CD, MR
Women's Institutes	EA, SCH, JC

Bibliography

Archives and Manuscripts

The Box (Plymouth) File 185 (Plymouth City Council [Plymouth Borough Council till 1928]: Public Health Committee; Special Purposes Committee) [incorporates the former Plymouth and West Devon Record Office]

The Box (Plymouth) File 1670/18–20 and 1670/30 (Plymouth Medical Society Papers)

The Box (Plymouth) File 3071/9 (St Budeaux Branch Co-operative Women's Guild)

British Red Cross Archive (London) Files 1293/1 & 1293/6

Cumbria Record Office (Carlisle) File DMAR/3/5 (Catherine Marshall Papers)

Devon Heritage Centre (Exeter) File 1148M/14/Series II (Acland Family Papers)

Devon Heritage Centre (Exeter) File 1262 M/O/LD/141 (Fortescue Family Papers, Lord Lieutenant of Devon File: Devon Women's War Service Committee)

Devon Heritage Centre (Exeter) File 1262 M/O/LD/142 (Fortescue Family Papers, Lord Lieutenant of Devon File: Devon County Council Agricultural Executive Committee Minutes)

Devon Heritage Centre (Exeter) File 1262 M/O/LD/145 (Fortescue Family Papers, Lord Lieutenant of Devon File: Devonshire Red Cross and Voluntary Aid Organisations)

Devon Heritage Centre (Exeter) File 2065M (Buller Family Papers)

Devon Heritage Centre (Exeter) File 2065M Add 7 Box 2767 (Buller Family Papers: Details of First World War Convoys)

Devon Heritage Centre (Exeter) File 2065M Add F357 (Buller Family Papers: Red Cross, Devonshire Branch, Minutes Book; *Tittle-Tattle, Hospital No. 1 Magazine*, June 1916; 'Exeter War Hospitals')

Devon Heritage Centre (Exeter) File 3169C/EFG1 (Bishop Blackall School Governors' Minutes)

Devon Heritage Centre (Exeter) File 4110Z/27/9/5/8/3 (Michael Sadler, 'Report on Secondary and Higher Education in Exeter', 1905)

Devon Heritage Centre (Exeter) File 6181G (Devonian Orthopaedic Organisation)

Devon Heritage Centre (Exeter) File 7137G (Mothers' Union, Diocese of Exeter)

Devon Heritage Centre (Exeter) File DCM (Devon County Council Minutes, 1905–1974)

Devon Heritage Centre (Exeter) File ZAKZ (St Loye's College and School of Occupational Therapy)

Devon Heritage Centre (Exeter) Westcountry Studies Collection, Special Collections F6 (The Scrapbooks of Juanita Maxwell Phillips)

The National Archives (Kew) File MAF 59/1 (Ministry of Agriculture and Food, Women's County Committees)

The National Archives (Kew) File MH 66–58 (Devonshire Public Health Survey)

The National Archives (Kew) File MH 66–618 (Local Government Surveys: Report for the City of Plymouth)

Parliamentary Archives (London) File LG/C/10/2/12 (David Lloyd George Papers)

Royal College of Physicians (London) File MS87 (Mabel Ramsay, 'A Doctor's Zig-Zag Road')

Wellcome Library (London) File SA/MWF/B.2/8-9 (*Medical Women's Federation Quarterly Review*)

Wellcome Library (London) File SA/MWF/D.7 (Home Office Committee to Enquire into Sexual Offences Against Young Persons)

Contemporary Newspapers and Magazines

Aberdeen Daily Journal

Bishop Blackall School Commemorative Magazine

Brechin Advertiser

British Medical Journal

Church Militant

Church Times

Common Cause [previously *The Common Cause of Humanity*; later *The Woman's Leader*]

The Cornishman
Daily Herald
Daily News [London]
Derby Daily Telegraph
Devon and Exeter [Daily] Gazette
Dundee Courier
The Evening Post [Exeter]
Exeter Diocesan Gazette
Exmouth Journal
Express and Echo [Exeter]
Gloucester Citizen
Gloucester Journal
Grantham Journal
Home and Country
Hull Daily Mail
Kent and Sussex Courier
Liberal Federation Women's News [later Federation News; then Liberal Women's
    News]
London Gazette
London Monitor and New Era
Manchester Courier and Lancashire General Advertiser
Manchester Guardian [later The Guardian]
Medical Women's Federation Quarterly Review
North Devon Gazette
North Devon Journal
Nottingham Journal
The Observer
Pall Mall Gazette
The People
The Tablet
Taunton Courier
The Times
The Vote
Walsall Advertiser
West Briton and Cornwall Advertiser
Western Chronicle
Western Daily Mercury
Western Daily Press
Western Evening Herald

Western Mail

Western Morning News [later *Western Morning News and Western Daily Mercury*; then *Western Morning News and Devon and Exeter Daily Gazette*]

Western Times

Books

Acland, Anne, *A Devon Family: The Story of the Aclands* (London and Chichester: Phillimore, 1981)

Acland, Eleanor, *Dark Side Out* (London: Sidgwick & Jackson, 1921)

Acland, Eleanor [writing as Margaret Burneside], *The Delusion of Diana* (London: Arnold, 1898)

Acland, Eleanor, *Good-bye for the Present: The Story of Two Childhoods, Milly 1878–88 & Ellen, 1913–24* (London: Hodder & Stoughton, 1935)

Acland, Eleanor [writing as Eleanor Cropper], *In the Straits of Hope* (London: Murray, 1904)

Acland, Eleanor, *A Report of a Fortnight's Tour in Ireland: Drawn Up for the Women's National Liberal Federation* (London: WNLF, [1921?])

Andrews, Maggie, *The Acceptable Face of Feminism: The Women's Institute as a Social Movement* (London: Lawrence and Wishart, 1997)

Atkinson, Diane, *Elsie and Mairi Go to War: Two Extraordinary Women on the Western Front* (London: Preface, 2009)

Austin, Anne, *The History of the Clinton Barony, 1299–1999* ([Exeter]: Lord Clinton, 1999)

Baden-Powell, Agnes, *The Handbook for Girl Guides, or, How Girls can Build the Empire*, by Agnes Baden-Powell in collaboration with Sir Robert Baden-Powell (London: Nelson, 1912)

Baden-Powell, Robert Stephenson Smyth, *Scouting for Boys: A Handbook for Instruction in Good Citizenship*, complete edn, rev. (London: Pearson, 1908)

Ball, Stuart, *Portrait of a Party: The Conservative Party in Britain, 1918–1945* (Oxford: Oxford University Press, 2013) https://doi.org/10.1093/acpr of:oso/9780199667987.001.0001

Banks, Olive, *Faces of Feminism: A Study of Feminism as a Social Movement* (Oxford: Robertson, 1981; repr. Oxford: Blackwell, 1986)

Batten, Richard, ed., *A Lord Lieutenant in Wartime: The Experiences of the Fourth Earl Fortescue during the First World War*, Devon and Cornwall Record Society, new series, 61 (Woodbridge: Boydell, 2018) https://doi.org/10.1017/9781787444423

Beaumont, Caitríona, *Housewives and Citizens: Domesticity and the Women's Movement in England, 1928–64* (Manchester: Manchester University Press, 2013) https://doi.org/10.7228/manchester/9780719086076.001.0001

Beddoe, Deirdre, *Back to Home and Duty: Women between the Wars, 1918–1939* (London: HarperCollins, 1989)

Board of Education, *Report of Consultative Committee on the Differentiation of the Curriculum for Boys and Girls Respectively in Secondary Schools* (London: HMSO, 1923)

Borsay, Anne, *Disability and Social Policy in Britain since 1750: A History of Exclusion* (Basingstoke: Palgrave Macmillan, 2005) https://doi.org/10.1007/978-1-137-18109-1

Bowser, Thekla, *The Story of British VAD Work in the Great War* (London: Imperial War Museum, 1917)

Boyce, D.G., *Englishmen and Irish Troubles: British Public Opinion and the Making of Irish Policy, 1918–1922* (London: Cape, 1971)

Brown, Jane, *Angel Dorothy: How an American Progressive Came to Devon* (London: Unbound, 2017)

Caine, Barbara, *Biography and History*, 2nd edn (London: Red Globe Press; Macmillan International, 2019)

Calendar of the Association for Promoting the Education of Women in Oxford for the year 1909–1910 (Oxford: The Association, 1910)

Calmady-Hamlyn, Mary Sylvia, *The Dartmoor Pony* (London: British Horse Society; Buckfast, Devon: Dartmoor Pony Society, 1949) [2nd edn, 1952]

Cartwright, Colin, *Burning to Get the Vote: The Women's Suffrage Movement in Central Buckinghamshire, 1904–1914* (Buckingham: University of Buckingham Press, 2013)

Chanter, John Frederick, *The Bishop's Palace, Exeter, and its Story* (London: SPCK, 1932)

Collis, Maurice, *Nancy Astor: An Informal Biography* (London: Faber, 1960)

Cooter, Roger, *Surgery and Society in Peace and War: Orthopaedics and the Organization of Modern Medicine, 1880–1948* (Basingstoke: Palgrave Macmillan, 1993)

Crawford, Elizabeth, *The Women's Suffrage Movement: A Reference Guide, 1866–1918* (London: Routledge, 1999)

Crawford, Elizabeth, *The Women's Suffrage Movement in Britain and Ireland: A Regional Survey* (London: Routledge, 2006)

Crump, Melanie, *Struggle and Suffrage in Torbay: Women's Lives and the Fight for Equality* (Barnsley: Pen and Sword, 2019)

Delafield, E.M., *The War Workers* (London: Heinemann, 1918)

Exeter Heritage Project, *Working Lives: The Careers of Seven Exeter Women* (Exeter: Exeter City Council, 1987)

Dyhouse, Carol, *Girls Growing up in late Victorian and Edwardian England* (London: Routledge and Kegan Paul, 1981; repr. Abingdon: Routledge, 2013) https://doi.org/10.4324/9780203104101

Dyhouse, Carol, *No Distinction of Sex?: Women in British Universities, 1870–1939* (London: Routledge, 1995)

Fawcett, Millicent Garrett, *The Women's Victory and After: Personal Reminiscences, 1911–1918* (London: Sidgwick & Jackson, 1920)

Fort, Adrian, *Nancy: The Story of Lady Astor* (London: Cape, 2012)

French, Henry and Rothery, Mark, *Man's Estate: Landed Gentry Masculinities, c.1660–c.1900* (Oxford: Oxford University Press, 2012) https://doi.org/10.1093/acprof:oso/9780199576692.001.0001

Furniss, Averil D.S. and Phillips, Marion, *The Working Woman's House* (London: Swarthmore Press, [1920])

Gardner, Helen D., *The First Girl Guide: The Story of Agnes Baden-Powell* (Stroud: Amberley, 2010)

Gascoyne-Cecil, Lord William, *Changing China*, by Lord William Gascoyne-Cecil, assisted by Lady Florence Cecil (London: Nisbet, 1911)

Girdlestone, G.R., *The Care and Cure of Crippled Children* (Bristol: Wright, 1924)

Glasby, Jon, *Poverty and Opportunity: 100 Years of the Birmingham Settlement* (Studley, Warwickshire: Brewin Books, 1999)

Glasspool, Tracey, *Struggle and Suffrage in Plymouth: Women's Lives and the Fight for Equality* (Barnsley: Pen and Sword, 2019)

Glew, Helen, *Gender, Rhetoric and Regulation: Women's Work in the Civil Service and London County Council, 1900–1955* (Manchester: Manchester University Press, 2016)

Goronwy-Roberts, Marian, *A Woman of Vision: A Life of Marion Phillips, MP* (Wrexham: Bridge Books, 2000)

Graves, Pamela, *Labour Women: Women in British Working-Class Politics, 1918–1939* (Cambridge: Cambridge University Press, 1994) https://doi.org/10.1080/03612759.1995.9949166

Gray, Todd, *Remarkable Women of Devon* (Exeter: Mint Press, 2009)

Hadden, M.L.E., *Bishop Blackall School, Exeter (1877–1983)* (Exeter: the author, 1983)

Hamilton, Cicely, *Life Errant* (London: Dent, 1935)

Hannam, June and Hunt, Karen, *Socialist Women: Britain, 1880s to 1920s* (London: Routledge, 2002)

Harrison, Brian, *Prudent Revolutionaries: Portraits of British Feminists between the Wars* (Oxford: Clarendon Press, 1987)

Harvey, Hazel, *The Royal Devon & Exeter Hospital 1948–1998: A Better Provision: Fifty Years On* (Exeter: Royal Devon & Exeter Healthcare NHS Trust, 1998)

Headridge, Jessie [writing as J.H.], *Labuntur Anni* (Exeter: Wheaton, 1932)

Hepburn-Stuart-Forbes-Trefusis, Jane Grey, Baroness Clinton, *Happy Hours in an Irish Home* (Edinburgh: William Brown, 1938)

Hepburn-Stuart-Forbes-Trefusis, Jane Grey, Baroness Clinton, *Stories to Tell: Written or Remembered* (London: Robert Scott, 1930)

Holton, Sandra Stanley, *Feminism and Democracy: Women's Suffrage and Reform Politics in Britain, 1900–1918* (Cambridge: Cambridge University Press, 1986)

Howell, Rosemary, *Splendid Fun: The Story of One Hundred Years of Devon Girl Guides* (Ivybridge, Devon: Howell, 2019)

Jenkins, Inez, *The History of the Women's Institute Movement of England and Wales* (Oxford: Oxford University Press, 1953)

Jones, Helen, ed., *Duty and Citizenship: The Correspondence and Political Papers of Violet Markham, 1896–1953* (London: Historians' Press, 1994)

Kean, Hilda, *Deeds not Words: Lives of Suffragette Teachers* (London: Pluto Press, 1990)

Kerr, Rose, *Story of the Girl Guides, 1908–1938*, rev. edn (London: Girl Guides Association, 1976)

King, Steven, *Women, Welfare and Local Politics, 1880–1920: We Might Be Trusted* (Brighton: Sussex Academic Press, 2006)

Law, Cheryl, *Suffrage and Power: The Women's Movement, 1918–1928* (London: I.B.Tauris, 1997)

Law, Cheryl, *Women, a Modern Political Dictionary* (London: I.B.Tauris, 2000)

Lawson, John and Silver, Harold, *A Social History of Education in England* (London: Methuen, 1973)

Liberal Party, *Britain's Industrial Future: Being the Report of the Liberal Industrial Inquiry* (London: Benn, 1928)

Liberal Party, *The Land and the Nation: Rural Report of the Liberal Land Committee, 1923–1925* (London: Hodder and Stoughton, [1925])

Liddington, Jill, *Vanishing for the Vote: Suffrage, Citizenship and the Battle for the Census* (Manchester: Manchester University Press, 2014) https://doi.org/10.7228/manchester/9780719087486.001.0001

Longworth, Philip, *The Unending Vigil: A History of the Commonwealth War Graves Commission*, new edn (London: Secker & Warburg, 1986; repr. Barnsley: Leo Cooper, 2003)

Macadam, Elizabeth, *The New Philanthropy: A Study of the Relations between the Statutory and Voluntary Social Services* (London: Allen & Unwin, 1934)

McCarthy, Helen, *The British People and the League of Nations: Democracy, Citizenship and Internationalism, c.1918–1945* (Manchester: Manchester University Press, 2011) https://doi.org/10.7228/manchester/9780719086168.001.0001

Marjoram, April, *The Women's Suffrage Movement in Exmouth* (Exmouth: Exmouth Historical and Archaeological Society, 2018)

The Maynard School: A Celebration of 350 Years, 1658–2008 (Exeter: Maynard School, 2008)

Melville, C.H., *Life of General the Right Hon. Sir Redvers Buller, V.C., G.C.B., G.C.M.G.* 2 vols (London: Arnold, 1923)

Ministry of Reconstruction, *The Aims of Reconstruction* (London: HMSO, 1918)

Ministry of Reconstruction, Adult Education Committee, *Final Report*, Cmd 321 (London: HMSO, 1919)

Moffat, Ian C.D., *The Allied Intervention in Russia, 1918–1920: The Diplomacy of Chaos* (Basingstoke: Palgrave Macmillan, 2015) https://doi.org/10.1057/9781137435736

Moyse, Cordelia, *A History of the Mothers' Union: Women, Anglicanism and Globalisation, 1876–2008* (Woodbridge: Boydell & Brewer, 2009)

National Trust, *Killerton, Devon: A Souvenir Guide* (Swindon: National Trust, 2014)

Neville, Julia, *Juanita Phillips: Champion for Change in East Devon between the Wars* (Exeter: Short Run Press, 2012)

Norman, Vicky, *Scattered Homes, Broken Hearts* (Plymouth: Foxfield Publications, 2003)

Pankhurst, Sylvia, *The Suffragette Movement: An Intimate Account of Persons and Ideals* (London: Longmans, Green, 1931; repr. London: Virago, 1977)

Powell, Violet, *The Life of a Provincial Lady: A Study of E.M. Delafield and her World* (London: Heinemann, 1988)

Pugh, Martin, *Women and the Women's Movement in Britain, 1914–1959* (Basingstoke: Macmillan, 1992)

Robb, Janet Henderson, *The Primrose League, 1883–1906* (New York: Columbia University Press, 1942) https://doi.org/10.7312/robb94004

Robinson, Jane, *A Force to be Reckoned With: A History of the Women's Institute* (London: Virago, 2011)

Robinson, Jane, *Ladies Can't Climb Ladders: The Pioneering Adventures of the First Professional Women* (London: Doubleday, 2020)

Schools Inquiry Commission, *Report of the Commissioners* (London: HMSO, 1868) [Vol. 1 of the Taunton Report]

Scott, Gillian, *Feminism and the Politics of Working Women: The Women's Co-operative Guild, 1880s to the Second World War* (London: UCL Press, 1998)

Storr, Katherine, *Excluded from the Record: Women, Refugees and Relief, 1914–1929* (London: Peter Lang, 2009)

Sutcliff, Rosemary, *Blue Remembered Hills: A Recollection* (London: Bodley Head, 1983; repr. Oxford: Oxford University Press, 1984)

Thomas, F.G., *The Changing Village: An Essay in Rural Reconstruction* (London: Nelson, 1939)

Thorpe, Andrew, *The British General Election of 1931* (Oxford: Clarendon Press, 1991) https://doi.org/10.1093/acprof:oso/9780198202189.001.0001

Tregidga, Garry, ed., *Killerton, Camborne and Westminster: The Political Correspondence of Sir Francis and Lady Acland, 1910–1929*, Devon and Cornwall Record Society, new series, 48 (Exeter: Devon and Cornwall Record Society, 2006)

Tregidga, Garry, *The Liberal Party in South-West Britain since 1918: Political Decline, Dormancy and Rebirth* (Exeter: University of Exeter Press, 2000)

Vass, Pamela, *Breaking the Mould: The Suffragette Story in North Devon* (Littleham, Bideford: Boundstone Books, 2017)

Vellacott, Jo, *From Liberal to Labour: The Story of Catherine Marshall* (Montreal: McGill-Queen's University Press, 1993)

Vellacott, Jo, *Pacifists, Patriots and the Vote: The Erosion of Democratic Suffragism in Britain during the First World War* (Basingstoke: Palgrave Macmillan, 2007) https://doi.org/10.1057/9780230592063

White, Bonnie, *The Women's Land Army in First World War Britain* (Basingstoke: Palgrave Macmillan, 2014) https://doi.org/10.1057/9781137363909

Articles and Chapters in Books

Auchterlonie, Mitzi, 'Acland (*née* Cropper), Eleanor Mary, Lady Acland', *Oxford Dictionary of National Biography*. https://doi.org/10.1093/odnb/9780198614128.013.56214

Auchterlonie, Mitzi, 'Pratt, Edith Helen', *Oxford Dictionary of National Biography*. https://doi.org/10.1093/odnb/9780198614128.013.109632

Bayer, Penny, 'The Contribution of NUWSS Organisers in Devon to the Campaign for Women's Suffrage', *The Devon Historian*, 90 (2020), 53–67

Bayer, Penny, 'Participation in the Female Community by Women of the Frood Family of Topsham: Gentility, Suffrage, WW1 and Afterwards', *The Devon Historian*, 87 (2018), 71–84

Beauman, Nicola, 'Dashwood (*née* de la Pasture), Edmée Elizabeth Monica

(pseud of E.M. Delafield)', *Oxford Dictionary of National Biography*. https://
doi.org/10.1093/ref:odnb/32720

Beaumont, Caitríona, 'Citizens not Feminists: The Boundary Negotiated
between Citizenship and Feminism by Mainstream Women's Organisations
in England, 1928–39', *Women's History Review*, 9 (2000), 411–29. https://
doi.org/10.1080/09612020000200240

Beaumont, Caitríona, 'The Women's Movement: Politics and Citizenship,
1918–1950s', in *Women in Twentieth-Century Britain*, ed. by Ina Zweiniger-
Bargielowska (Harlow: Longmans, 2001), 262–77

Berthezène, Clarisse, 'The Middlebrow and the Making of a "New Common
Sense": Women's Voluntarism, Conservative Politics and Representations of
Womanhood', in *Rethinking Right-Wing Women: Gender and the Conservative
Party, 1880s to the Present*, ed. by Clarisse Berthezène and Julia V. Gottlieb
(Manchester: Manchester University Press, 2018), 104–21. https://doi.
org/10.7228/manchester/9781784994389.003.0007

Bingham, Adrian, '"An Era of Domesticity?": Histories of Women and Gender in
Interwar Britain', *Cultural and Social History*, 1 (2004), 225–33. https://doi.
org/10.1191/1478003804cs0014ra

Breitenbach, Esther and Wright, Valerie, 'Women as Active Citizens: Glasgow
and Edinburgh, c.1918–1939', *Women's History Review*, 23 (2014), 401–20.
http://dx.doi.org/10.1080/09612025.2013.820602

Calmady-Hamlyn, Sylvia, 'A Woman's Farm in Devon', *Journal of the Board of
Agriculture*, 25.7 (1918), 834–39

Capener, Norman, 'In Memoriam Dame Georgiana Buller', *Journal of Bone
and Joint Surgery*, 35 (1953), 573–74. https://doi.org/10.2106/00004623-
195335030-00005

DiCenzo, Maria, '"Our Freedom and its Results": Measuring Progress in the
Aftermath of Suffrage', *Women's History Review*, 23 (2014), 421–40. http://
dx.doi.org/10.1080/09612025.2013.820598

Condell, Diana and Liddiard, Jean, 'T'Serclaes, Elizabeth Blackall de (*née*
Elizabeth Blackall Shapter; other married name, Elizabeth Blackall
Knocker)', *Oxford Dictionary of National Biography*. https://doi.org/10.1093/
ref:odnb/67675

Finlayson, Geoffrey, 'A Moving Frontier: Voluntarism and the State in British
Social Welfare, 1911–1949', *Twentieth-Century British History*, 2 (1990)
183–206, https://doi.org.uoelibrary.idm.oclc.org/10.1093/tcbh/1.2.183

Geddes, J.F., 'The Doctors' Dilemma: Medical Woman and the British Suffrage
Movement', *Women's History Review*, 18 (2009), 203–18. https://doi.
org/10.1080/09612020902770691

Haines, Catherine M.C., 'Buller, Dame (Audrey Charlotte) Georgiana', *Oxford Dictionary of National Biography*. https://doi.org/10.1093/ref:odnb/51969

Hannam, June, '"I Had Not Been to London": Women's Suffrage, a View from the Regions', in *Votes for Women*, ed. by June Purvis and Sandra Stanley Holton (London: Routledge, 2000), 226–45

Hilson, Mary, 'Consumers and Politics: The Co-operative Movement in Plymouth, 1890–1920', *Labour History Review*, 67 (2002), 7–27. https://doi.org/10.3828/lhr.67.1.7

Hirshfield, Claire, 'Fractured Faith: Liberal Party Women and the Suffrage Issue in Britain, 1892–1914', *Gender and History*, 2 (1990), 173–97. https://doi.org/10.1111/j.1468-0424.1990.tb00092.x

Hunt, Catherine, 'Success with the Ladies: An Examination of Women's Experiences as Labour Councillors in Inter War Coventry', *Midland History*, 32 (2007), 141–59. https://doi.org/10.1179/mdh.2007.32.1.141

Hunt, Karen and Hannam, June, 'Towards an Archaeology of Interwar Women's Politics: The Local and the Everyday', in *The Aftermath of Suffrage: Women, Gender and Politics in Britain, 1918–1945*, ed. by Julie V. Gottlieb and Richard Toye (Basingstoke: Palgrave Macmillan, 2013), 124–41. https://doi.org/10.1057/9781137333001_8

Innes, Sue, 'Constructing Women's Citizenship in the Inter-War Period: the Edinburgh Women Citizens' Association', *Women's History Review*, 13 (2004), 621–47. https://doi.org/10.1080/09612020400200414

Irvine, E.D., 'A Century of Voluntary Service: The Exeter Diocesan Association for the Care of Girls (St Olave's Trust)', *Report and Transactions of the Devonshire Association for the Advancement of Science*, 113 (1981), 133–45.

Jones, Sir Robert and Girdlestone, G.R., 'The Care of Crippled Children: Proposed National Scheme', *British Medical Journal*, 3067 (11 October 1919), 457–60. https://doi.org/10.1136/bmj.2.3067.457

Kean, Hilda, 'Phipps, Emily Frost', *Oxford Dictionary of National Biography*. https://doi.org/10.1093/ref:odnb/51782

Keating, Jenny, 'Andrew, Clara', *Oxford Dictionary of National Biography*. https://doi.org/10.1093/odnb/9780198614128.013.369168

Krafchik, Max, 'Unemployment and Vagrancy in the 1930s: Deterrence, Rehabilitation and the Depression', *Journal of Social Policy*, 12 (1983), 195–213. https://doi.org/10.1017/S0047279400012605

Leneman, Leah, 'Inglis, Elsie Maud', *Oxford Dictionary of National Biography*. https://doi.org/10.1093/ref:odnb/34101

Locker, Anne, 'Partridge, Margaret Mary', *Oxford Dictionary of National Biography*. https://doi.org/10.1093/odnb/9780198614128.013.110230

Logan, Anne, 'In Search of Equal Citizenship: The Campaign for Women Magistrates in England and Wales, 1910–1939', *Women's History Review*, 16 (2007), 501–18. https://doi.org/10.1080/09612020701445784

Logan, Anne, 'MP and/or JP: An Examination of the Public Work of Selected Women during the Early Years of Women's Enfranchisement (c.1920–1931)', *Open Library of Humanities*, 6.2 (2020), 1–29. https://doi.org/10.16995/olh.565

'Mabel L. Ramsay [Obituary]', *British Medical Journal*, 4872 (22 May 1954), 1212

McCarthy, Helen, 'Associational Voluntarism in Interwar Britain', in *The Ages of Voluntarism: How We Got to the Big Society*, ed. by Matthew Hilton and James McKay (Oxford: Oxford University Press for the British Academy, 2011), 47–69. https://doi.org/10.5871/bacad/9780197264829.003.0003

Marjoram, April, 'Two Suffrage Actresses with Exmouth Connections', *Report and Transactions of the Devonshire Association for the Advancement of Science*, 151 (2019), 179–200

Marland, Hilary, 'A Pioneer in Infant Welfare: The Huddersfield Scheme 1903–1920', *Social History of Medicine*, 6 (1993), 25–50. https://doi.org.uoelibrary.idm.oclc.org/10.1093/sochis/6.1.25

Neville, Julia, 'Challenge, Conformity and Casework in Interwar England: The First Women Councillors in Devon', in *Women's History Review*, 22 (2013), 971–94. https://doi.org/10.1080/09612025.2013.780846

Neville, Julia, 'Noblesse Oblige: Dame Georgiana Buller and Services for Disabled People in Twentieth-Century Devon', in *Aspects of Devon History: People, Places, Landscapes*, ed. by Jane Bliss, Christopher Jago and Elizabeth Maycock (Exeter: Devon History Society, 2012), 387–99

Neville, Julia, '"They Women Have Done Well": Sylvia Calmady-Hamlyn and Women Working on the Land', in *Food, Farming and Fishing in Devon during the First World War* (Exeter: Short Run Press, 2016), 129–33. [Also available at <http://www.devonhistorysociety.org.uk/research/food-farming-fishing-devon-first-world-war/>]

Ockwell, Anne, 'Acland, Sir Arthur Herbert Dyke, Thirteenth Baronet', *Oxford Dictionary of National Biography*. https://doi.org/10.1093/ref:odnb/30327

Parkes, S.M., 'Steamboat Ladies', *Oxford Dictionary of National Biography*. https://doi.org/10.1093/ref:odnb/61643

Phillips, David, 'Michael Sadler and Comparative Education', *Oxford Review of Education*, 32 (2006), 39–54. https://doi.org/10.1080/03054980500496346

Pugh, Martin, 'The Limits of Liberalism: Liberals and Women's Suffrage, 1867–1914', in *Citizenship and Community: Liberals, Radicals and Collective Identities in the British Isles, 1865–1931*, ed. by Eugenio F. Biagini (Cambridge:

Cambridge University Press, 1996), 45–65. https://doi.org/10.1017/CBO9780511522475.003

Purvis, June, '"A Glass Half Full?": Women's History in the UK', *Women's History Review*, 27 (2018), 88–108. https://doi.org/10.1080/09612025.2016.1250544

Purvis, Martin, 'Acland (*née* Cunningham), Alice Sophia, Lady Acland', *Oxford Dictionary of National Biography*. https://doi.org/10.1093/ref:odnb/56454

Rathbone, Eleanor, 'Changes in Public Life', in *Our Freedom and its Results*, ed. by Ray Strachey (London: Hogarth Press, 1936), 13–76

Rendel, Margherita, 'The Campaign in Devon for Women's Suffrage, 1866–1908', *Report and Transactions of the Devonshire Association for the Advancement of Science*, 140 (2008), 111–51

Roberts, Kryztina, 'Gender, Class and Patriotism in Britain: Women's Paramilitary Units in First World War Britain', *International History Review*, 19 (1997), 52–65. https://doi.org/10.1080/07075332.1997.9640774

Rowbotham, Judith and Stevenson, Kim, 'A Point of Justice – Granted or Fought For?: Women's Suffrage Campaigns in Plymouth and the South West', *Plymouth Law and Criminal Justice Review*, 1 (2016), 84–98

Russell, Iain F., 'Macewen, Sir William', *Oxford Dictionary of National Biography*. https://doi.org/10.1093/ref:odnb/34720

Schlesinger, Arthur M., Jr., 'Editor's note', in *Thomas Jefferson*, ed. by Joyce Appleby (New York: Henry Holt, 2001)

Scott, Jean M., 'Women and the GMC: The Struggle for Representation', *Journal of the Royal Society of Medicine*, 81 (March 1988), 164–66. https://doi.org/10.1177/014107688808100315

Simms, Madeleine, 'Parliament and Birth Control in the 1920s', *Journal of the Royal College of General Practitioners*, 28 (1978), 83–88

Smith, Harold, 'British Feminism and the Equal Pay Issue in the 1930s', *Women's History Review*, 5 (1996), 97–110. https://doi.org/10.1080/09612029600200102

Smith, Harold, 'British Feminism in the 1920s', in *British Feminism in the Twentieth Century*, ed. by Harold Smith (Aldershot: Elgar, 1990), 47–65

Strachey, Oliver, 'What Next?', *The Common Cause of Humanity: The Organ of the National Union of Women's Suffrage Societies*, 6 July 1917, 167

Takayanagi, Mari, 'Sacred Year or Broken Reed?: the Sex Disqualification (Removal) Act 1919', *Women's History Review*, 29 (2020), 563–82. https://doi.org/10.1080/09612025.2019.1702782

Thane, Pat, 'The Impact of Mass Democracy on British Political Culture, 1918–1939', in *The Aftermath of Suffrage: Women, Gender and Politics in Britain,*

1918–1945, ed. by Julie V. Gottlieb and Richard Toye (Basingstoke: Palgrave Macmillan, 2013), 54–69. https://doi.org/10.1057/9781137333001_4

Thane, Pat, 'What Difference Did the Vote Make?', in *Women, Privilege and Power: British Politics 1750 to the Present*, ed. by Amanda Vickery (Stanford: Stanford University Press, 2001), 253–88

Thane, Pat, 'What Difference Did the Vote Make?: Women in Public and Private Life in Britain since 1918', *Historical Research*, 76 (2003), 268–85. https://doi.org/10.1111/1468-2281.00175

Thane, Pat, 'Women, Liberalism and Citizenship', in *Citizenship and Community: Liberals, Radicals and Collective Identities, in the British Isles, 1865–1931*, ed. by Eugenio F. Biagini (Cambridge: Cambridge University Press, 1996), 66–92. https://doi.org/10.1017/CBO9780511522475.004

Thane, Pat, 'The Women of the British Labour Party and Feminism, 1906–1945', in *British Feminism in the Twentieth Century*, ed. by Harold Smith (Aldershot: Elgar, 1990), 124–43

Thompson, A.F., 'Acland, Sir Richard Thomas Dyke, Fifteenth Baronet', *Oxford Dictionary of National Biography*. https://doi.org/10.1093/ref:odnb/39848

Walker, Linda, 'Gender, Suffrage and Party: Liberal Women's Organisations, 1880–1914', in *Suffrage outside Suffragism: Women's Vote in Britain, 1880–1914*, ed. by Myriam Boussahba-Bravard (Basingstoke: Palgrave Macmillan, 2007), 77–101. https://doi.org/10.1057/9780230801318_4

'War Hospitals in Exeter', *British Medical Journal*, 2852 (28 August 1915), 336–38

Warren, Allen, 'Sir Robert Baden-Powell, the Scout Movement and Citizen Training in Great Britain, 1900–1920', *English Historical Review*, 101 (1986), 376–98, https://doi.org.uoelibrary.idm.oclc.org/10.1093/ehr/CI.CCCXCIX.376

White, Bonnie, 'Sowing the Seeds of Patriotism?: The Women's Land Army in Devon, 1916–1918', *The Local Historian*, 41.1 (2011), 13–27

Workman, Joanne, 'Wading through the Mire: An Historiographical Study of the British Women's Movement between the Wars', *University of Sussex Journal of Contemporary History*, 2 (2001), 1–12

Reference Works

The Magistrates of England and Wales: Western Circuit: Cornwall, Devonshire, Dorsetshire, Hampshire, Somersetshire, Wiltshire (Hereford: Jakemans, 1940)

The Medical Directory (London: Churchill)

Oxford Dictionary of National Biography (Oxford: Oxford University Press)

Oxford English Dictionary Online

Who's Who in Devonshire (Hereford: Wilson & Phillips, 1934)

Unpublished Theses and Dissertations

Clements, Samantha, 'Feminism, Citizenship and Social Activity: The Role and Importance of Local Women's Organisations, Nottingham, 1918–1969' (unpublished doctoral thesis, University of Nottingham, 2008)

Davidson, Ruth, 'Citizens at last: Women's Political Culture and Civil Society, Croydon and East Surrey, 1914–39' (unpublished doctoral thesis, University of London, Royal Holloway College, 2010)

Dawson, Anthony Michael, 'Politics in Devon and Cornwall, 1900–1931' (unpublished doctoral thesis, University of London, London School of Economics and Political Science, 1991)

Neville, Julia, 'Explaining Variations in Municipal Hospital Provision in the 1930s: A Study of Councils in the Far South-West' (unpublished doctoral thesis, University of Exeter, 2009)

Websites

Ancestry <www.ancestry.co.uk> [accessed 29 September 2020]

Bermuda Bios, 'Gladys Misick Morrell' <http://www.bermudabiographies.bm/Biographies/Biography-Gladys%20Morrell.html> [accessed 25 September 2020]

Bradley, Kate, *Juvenile Delinquency and the Evolution of the British Juvenile Courts, c.1900–1950* <https://archives.history.ac.uk/history-in-focus/welfare/articles/bradleyk.html> [accessed 29 September 2020]

Commonwealth War Graves Commission, *Shaping Our Sorrow: Petition to the Prince of Wales from Lady Florence Cecil* <https://shapingoursorrow.cwgc.org/news-and-events/collection-item/petition-to-the-prince-of-wales-from-lady-florence-cecil-wife-of-the-bishop-of-exeter-presented-in-1919> [accessed 29 September 2020]

Courage Copse Creatives, *The Timber Girls Heritage Project*, 'Miss Sylvia Calmady-Hamlyn and Timber Girls in Devon', <http://www.local-devon-biochar-charcoal.co.uk/project/timber-girls-heritage-project> [accessed 30 September 2020]

The Davis Historical Archive: Mathematical Women in the British Isles, 1878–1940 <https://mathshistory.st-andrews.ac.uk/Davis/Indexes/alphname_H.html> [accessed 26 September 2020]

Devon History Society, *Lives of Devon Women Suffrage Activists, 1866–1918* <https://www.devonhistorysociety.org.uk/news/lives-of-devons-women-suffrage-activists-1866-1918/> [accessed 25 September 2020]

Findmypast <www.findmypast.co.uk> [accessed 25 September 2020]

Foxhams Stud, 'Heather Mixture', <http://www.foxhamsstud.co.uk/horses/
heather-mixture> [accessed 30 September 2020] and, 'The Leat', <http://
www.foxhamsstud.co.uk/other-stallions/the-leat> [accessed 30 September
2020]

Gillard, Derek, *Education in England: The History of Our Schools* <http://www.
educationengland.org.uk> [accessed 26 September 2020]

Girlguiding, 'The Guide Association: Royal Charter and Bye-Laws' <https://
www.girlguiding.org.uk/globalassets/docs-and-resources/quality-and-
compliance/royal-charter.pdf> [accessed 30 September 2020]

Kelly, Margaret, *Margaret's WW1 Diary* <https://kelly-house.co.uk/margarets-
ww1-diary-100-years> [accessed 29 September 2020]

Luscombe, Stephen, *The British Empire: The Primrose League* <https://www.
britishempire.co.uk/article/primroseleague.htm> [accessed 30 September
2020]

Manchester High School for Girls. *Archive* <http://www.mhsgarchive.org>
[accessed 26 September 2020]

Mandler, Peter, *Secondary Education and Social Change in the United Kingdom since
1945* <https://sesc.hist.cam.ac.uk/2018/06/20/the-centenary-of-the-
fisher-act-1918> [accessed 26 September 2020]

Medical Women's Federation, *Our History* <https://www.medicalwomens
federation.org.uk/about/our-history> [accessed 25 September 2020]

Medical Women's International Association, *History* <https://mwia.net/
about/history> [accessed 25 September 2020]

Royal College of Surgeons in England, *History of Women in Surgery* <https://
www.rcseng.ac.uk/careers-in-surgery/women-in-surgery/history>
[accessed 25 September 2020]

Wilson, Helen, *The Pinwill Woodcarving Catalogue: Plymouth Medical Society*
<http://www.pinwillwoodcarving.org.uk/catalogue.htm#_Toc32766374>
[accessed 25 September 2020]

Index

Cecil, Lord William, Bishop of Exeter 19,
  20, 24, 52, 135–40, 144, 150, 154,
  170, 228–29
census boycott (1911) 23n100, 90–91
Central Committee for the Care of Cripples
  167, 174
Central Council for Cripples' Aid 230
Central Society for Women's Suffrage 30n5
Chamberlain, Austen 45
charitable giving (schools) 112–13
Chelsea Committee for Belgian Refugees
  36
Cherbourg 92
Chichester, Rosalie 168
Children Act (1908) 62
Children and Young Persons Act (1933)
  170
children's homes 22, 24, 71–72, 74–75,
  141, 159
children's welfare 8, 23, 62–63, 71–72
  see also infant welfare
China 136
Chisholm, Catherine 99
Chorlton 110, 111
Christmas Appeal Committee 161
Chulmleigh 189
Church Army Housing Scheme 152, 169,
  235
Church League for Women's Suffrage 142
Church of England 112, 135–56, 205, 229
Church of England Children's Society see
  under Waifs and Strays Society
Church of England Pensions Board 146
Church of England Synod 230
citizenship 14, 16, 21, 27, 231
  Acland, Eleanor 34, 47, 56
  Baden-Powell, Sir Robert 183
  Buller, Georgiana 170
  Clinton, Jane Grey 192
  Fawcett, Millicent 7
  Ministry of Reconstruction 213
  Women Citizens' Associations 11
  see also National Union of Societies for
    Equal Citizenship
City Hospital (Plymouth) 94

Clarence House (Plymouth) 74
Clarke, Basil 44
Clarry, Reginald 49
class size (schools) 115–17
Clements, Samantha 4
Clifford, Hilda 67
Clinton, Jane Grey
  Acland, Francis 26, 194–95
  Agricultural Committee (Devon County
    Council) 193–95
  agricultural training (women) 26,
    193–96
  birth of 179
  Budleigh Salterton Nursing Association
    20, 182, 197
  Calmady-Hamlyn, Mary Sylvia 188, 189,
    218
  on citizenship 192
  Clinton, Lord 180–81, 229
  created Commander of the Order of St
    John 200
  Conservative Party 26, 190–91, 196,
    229
  death of 200
  Devon County Council 193–95, 198–99
  Devon Nursing Association 26, 180n5,
    181–82, 196–99, 200
  Devon Women's War Agricultural
    Committee 187
  Devonshire Association for Cripple's Aid
    167
  education of 20, 180, 229
  elections 190–91
  English Folk Dance Society 191n72
  family of 179–80, 182, 185–86,
    199–200
  First World War 185–87
  fundraising 180, 185, 197–98, 199
  Girl Guides 20, 25, 183–87, 188,
    191–92, 196, 198, 200–01, 218
  girls' education 25
  governesses 20, 180, 229
  Happy Hours in an Irish Home 179
  Headridge, Jessie 24
  health of 196, 199–200

www.ingramcontent.com/pod-product-compliance
Lightning Source LLC
Chambersburg PA
CBHW030644270326
41929CB00007B/193